# CHASING RAINBOWS: CHILDREN, DIVORCE & LOSS

## BRYNNA KROLL

PUBLISHING

Russell House Publishing Limited
38 Silver Street
Lyme Regis
Dorset
DT7 3HS

© Brynna Kroll 1994
Reprinted 1998

**British Library Cataloguing-in-Publication Data:**
A catalogue record for this book is available from the British
Library.

ISBN: 1-898924-10-4

*Typeset by:* EMS Phototypesetting, Berwick upon Tweed

*Printed by:* Ashford Press, Southampton

*Cover illustration by:* Xandi Rose

# CONTENTS

# The Author

Dr Brynna Kroll spent twelve years as a probation officer, court welfare officer and Guardian ad Litem, before joining the social work department at the West London Institute, a college of Brunel University. Currently a Senior Lecturer, specialising in probation practice, family work and direct work with children and adolescents, she has a particular interest in child-centred work in statutory settings. She is co-author of The Probation Handbook published by Longman in 1992.

# Acknowledgements

There are many people that I would like to thank for their kindness, support and encouragement.

First my thanks to the clients and staff with whom I worked, while undertaking this research, especially to all the children, who taught me so much. Particular thanks are due to my colleagues Annie Foden, for support both then and now, Jim Gritton, Steve Niechcial, Bosie Swanton, and Helen Sears, as well as to Sheila Himmel, the then Chief Probation Officer who supported the research wholeheartedly. Thanks, too, to my secretary, the late Anne Holloway.

I am eternally grateful to Professor Michael Rustin, for endless support, patience and help, above and beyond the call of duty, during the nine years it took to undertake the PhD, which provided the basis for this book. Thanks also to Dr Amal Treacher, and Dr Carol Satyamurti from the University of East London, who provided invaluable help, encouragement and support, to Elizabeth Oliver-Bellasis, of the Tavistock Clinic, for help and guidance with the clinical material and to Dr Jane Aldgate. I also thank Barbara Prynn and Katie Prince, for encouragement, support and sympathy. Mr David Millar's part in this is too complex to explain, but he has my heartfelt thanks and gratitude.

Friends and colleagues at the West London Institute have also given me help and support. Thank you to Dr John Pitts for guidance, wisdom, jokes and endless editorial assistance, to Dr David Barrett, and to Robin Solomon. Thanks too to Alan Dearling and Geoffrey Mann at Russell House Publishing.

Andy cannot be thanked enough. His constant support, encouragement, and love have kept me going, as has his constructive criticism and willingness to help in any way.

A special thank you is due to my nephews Oliver, Xandi, Simon and Tom who, among other things, enable me to continue to explore (and frequently to inhabit) the world of children, even though I am no longer in professional contact with them. Thanks also to my parents, Pamela and David Kroll, and to my sisters Jude – who consistently encouraged me and always believed it would happen – and Leanda, for buying me the anteaters and lending me her dolls' house.

Finally, my thanks to Nick Segal, for his patience, help and guidance. I will always remember his immortal acronym, RTFM.

# Introduction: Exploring the Rainbow

She looked from one to the other and she saw them established to her safety and she was free. She played between the pillar of fire and the pillar of cloud in confidence, having the assurance on her right hand and the assurance on her left. She was no longer called upon to uphold with her childish might the broken end of the arch. Her father and mother now met to the span of the heavens and she, the child, was free to play in the space beneath, between.

D. H. Lawrence: The Rainbow

When one end of your rainbow suddenly disappears, often without explanation, the consequences can be both manifold and complex. Children of divorce have to deal with a range of emotions, as well as with the radical changes that often take place both in the behaviour and state of mind of their parents and in their life styles. The pillars of fire and cloud can frequently be seen to be rocking dangerously at their foundations. Sometimes they crumble or fall apart altogether; children may be accidentally or deliberately hit by falling rubble. The security and containment provided by the rainbow is no longer present, and considerable anxiety is engendered by the sight of one end of it flapping haphazardly in the breeze. Often the divorced child is indeed called upon "to uphold with her childish might the broken end of the arch", becoming support instead of supported and taking on a prematurely responsible adult role. Sometimes the child is overcome by despair at the loss of the rainbow, or searches frantically for it. Some children rage at the "pillar of fire and the pillar of cloud" because they feel that neither of these sources of support has held onto the rainbow firmly enough.

- How do these children cope with parental conflict that so often accompanies the breakdown of relationships?
- What do they feel, and how do they convey this to those around them?
- Is it appropriate to offer such children short term therapeutic help at a time of crisis, and if so, how can it help both them and their parents?
- What techniques are available to use in such work, and what is the general practice and opinion about this in social work circles?
- How can direct work with children undertaken in the course of preparing a welfare report assist the process of assessment, and how can such work be translated into 'courtspeak', the language in which reports must be written?

1

It was as a result of asking myself these questions that this book evolved. What follows is my attempt to answer them at a time when divorce statistics continue to soar. Concern is regularly expressed in the media about the plight of single parent families and their children have become the objects of political consternation. Despite this, little is known about how children in Britain deal with divorce while it is happening, and even less is heard from the children themselves, except in retrospect.

I first became interested in the effects on children of parental conflict and separation or divorce when I was a field probation officer. Many of my clients – particularly adolescents and young adults – seemed to have suffered as a result of the breakdown in the relationships between their parents, leaving many of them angry and depressed, conveying a sense of loss and rejection which often manifested itself in offending. Many expressed little confidence in establishing their own relationships with partners, as well as feeling strong desires to compensate for what had happened to them, when they had children of their own. This, together with preparing welfare reports alongside the criminal work I was undertaking, led me to think about the problems involved in attempting to help people resolve the sense of loss that they were feeling. I also began to wonder whether, if at the time of separation, the child was heard, rather than simply seen, it might be possible to deal with some of the strong feelings engendered in such a way that they were not carried forward into the future with such apparent force.

At that time (1977-1982) divorce court welfare work was not a specialism in the sense that it now is; the welfare officer's role and tasks were squeezed in amongst the everyday responsibilities engendered by criminal work. There was no specialist training, and direct contact with children was neither expected nor encouraged, despite the paramountcy principle. The context in which this work had to be done and the lack of support for the development of skills within it had its frustrations and when the opportunity arose to join a specialist unit in 1982, I did so.

Once there, my interest in working directly with children, in an attempt to offer a service to them as well as to their parents, grew. However, there was a problem: although I could recognise a child when I saw one, I was not entirely clear where to go from there. I decided to try to develop the skills needed to talk to children, and to offer them an individual service in which they would be enabled to talk about their experiences and I would be helped to make a more accurate assessment of their needs.

I wanted to look at a number of interrelated issues. Firstly I wanted to try to gather together first hand information about children's experiences of their parents' predicament, so that I could build up some sense of what the different reactions were likely to be. I was particularly interested in the experiences of small children

since I considered them to be the most vulnerable a͏͏
able to articulate or express their views in a convention
was instantly accessible to an adult framework of t͏
consequence I decided to focus on children who were under eleven.

Closely related to this was the desire to explore the potential for
undertaking short term therapeutic work, within a statutory context,
with children 'in crisis' with a view to offering the child clients a
service at a time when research indicated that many had no one to
whom they felt they could turn (Wallerstein and Kelly 1980;
Walczak and Burns 1984; Mitchell 1985). My hope was that, if this
were possible, it would also assist parent/child communication so
that parents could appreciate and respond to their children's needs
more effectively, and thus minimise the trauma for the family as a
whole. This seemed particularly important in the light of my existing
experience in which parents and children often swapped roles,
changed places and became very tangled up in one another's worlds.
My intention was to try to facilitate an awareness of this and to offer
support while everyone worked towards relocating themselves.

At the same time, however, I was aware that this would not
necessarily be all that easy. Once again, my experience told me that
often parents were in such a state of distress themselves, so overcome
with anger, bitterness, grief and anxiety that they were unable to
respond to their children's needs, however effectively these might be
communicated to them. As a result, it was important to explore ways
of supporting children, without undermining their parents, so that
they could withstand some of the pressures they might be under. By
the same token, it seemed crucial to be aware of the fact that
children's wishes and parents' wishes did not always coincide –
especially regarding contact – and therefore it was important to give
children the opportunity to express their own point of view. I felt
strongly that, as the welfare of the child was the paramount
consideration for the court, the child's voice needed to be heard
since, only by this means, could a thorough assessment of the child's
needs be made.

The focus, then, was on direct work with children – brief,
focused, therapeutic work in a statutory setting at a time of crisis. As
a consequence, it was necessary to develop a range of useful play
techniques and games which could address children's fears and
fantasies, while also enabling them to express some of what they
were feeling. I was able to gather a collection of toys, animals,
figures, puppets and puzzles together, so that the same materials
would be available for each child. I was also fortunate in having
access to a play house big enough to contain both children and
welfare officer, and a dolls' house where domestic scenes could be
enacted at one step removed. My intention was to use what emerged
from play sessions to place alongside other information and
observations, to tell me both something about the child's feelings,

and contribute to an assessment. At the same time, I was placing behaviour in a developmental framework, analysing it from a psychodynamic perspective, and linking it to both attachment and mourning theory.

My hope was that I might be able to contribute to a greater understanding of the ways in which young children cope, at a critical point in the process of separation or divorce. This would ideally encompass an increased sense of their fears, preoccupations and concerns, as well as provide an indication of what they might need at this difficult time. In the course of this, I wanted to test out the possibility of developing a typology of children's adaptations, which might help both professionals and parents to appreciate and understand the meaning of certain types of behaviour, leading to a more considered and purposeful response to the child, at a time of crisis. This could then form a basis on which to construct a set of ideas which combined theoretical understanding, a knowledge base rooted in child development and practical suggestions for working with children, and that this would represent a set of transferable skills applicable to other areas of child care work.

The final strand of the project concentrated on two professional issues. The first of these related to current social work practice regarding the service being offered to children. The social workers I chose to interview to this end happened to be court welfare officers, selected because they had the most consistent experience of children of divorce and the service in this area was well established. The findings however could equally well apply to social workers everywhere, since they reflect the problems, tensions and conflicts that inevitably arise when getting to grips with children's raw experience. I was particularly interested in strategies for managing the feelings engendered by this type of work, and whether *not* working with children was one way of dealing with, or avoiding the pain that contact with distressed children can cause for the professional worker.

The second issue moved into the wider debate about the absence of, and need for direct work with children in the social work field. I wanted to develop a 'starter kit' for this kind of work which would be transferable, accessible and relevant to any professional involved with children experiencing separation or divorce, or indeed loss of any kind. I felt passionately that children were an increasingly disadvantaged group in social work, discriminated against on the basis of their size and their age, and a prey to all kinds of assumptions about their level of understanding and awareness. In short, I strongly suspected that they were not getting an equal service, that workers were both scared of them and at sea in relation to what to do with them.

The image of the rainbow forms the structure of the book. For me it represented the safe, containing place to which all children are entitled, in an ideal world, as well as a somewhat fragile structure, prey to many outside forces. As I began to explore "the space beneath, between" during the divorcing process and the attendant parental conflict, I began to see that there were four ways in which children tended to adapt, each with their own set of characteristics, and that these needed to be recognised for what they were and responded to appropriately. Of course some children exhibited characteristics that placed them in more than one category, and some moved back and forth; I chose to group them according to their principal way of adapting and tried to link this with stages in the mourning process.

I called the four types of adaptation that emerged parental, despairing, retreating and angry.

- The primary response of the **parental children** was to become more adult. They tended to be watchful, anxious, concerned, protective of their parents/brothers/sisters, exhibiting a constant preoccupation with adults' well being. They possessed a premature maturity and sense of responsibility, and were often beset by age-inappropriate concerns (finance, housework, housing, maintenance).
- The **despairing children** conveyed intense sadness, characterised by a forlorn and lost air. They were often tearful, distracted and wistful, with an inability to play, a reluctance to be stimulated, communicating a sense of yearning. Often, too, they would be preoccupied with order, as a way of coping with the chaos around them.
- **Retreating children** harked back to the idyllic state of babyhood. Their urge was to gallop backwards at a rate of knots to a safer period in their lives and their behaviour was often appropriate to a younger child – thumb sucking, using a bottle, making babylike sounds, primitive wailing, searching behaviour, and the return of separation anxiety which had been previously mastered.
- Finally, there were the **angry children**. Their response was to rage, to fight against what was happening, express anger, often through violent, aggressive or destructive play, in which danger, fire, flood, and demolition would feature.

**The first chapter focuses on the story so far – what we know about the effects of divorce on children**, both on a short term and a longer term basis.

**Chapter two considers the current state of face to face work with children of divorce**, in a particular statutory setting, with particular emphasis on the ways in which painful feelings are managed, and the relevance of my observations to child centred work in general.

**Chapters three and four focus on theories, techniques and games** and illustrate how I combined and applied them in practice. I then move on to an analysis of the way in which the play sessions were used in the assessment process and how what was learned was translated into 'courtspeak', the language of the court report. I also address some of the implications for the transferability of skills and techniques to other areas of child care practice.

**Chapters five to eight deal with the children themselves.** Grouped according to the four principal modes of adaptation to their situation, each chapter presents descriptions of direct work with the children, accounts of play sessions and my attempts to interpret what might be happening in their worlds. The names of all the parents and children who appear in the case studies are, of course, fictitious.

**The final chapter attempts to draw some conclusions about children's responses to parental separation,** as well as the implications for practice in child centred agencies, with particular reference to the demands placed on practitioners by the Children Act. Here I offer what I call a 'starter kit' for good child centred practice – four essential building blocks which interlock with the central principles and philosophy of the Children Act.

What follows will, I hope, have relevance and appeal to anyone who encounters children dealing with divorce, separation and loss, and encourage and inspire them to listen to children and allow them to tell their stories. It does not always make easy reading, since the children's strong emotions are often all too evident, but I make no apology for this. Knowing about how awful it really can be, and being able to acknowledge it and bear it, is what this work is all about....

# Chapter I: When the Rainbow Fades –
## Children and Divorce

"Custody? That's what they say when they take you to a prison," said Caddie, her eyes alarmed. "Will Father keep us in custody from Mother? Won't we ever see her?"

"Don't be such a goose, Caddie," said Philippa. "Mother has access."

"Access?" Caddie could only repeat these terrifying new words. "What's access?"

"It means we can be posted about like parcels," said Hugh, "to Italy or wherever Mother happens to be, when Father says we can visit her."

"*Visit* her?" The full meaning of this extraordinary conversation had at last reached Caddie and she sat appalled....

Rumer Godden: The Battle of The Villa Fiorita

This exchange highlights some of the fundamental dilemmas faced by children of separating parents, as well as reflecting some of the emotions engendered by it – whether distress as in Caddie's case, cynicism as in Hugh's or feigned maturity and savoir-faire as in Philippa's. Here we see the terrifying bewilderment of the youngest child in the face both of the loss of her mother, the sense of being literally imprisoned by the situation and the strange terminology which henceforth will direct her movements between her parents. Here we also recognise the curious notion of visiting a parent who, formerly, was always there. Hugh's awareness of the children's powerlessness is also evident, in his analogy with parcels; his disgust is apparent. Philippa, at seventeen, is perhaps able to temper her distress with the disdain of adolescence.

In this Chapter, I want to look at the story so far.

What do we know about the phenomenon of divorce?
- How does it affect children?
- What of the emotional, physical, and material consequences?
- Are boys and girls affected differently?
- Are children of different ages affected in different ways?
- What do children most need while caught up in the upheaval caused by parental separation and the attendant conflict?
- How can what we know inform child centred practice?

These are some of the questions which I hope to address, with the focus on the importance of the child's experience.

## Divorce: A Growing Problem

It is estimated that 160,000 children experience divorce each year. In the last thirty years there has been an increase of more than 400 per cent in the numbers of decree absolutes in England and Wales, with a slightly higher increase in Scotland (Mitchell 1985). About 60 per cent of divorces involve children under 16. Current figures indicate that there are 168,000 divorces every year, and that one in three marriages will not survive (Social Trends 1993). Approximately one in five children will experience divorce before they are 16, and one in eight before they are 10. Some children may experience divorce more than once, since second marriages which come to an end reach this point more quickly than first ones; a quarter of all divorces involve marriages where at least one partner has been married before. If current trends continue, by the twenty-first century 25% of children will have divorced parents and 50% of children will not grow up in what is described as a "traditional" family (Robinson 1991).

Divorce is a regular topic on television, the radio, and in newspapers. It is an experience which crosses every social and cultural barrier – as coverage of the recent 'Royal' divorces has demonstrated. It is an increasing focus of political concern, as Conservative party rhetoric of 'back to basics' and 'family values' indicates. Single parent families have been pilloried for producing delinquent children and draining the welfare state of resources. Divorce and its aftermath touches private life in tender places; few people do not have a friend, a colleague, or a member of their family who has not been through the experience

## Divorce as a Process

For many years, divorce was referred to as a 'life event' – something that happened, like marriage, birth and death, and then was over. It was supposed to take between two and five years to recover from the experience. Divorce often featured in lists of stressful life events, including moving house, and losing your job, implying that it was simply a transition from one state to another. At the same time, however, divorce was likened to bereavement, coming second only to the death of a partner, in terms of these 'stressful life events'. Like bereavement, there are definite stages that need to be passed through – denial, anger, depression – before the realisation and acceptance that the loved one is dead, or that the ex-partner is indeed ex

(Wallerstein and Kelly 1980; Clulow and Vincent 1987). Of course, the fundamental difference between death and divorce is the lack of a body to mourn. Somewhere there is the continued existence of the 'lost' person, who may be deeply mourned, intensely hated or a cause of sorrow, resentment or bitterness, for whatever reason. The rarest response to separation is indifference; loss, whether one initiated the separation or not leaves us lost, too, at least for a while. Continued contact with the lost partner, for the sake of the children, can, as a consequence be fraught with pain and emotional land mines. No wonder then, that the journey to recovery is often tortuous; no wonder children – and parents – are so distressed by contact in the early stages, stirring up, as it does, those initial feelings of loss and desolation.

As Wallerstein (1989:18) observes:

"Divorce is deceptive. Legally it is a single event but psychologically it is a chain – sometimes a never-ending chain – of events, relocations and radically shifting relationships strung through time, a process that forever changes the lives of the people involved."

Children and parents will often talk about the impact of the experience ten or fifteen years after it has happened, sometimes with such passion that it is hard to believe that it happened so long ago. Why did it happen? How did it happen? What went wrong? The process leading up to the separation is now increasingly seen as significant since prolonged conflict and uncertainty can be particularly damaging to children (Richards 1990). To ignore this is to oversimplify the whole phenomenon.

Equally important is the fact that the process takes different forms, and moves at different speeds depending on the people concerned. Our capacities to deal with painful situations vary depending on all the factors that make us different from one another. The time scale for recovery cannot be dictated by anyone – courts, lawyers, social workers, parents or children. An awareness of the complexities of this process can make us more effective in our responses to people in this situation.

## Children's Reactions to Divorce

When we consider children's reactions to separation and divorce we are faced with a number of tricky questions – who feels what and why? Does age matter? Are boys and girls affected differently? What about practical changes? What are the short and long term effects? What is the significance of parental conflict? How does this affect contact with the departed parent? Does remarriage help? These tricky questions are sometimes better explored than answered....

Children's first reaction to parental separation is usually intense fear – what will happen to me? What will happen next? One parent has gone – might the other go too? Age, gender and levels of understanding also have to be taken into account when considering reactions in detail. It is also important to bear in mind the kind of child they are, their relationship with their parents, and the ways in which they usually deal with difficulties (Burgoyne et al 1987).

Possible reactions include fear of being left alone or abandoned, clinging, regression, feelings of powerlessness, anger, sadness, loneliness, self blame or depression. Anger is often seen by children as a dangerous emotion which should be hidden and as a consequence it is often turned inward or displaced onto other people or objects. By the same token, it is obviously helpful if a safe place can be found for these strong feelings to be expressed as Burgoyne et al observe (1987):

> "Clinical experience suggests that in the longer term, it is better that such feelings are expressed and it may be important to provide a child with a situation or a person with whom they feel safe enough to air their feelings and anxieties more freely.... Trying to understand a child's complex feelings at these times may be of great importance in providing emotional support and making appropriate practical arrangements."

The need expressed by children for some independent, friendly adult to talk to at a time of crisis is manifest in many of the studies which focused on children's experiences. (Mitchell 1985; Walczak and Burns 1984).

As we already know, most children prefer their parents to stay together. This is a very difficult fact for parents to accept and they would rather not know about it. One of the rationales used when facing the awesome prospect of parting is that it will be better for children to have two separated but happy parents, rather than two unhappy ones that live together. Of course separation leads to at least one less than happy parent, since the decision to part is rarely mutual; children therefore may have to wait some time for the promised calm after the storm. The other thing we would rather not know about is children's pain and sorrow, particularly when we may be having a struggle dealing with our own powerful emotions.

What we know about how children feel has generally been gained from retrospective accounts from young people themselves, sometime after the event. Reflecting on their feelings at the time, they are able to recall with startling clarity some of the difficulties that faced them as well as some of their frustrations and this tells us a great deal about their needs at a difficult time. The sense of not knowing what was going on or why, was a particular source of uncertainty and stress. Lulu, aged eight, interviewed about her experiences, offers some particularly heartfelt advice to separating parents:

"The most important thing for parents to do is to help their children understand why they got a divorce. They should let them think about the divorce as much as they want and let them ask as many questions as they feel like." (Krementz 1984)

The need to be allowed to talk – about worries, about what will happen next – seemed particularly important. Reassurance that the child was not to blame was also needed in some cases; children frequently became convinced that it was something they had done that had caused the separation, but often did not dare to ask, in case their worst fears were realised.

Even more important, for many children, was permission to talk about the departed parent, however teeth-gritting this might be for the remaining parent. By the same token, children found it difficult when the departed parent was maligned or rubbished. After all, it takes two to tango, and the rubbishing of one half of the partnership implicitly rubbishes one half of the child. Knowing where the lost parent is, when they will be seen again, and that they are alright are all preoccupations. Maintaining contact without fear of upsetting the resident parent is a real worry for many.

Being allowed to be sad and for this to be accepted and understood as a normal reaction is also important. There is often a feeling that emotions are misunderstood by both parents and children, with regression being seen by parents as deliberate obstruction, and distress or anxiety on the part of the parent being misinterpreted by the child as anger (Mitchell 1984). Distress after visits to, or by, the departed parent was often seen as a sign that such contact was harming the child, rather than as a natural response to being reminded of a sad event; social workers as well as parents were often tempted to terminate contact as a consequence, rather than to support the child to manage the inevitable pain of the re-enactment of the parting.

Many children find themselves taking responsibility for their parents in the aftermath of separation, and express both sorrow and concern for their lost childhood (McCredie and Horrox 1985; Wallerstein 1984; 1985; 1989). Adult worries and concerns are transferred onto children leading to role reversal, at best for a brief period, at worst for many years (Wallerstein 1980; 1989). This often has longer term consequences, where strong emotions will suddenly surface long after the event, triggered by adolescence.

"....typically the child of divorce is a party to a continuum that begins with parental failure to sustain love and commitment, proceeds through the emotional turmoil and dislocation of the divorce process, and continues to overshadow the many years of the aftermath .... the long term, experienced psychological consequences emerge developmentally on centre stage when the young person is at the threshold of adulthood and contemplates

the major life decisions of love, commitment and marriage."
(Wallerstein 1991).

Clearly this has implications for the kinds of help and intervention
needed and the times when it might be required. We are reminded
yet again that divorce is not a time-limited crisis, but a process, in
which emotions wax and wane before a final resolution is achieved.

Emotional stress engendered by separation can lead to health
problems, particularly psychosomatic symptoms. Other reactions
include problems at school, poor concentration, tiredness and
tensions in other relationships. All these signs could be easily missed
or misinterpreted unless we keep in mind the far-reaching impact of
deep and difficult loss.

## The Effects of Conflict

It is perhaps stating the obvious to say that relationships rarely end
without some conflict. Not only are adults in conflict with one
another, but children are in conflict with their parents. One of the
fundamental problems for children of separating parents is that, very
often, what they want is at odds with what at least one of their
parents wants since almost all children want their parents to stay
together. Many people who separate feel that it would be better for
their children to live with one happier parent than two unhappy
ones; research, however, indicates that most children would have
preferred their parents to have stayed together, even though they
may have been aware of conflict and violence. If this was not
possible, there was a clearly expressed need to retain positive links
with both parents, to avoid feeling rejected or cast off (Wallerstein
and Kelly 1980; Walczak and Burns 1984; Mitchell 1985).

A crucial factor in the adjustment of children to the separation is
the degree of conflict between the parents. Rather than the
separation itself being the cause of psychological difficulty, it is the
continued disturbance in relationships in the family that actually
does the damage (Rutter 1971; 1975; Kline 1991). Behavioural or
emotional problems experienced by children are most likely to be
attributable to parental conflict in the present, rather than marital
conflict in the past (Hetherington and Cox 1982).

## Conflict and the Implications for Contact

This idea – that it was conflict that mattered more than separation
per se – led to the development of a view that if parents were in
conflict after separating, it was better for a child not to see the
departed parent than to move between them in an atmosphere of
acrimony, since contact between a child and the non custodial parent
could be positively damaging unless the parents were on good terms

(Goldstein et al 1973; 1980). Children whose parents were able to work harmoniously together were seen as having fewer emotional problems, as well as problems of other kinds, than children whose parents were still in conflict (Lund 1984).

The presence of conflict is often offered as a reason both to stop contact with the departed parent, and for the visiting parent to stop visiting. The assumption is that the conflict is impossible to manage and will last forever, rather than being part of the process that we call divorce. After all, as Richards (1982) observes:

> "Anger between spouses is almost universal, at least for a short period. The parent with whom the child is living is often tempted to express this by minimising the other spouse's contact with the children. Children, too, may find access visits upsetting in the early stages."

The greatest difficulty for children is how to hold on to the love of both their parents, once they no longer love one another. Critical to children's adjustment to separation is the parents' ability to manage contact and to create an atmosphere in which children can move between them with relative ease (Wallerstein 1980; Mitchell 1985). Children who had lost contact with the departed parent were often prone to emotional problems, as well as showing signs of withdrawal and depression (Lund 1984). Contact at almost any price was better than no contact at all. The importance of access is confirmed by children themselves. Most had a desperate desire to hold on, in any way, to the departed parent, and their sorrow and sense of loss when this proved not to be possible was both intense and often lasting.


## Practical Changes

Divorce is not simply the loss of one parent. It brings other losses in its wake which also have to be taken into account. Continuity is important to children and they hate change and upheaval. Separation often means changes in home, school, lifestyle, standard of living (Wadsworth et al 1990). Finances are often stretched; parents who formerly may not have worked and were available to children, may have to obtain employment. All these practical changes take their toll, at a time when the world does not seem to be a particularly safe and reliable place. Changes of address may often mean reduced or total lack of contact with important people in a child's world – friends, family, neighbours. If acrimony between parents is particularly fearsome, children may lose contact not only with the lost parent but with family members too.

## Age and Gender

For children there is no 'good' age to experience divorce. The most vulnerable, however, are the very young – pre-school – and adolescents (Wallerstein 1984). This is perhaps not as surprising as it may seem, at first sight, since both age groups are dealing with issues of attachment and separation, and any further separation is likely to make this more difficult. At both stages children and young people are coping not only with separation and independence, but also major physical, social and emotional changes. Both groups are also prone to periods of regression. In addition, adolescents are dealing with the formation of their own adult relationships, and often become fearful that their parents' difficulties might be contagious. They also tend to find their parents' behaviour even more embarrassing than usual, and tend to be very troubled by any signs of regression in them, frequently adopting the moral high ground.

Younger primary school aged children (5-8 years) tend to become particularly concerned about the welfare of the departed parent. They also retain a deep and abiding conviction that their parents will be united one day, and no amount of remarrying on either side will dissuade them. Between the ages of 8-11 years, children are more prone to taking sides in the marital battle, marching into the fray to defend one or other of their parents. They find it particularly hard to hold on to the idea that parents can be several things at once – that they can love them, but leave them, for example – and they have a need for things to be unambiguous.

The ability to cope is inevitably linked to the ability to understand, and older children tend to receive more of an explanation than younger ones, and therefore appear to have more of a grip on things – at least in theory. Younger children tend to make more definite links between their behaviour and the departure of the parent – I was bad, my parent disappeared – as well as a clear link between physical and emotional proximity (Neal 1983). Smaller children seem to find it easier to retain a continuing sense of mothers as mothers, than of fathers as fathers, because of their awareness that they came out of mummy's tummy (McGurk and Glashan 1987). More questions tended to be asked of fathers, such as "is he still my daddy now he doesn't live here?" – a dilemma posed less in relation to mothers, most obviously due to the fact that statistically children are more likely to remain in their care after separation.

From what we know, it seems that boys are more vulnerable to the effects of any kind of separation, and divorce is no exception. There could be all sorts of reasons for this, including the fact that boys are still generally socialised into either hiding their feelings or expressing them in physically dramatic ways which may not gain them access to the right kind of attention, or to sympathy and understanding. It is also useful to reflect on the fact that as children generally remain in the care of their mothers, for boys the loss of the same sex parent has a greater impact. Add to this the fact that boys often manage this loss by assuming the role of the man of the house – a role that brings both kudos and resentment – and that discipline after separation tends to become muddled and inconsistent, at least for a while, and you have quite a heady mixture.

Girls do not get off lightly, though. Many appear to manage the separation reasonably well, with very few indications that anything is amiss. Girls are also more likely to gain access to support and sympathy, since they are seen to be better at expressing their feelings, and equally importantly, talking to people about them. However, with girls there is sometimes a 'sleeper' effect – young women who had previously seemed to adjust to parental separation become beset by anxieties and difficulties when entering into relationships and commitments of their own (Wallerstein 1989). Once again, we see evidence of the lengthy process of adjustment and the ways in which the experience can be triggered by ordinary developmental stages.

## Remarriage: Is this the Answer?

It was long believed that remarriage might be the answer to children's sadness about divorce. If the departed parent remarried, the child could gain reassurance from the fact that they were no longer alone and had someone to care for and to care for them. If the resident parent remarried, the same might apply. There would once again be two adults to ground the rainbow and, to the outside eye, the family would look 'normal' again. A brief reflection on the complexities of remarriage, however, soon reveal that, if anything, this event is likely to exacerbate things, at least for a while. For many children remarriage may finally bring it home to them that their parents' relationship is really over. (Although, as I have indicated, some children retain the hope of reconciliation despite this.) An incoming adult, with no rights, because they are not a 'real' mother or father, is likely to be tested to breaking point. Children may have to learn to share a parent for the first time in many years. Cosy mornings all snuggled up together eating toast in bed may suddenly become an 'adults only' affair. New partners may of course bring their own children with them, thus producing what are now called 'reordered' or 'reconstituted' families. However, some children would rather not have their family reordered or reconstituted. Discussion, preparation, tolerance and negotiation are required on all sides and conflicts of loyalties abound in endless permutations.

Support and guidance are essential if adverse effects on behaviour, school performance and ability to form relationships are to be minimised. Newly evolving families give rise to a range of complex relationships, losses and gains; an awareness of this makes a crucial difference (Robinson 1991). Pessimistic findings about the effects of family change make sobering reading; if children can be helped to make sense of change, be included and continue to feel a valued part of the process, these can be minimised. When you have a complicated story, it helps if there is someone around to help you with the narrative, so you can put the chapters together....

## Summary: Children and Divorce

What, then, is the story so far? What do we know about children and divorce, and how does it help us think about their experience?

There are profound consequences of divorce, especially for children. The child emerges as the innocent victim of a common but, for many, a devastating phenomenon. Despite the fact that many couples manage divorce amicably, thus minimising distress to all concerned, a significant number of families do not and this has serious implications for the next generation. The overall picture suggests that children are often confused and distressed, rarely given information about what is happening and feel unimportant and forgotten. Providing an opportunity for children to express their feelings, the importance of someone to talk to and the need for support for children who are experiencing their parents' separation, either at the time or afterwards, are clear requirements.

Divorce is a complex process, not an event, and like any other process, it takes longer in some cases than others. Divorce can cast a long shadow over children's lives. Its effects can be seen and felt for many years afterwards, often affecting the successful development of adult relationships. Children can become overburdened by the responsibility of supporting a lone parent, miss developmental stages in their own childhoods, and this can lead to delayed reaction in later life. Boys will often suffer more than girls, but girls may be prone to a 'sleeper' effect, whereby reactions lie dormant, often for many years, only to emerge later in a dramatic form. Intervention has to address this fact; the behaviour of children and young people may have to be interpreted in this light, long after the physical separation of the parents has taken place.

What also emerges is the constellation of factors which can affect children's adaptation and ability to cope. Age, developmental stage and cognitive ability are all relevant here, with smaller children finding it harder than older ones, although adolescents seem to suffer considerably too, perhaps because of the sensitive nature of that stage of development. A continued relationship with both parents, explanations of what is happening and the minimising of parental conflict are also crucial. Continued access to the 'lost' parent is also important, as is the presence of mentors, people to whom children can turn, who are outside the situation.

Over and over again, then, we see confirmation of the significance of parental separation, how hard it is to manage both practically and emotionally, and how problematic it can be for children long after the dust should ideally have settled. What seems to be missing, however, is children's on-the-spot-accounts of what it is like to be there while it is happening, what they think, what they need at that stage, and what appropriate resources either are available or should be provided for children at such a time. I felt that, if such accounts were available, this would fill a significant gap in our knowledge about children experiencing parental separation in general, and separation accompanied by conflict, in particular.

Ideally of course, children should be able to talk to their parents when things go wrong. What we know, however, is that due to their own distress, most parents who are separating become less accessible to their children, and also have a reduced capacity to deal with either their children's pain or their children's anger. They are also less likely to explain things to their children, particularly if they are very young. Given the fact that young children tend to experience the most damaging effects, it seemed particularly important to find a way of enabling parents to 'hear' them, so that they could respond more appropriately.

I was aware that social workers in a range of different agencies were increasingly dealing with the emotional consequences of separation and divorce. An approach was clearly needed which combined theoretical understanding with play techniques, so that the potential for such work could be explored. I wanted to develop and try out such an approach and see not only whether accounts from children could assist parents and professionals to understand their needs, but also to find out whether such intervention helped.

This book describes how I tried to do this.

# Chapter II: Dealing with Children's Sadness: Workers at The Rainbow's End

The litigation had seemed interminable and had in fact been complicated; but by the decision on appeal the judgement of the divorce court was confirmed as to the assignment of the child....and the little girl disposed of in a manner worthy of the judgement-seat of Solomon. She was divided in two and the portions tossed impartially to the disputants.... She was abandoned to her fate. What was clear to any spectator was that the only link binding her to either parent was this lamentable fact of her being a ready vessel for bitterness, a deep little porcelain cup in which biting acids could be mixed.

Henry James: What Maisie Knew

It isn't his parents' divorce that bothers him. He could have lived with that. It was the way things just happened to him. He wanted to live with his father, but who asked him? His parents argued with each other until they came to a decision, and now his mother is stuck with him, when everyone knows they have never gotten along.... His mother can pretend to want him all she likes, but all he wants is to go back to where....every restaurant doesn't serve grits and Alligator salad and some people have fathers.

Alice Hoffman: Turtle Moon

If anyone had ever been in need of a little sensitive professional intervention, it must surely have been poor Maisie, although one would have had the deepest sympathy for the unfortunate worker allocated to the case of Farange - v - Farange. In Maisie we have the epitome of all that is most distressing in the predicament of the child of divorce – the sense that she is a parcel to be "assigned", "disposed of " and "divided in two", with neither parent considering her needs, due to their more pressing preoccupation with hurting and punishing one another. One can only speculate on what her wishes and feelings would have been, had she been in a position to express them. Almost a century later, Keith Rosen, the hero of 'Turtle Moon', could also have done with someone to talk to, at the time of

19

his parents' acrimonious separation. He echoes the feelings of many such children, never asked or consulted. It does indeed require Solomon-like wisdom to make decisions about children trapped in such circumstances.

What is the legal context in which decisions about the Maisies and Keiths of this world and their parents are made? How is social work intervention seen and how are social workers experienced, by both parents and children? What of the workers themselves – what kind of service do they provide, as far as children are concerned? What are their strategies for managing the feelings engendered by this type of work? Much of the practice that I heard about was characterised by muddle and avoidance, and, as a consequence, I had to conclude that little attention or regard is currently being paid to the feelings or experience of the child.

## The Legal Context

Prior to the 1989 Children Act, English law required the court to be satisfied with the arrangements made for the children or assured that the arrangements made were "the best that could be devised in the circumstances" (Matrimonial Causes Act 1973 s.41.1) before the tie between the adults could be officially severed. An order for custody and access would then be made on this basis and if the court felt that further intervention was necessary, a Matrimonial Supervision Order could be made, theoretically lasting until a child was sixteen. The 1989 Act, with its principle of the presumption of no order, means that now an order is only made if to do so would be more beneficial to the child then not to do so (Children Act 1989 s.1.5) and if further support is deemed appropriate, this finds expression in the Family Assistance Order, lasting six months.

The Children Act has reinforced the principle of parental responsibility with the added emphasis that this will be shared, despite separation or divorce. Court scrutiny of the arrangements for children takes place at an earlier stage and parents are required to complete a detailed "M4" statement. The welfare "check list" in s.1.3 of the Act is designed to provide a guideline for establishing the point at which intervention should take place. This checklist, argues Clulow (1990):

> "is likely to be scrutinised carefully....because it spells out the rules by which the judicial game will be played."

It is significant that establishing "the ascertainable wishes and feelings of the child concerned, considered in the light of his (sic) age and understanding" comes at the top of the list.

The idea is that parents are encouraged to make voluntary arrangements about contact with the departed parent, and that this, coupled with the possibility of a cooling-off period and 'no fault divorce' removes much of the conflict that currently frequently surrounds divorce. Unfortunately, however, as Lord Mackay, the Lord Chancellor, has observed, legislation alone cannot encourage people either to stay married or, if they decide to separate, remove the strong, primitive and all-consuming need which some people feel for vindication, revenge and blame. I suspect that the same people who used their children as a battleground under the old legislation continue to do so under the new. In such cases, a sense of shared parental responsibility may not save the day, and other steps may need to be taken.

## The Role of The Professional Worker

It is at this point in the legal drama, where there is no agreement and where conflict is at its height, that professionals may get drawn into the fray. As the previous chapter illustrated, the effects of family breakdown can have manifold consequences for all concerned, with children presenting behavioural problems at school or at nursery, and parents seeking medical help, advice or support, either for themselves, their children, or both.

Whatever the role of the professional, the emotions encountered are often very similar – rage, despair, depression, distress, feelings of loss and grief, revenge, bitterness. In short very primitive reactions to pain, disappointment and fear. Encountering such emotions is a test for any one; the sense of powerlessness, sadness, anxiety, not to mention irritation, frustration, and stuckness tend to be contagious. There is competition for attention, since the adults are as needy as the children and it is easy to concentrate on the former to the detriment of the latter. It is not only essential to know how individuals work, but to have a grasp of marital and family dynamics as well. Pottering about in other people's lives can be a very taxing business....

Social work qualifying courses never equipped workers adequately for marital and family work. Many experienced qualified professionals continue to bemoan their lack of clarity in relation to the skills and approaches particularly necessary for effective work with children in crisis. An awareness of child development, and family systems, related to principles, methods and skills, as well as joint work with other agencies is required. This is an essential tool kit for any professionals coming into contact with divorcing families.

## Perceptions of Social Workers

Parents' views about the value of social work intervention vary. On the whole, most were glad of the chance to talk about what had been happening, although many would have preferred contact at the time of the separation, when the need for emotional and practical help is often more acute. Clearly the point at which one is seen, as well as the setting, make a difference – bargaining in the shadow of the courtroom is the most stressful and pressurising, seeing a conciliator in a relaxed setting is preferable. A few parents felt that more information should have been sought by the court – as one parent put it (Mitchell 1985):

> "No one looked into whether the children were happy. All that mattered to the court was that I was prepared to keep the children and that I could provide adequate housing."

Children's views about social workers are very hard to come by. Mitchell (1985) asked children about what their reactions might be to a hypothetical visitor who called on separated families. She found that twice as many approved as disapproved, some would have very much appreciated someone to talk to, although some children felt they would have been too shy to talk, and others that it would be prying. It was suggested that any visit that took place would be more useful at some distance from the separation, when feelings had had time to settle; follow up visits might also be useful to 'keep an eye on the children'. There was also some scepticism about the likely quality of social work intervention. As one child reflected (Mitchell 1985):

> "I have a real thing about social workers and I've met so many fools of professional people.... If you ask children questions, they'll start thinking about it and blow it up in their minds."

What emerged from Mitchell's account were the children's mixed feelings about whether they wanted to talk about what was happening, whether they wanted outsiders to know, and how they wanted them to react, if they were told. She concludes that, like prisoners' children, children of divorce have their financial needs attended to more assiduously than their psychological problems.

## 'Solomon's Servants'

I would now like to turn to the social workers themselves – professionals engaged in working with divorcing families in a statutory setting, who assist the courts to make Solomon-like decisions about children. In a research project I undertook with divorce court welfare officers most described being "thrown in at the deep end" and developing expertise by "learning on the job", and watching colleagues. Several described training for this area of work as "minimal", "a pathetically small amount", much of it coming rather too late in the day to be useful.

The areas of practice which interested me most were the service offered to children and the management of feelings generated by the work, both of which highlight the dilemmas, tensions and conflicts presented by this area of practice.

## Role, Task and Function

"I think we walk a tightrope" said one very experienced worker. "It's a minefield."

All the workers saw their main task as supporting and enabling parents to make their own decisions about their children, and resolve their conflicts. The main client was seen, by the majority, as either the couple or the family. A few saw the child as their main client "both emotionally and professionally", whilst also acknowledging the importance of helping parents reach agreement, and their task as investigators and reporters to the court. This group felt that, in seeing their role this way, they were accurately meeting the court's expectations of their role:

"I think our job is to represent the Judge in looking after the child's interests....to represent the children's interests to the Judge, to get the parents to reach an agreement....but if you fail, to tell the Judge what the options are....I think they (the courts) think we're there to do that."

What emerged was a sense of continual struggle to reconcile the various demands, expectations and tensions springing from courts, colleagues developing other approaches, management, in terms of speed of 'throughput' of reports, and individuals' own sense of personal and professional integrity. It was important to feel free to do the work in whatever way seemed best to the individual worker. This level of autonomy at times appeared to me a defence against uncertainty; at other times it seemed like a denial of some of the complexities of the work and their implications for worker survival.

## Service to Children: Principles and Practice

What of the prevailing philosophy and practice in relation to the service offered to children? Once again, the people to whom I spoke provided me with a range of views, frequently highlighting their uncertainty about what they could – or should – offer children, and in many cases their lack of confidence in this area of work, due to what they saw as inadequate training and the lack of importance attached to this aspect of the work. As one person said:

"We find it easier to focus on adults than to deal with children."

– an observation which was echoed several times.

Most were conscious of the need to develop skills in working with children and were grappling with this, within the time constraints imposed upon them. Three of the offices where workers were based were equipped with a play area/room, toys, games, and in two cases a dolls' house and play house, creating an environment intended to put a child at ease. The fourth did not have such resources, since most of their contact with children took place at parents' homes. At the time we met, many had recently undertaken specific child-centred training in the areas of physical and sexual abuse as well as short 'Communicating with Children' courses. Many were experimenting with games, play, drawing, fantasy and other techniques.

Views about the service that should be offered to children were linked to workers' perceptions of their role and task. In keeping with this, those committed to a family systems approach in which the client was the whole family, believed in "helping the children through the parents". Generally, children were brought to one meeting at the office, and often "they'd just play around" while the significant work went on with the parents, although, at various points, they would be involved in discussion, play and fantasy games. Observations would be made about the children's perceptions of their family and its problems, and workers were confident that an assessment or understanding of the child's position could be accomplished during that session. There was acknowledgement, however, that under some circumstances, this might not be the best way to see a child and that "sometimes we are not very well thought out on that".

The general view expressed by this group was that it was "unprofessional" – indeed "dangerous" – to attempt to form a relationship with children who would only have brief contact with the worker. The fear was that intense contact would set up a dependency in the child, cause problems concerning confidentiality, raise expectations of what the officer could do for them, undermine parental links, and be seen as competitive.

There was also concern that, in one meeting, children are only likely to reveal a few facets of themselves, and a full, realistic picture would be difficult to obtain, without recourse to other sources (schools nurseries, extended family, and so on). Interpreting children's behaviour, therefore, was seen as not only "very difficult" but invalid, under the circumstances.

This group conveyed a very distinct rationale for their practice, in terms of the service offered to children. Indeed, so passionately did they feel on this issue, that they expressed considerable criticism of others working differently. As one officer said:

"We've all come across cases where....a lot of attention is given to developing a relationship with a child in order to understand how a child ticks....I think that is....quite dishonest towards children, leads them very much up the garden path, and at the end of the day, when the piece of work is finished, you leave them....I would like to feel that that type of work is not carried out under the court welfare service, because it doesn't strike me as being very professional. I'd prefer the methods we use to be more widely followed...."

The majority however, were committed to the idea that children should be offered a service in their own right, some private time

"....to try and establish a relationship with the children in such a way as to create a safe space in this kind of chaos around them where....they can explore their own feelings and thoughts in a way they can't do with their parents, who are very much involved with each other."

Alongside this, was another shared concern about keeping the children in mind, not forgetting about them, and that the work was fundamentally about their future. One person put it this way:

"....sometimes the children get lost; the parents lose them in their argument, and then the welfare officer loses them in trying to sort out the parental argument. The welfare officer, if you like, makes the same mistake as the parents. I'd like people to be reminded that our job, at the end of the day is for those kids....I don't think we emphasise that bit enough....we have endless discussions about adults, but we don't remind ourselves about the children."

There was some acknowledgement of the importance of "hearing what children say", "listening to children" in the firm belief that:

"Children need someone to understand what it's like to be torn between two parents."

Tensions occurred, however, in relation to decisions about how much time it was possible to spend in direct contact with the children, notwithstanding a firm commitment to the value of this as time well spent. Several voiced their frustration with this state of affairs:

"On average, the children are seen maybe once or twice. It's ridiculous and I know it's ridiculous to try and get to know a child so a child can really tell you how they are feeling, in one or two sessions – it's daft. But we do it, and we do it because we are not given sufficient space to do otherwise."

This limited contact was reflected in the practice of many, giving rise to "a feeling of impotence about wanting to do more for children than is realistically in our power".

Concerns abounded about issues of confidentiality, raising children's expectations, encouraging dependence. Most felt that they offered children confidentiality, with the proviso that, if there were things they felt parents should know, they would tell the child this and find ways of conveying the information without incriminating the child. It was apparent that this was a problem with which workers were still grappling. What was agreed however, was that any allegation of abuse would be conveyed, irrespective of the child's wishes.

Dealing with children's expectations and the feelings of dependence that may be engendered revealed similar struggles: providing something human and meaningful, whilst not encouraging children to believe they had made a life-long friend. One worker felt strongly that it was essential to respond to a child's pain by acknowledging it, but was guided by the dictum 'never start anything you can't finish'. Another put it this way:

> "I think you have to be very honest in your approach towards children and let them know you are here today and gone tomorrow. Don't let them build up hopes unnecessarily that you are going to solve their problems...."

It was clear that the children who posed the greatest problems in terms of any form of communication were those of pre-school age. What was also interesting was that many workers made the same assumptions about them that divorcing parents tend to make – that they were too young to understand or have a response. As one put it:

> "...obviously if they're toddlers – under five, say – then they are not going to have much to say about what's happening."

Some were, however, mindful of the danger of such assumptions, and felt they needed more training in enabling them to work more effectively with smaller children:

> "It's hard with small children to interpret what they say and I still find it very difficult....and to be able to recognise when they have been coached and when they're saying what they really feel....(I'd like) just a greater sensitivity to them really."

Most felt that, with very small children (under four), they would be less likely to see them alone, and would rely mainly on observation and child/parent interaction, in order to make an assessment.

The feeling was that there was a lack of training in this area, a need for expertise, but some anxiety about how such work could be most effectively undertaken. It was clear that some felt more comfortable with children than others, and that, for some, contact with children was a tense, uncomfortable experience. Despite an increase in training in communicating with children, this had been more geared towards people who were working with children longer term, and that the particular problems of short term, constructive intervention with children were not being addressed. As one worker remarked, about this particular aspect of the work:

> "It's like walking on broken glass....it's a very difficult one to contend with."

## The Management of Feelings

> "Divorce is unique in that it unleashes our most primitive and most profound human passions – love, hate and jealousy." (Wallerstein 1989)

Being constantly assailed by these powerful emotions was an unenviable state of affairs. The problems inherent in working with loss and depression, manipulative and unreasonable adults, and intense infantile feelings emanating from parents were numerous. Two workers particularly highlighted the painful feelings engendered by specific situations:

> "It can be awful....for fathers to accept that they can't see the children, it just isn't going to work, the level of conflict is such that access just can't work and maybe it's best for the children for them to give up. It can also be awful for children if one parent does give up and they want to go on seeing them."

Some people explicitly stated that the painful feelings for them emanated from contact with the children and their distress:

> "....the emotions have hit me hard....I can think of one little boy who....just came up and held onto my legs and it was as if he was trying to say something to me and I couldn't work it out....I found that very distressing....I think it (contact with children) opens up holes in you – I'm getting emotional just talking about it....it makes you look at things that you would really rather have left tucked away".

Another, with nearly ten years experience of the job, said:

> 'I'm affected by the pain of the children in a way that I sometimes find unbearable."

Some were aware that, for this reason, they tended to limit their contact with children, despite their commitment to offering a service. As one said "there are only certain things I want to hear from children."

Strategies for managing feelings varied. Co-working and team working were seen as excellent ways of sharing the strain and tension engendered by getting tangled up in the dynamics of other people's families. Co-working was also seen by several officers as a necessary safeguard against getting too upset or over involved.

Senior managers who would provide support on request were valued, although one worker was slightly wary about sharing too much in this forum:

> "There's a natural reticence on my part....about how much you open up your heart....to your senior because you are showing the vulnerable part of you....my reaction is to smile grimly, say everything is wonderful and I'm coping fine....those who survive....are those who are expected to stand on their own two feet."

Usually, however, there was no structure for managing and containing feelings – "you've got to get on with the next one and that helps you forget about the last". Colleagues were rarely available for support as they were busy too, and at the end of the day feelings just had to be absorbed, so that the show could go on.

My impression was that, for workers who were prepared to engage with children, there were major issues to consider. One was related to the management of their own pain, as a consequence of exposing themselves to the child's pain. This led on to issues of support, the 'official' acceptance of emotion, and freedom to express it to management. For those working as a team, using an exclusively family-systems approach, the issue of painful feelings did not appear to arise, and in my view this was not unconnected to their practice with children.

## Summary: Dealing with Children's Sadness

Practice with children seemed inconsistent and confused. Most people were attempting to provide some individual time for children, whilst being aware that they could offer very little, and were, in some cases, uncertain, about what to do with them – particularly small ones – when they did see them. Training was felt to be important; workers often felt at a loss regarding the interpretation and understanding of children's communication, and few, if any, felt confident or competent in this area, in contrast to the considerable skills they felt they demonstrated in the work as a whole.

Most felt it was important to offer children a service but felt constrained by pressures, workload, and time. Equally clear was the fact that contact with children was often painful, and I gained a sense that restricting this contact was a way of coping with feelings which, even for experienced workers, were frequently unbearable. Most surprising was the hostility expressed by some to the idea of working directly with children. This highly professional group had, in my view, adopted an institutionalised defence against this, the most sensitive, threatening, difficult and distressing element of the work.

Their hostility to those struggling in this area perhaps betrayed more effectively than anything else could their fear of becoming vulnerable to very primitive feelings, and their uncertainty about dealing with them.

They were not alone in adopting defences against the onslaught of the pain and difficulty inherent in the work, however. Some were frank about about the fact that they tended to avoid or shy away from work with children which was too personally threatening. For others the sheer pressure of work enabled them to escape through very convenient, albeit real, busyness. A denial that there was time to attend to children operated in the same way, as did a denial that it was part of the workers' brief to engage with children.

Alongside this, however, was the strong sense that many were uncomfortable about the service they were offering children, feeling that, despite the fact that their welfare was the paramount consideration, they received the least time and attention. This state of affairs brought many frustrations in its wake, as well as a sense of impotence about being able to do anything about this situation. There was concern about encouraging dependence in children, and fear of abandoning them, since officers could only be involved for a short time – a curious argument in view of the fact that short term crisis intervention was a recognised approach in relation to the service offered to adults. All in all, what I learned served to confirm Hopkirk's view that:

> "...the pain of children is so distressing that it is very much easier to devote our energies to working around them than to working directly with them." (1988)

Many of these concerns were echoed in subsequent discussions with other workers in statutory settings, struggling to provide a child-centred service. Issues also emerged concerning how to make the best use of limited contact with a child, and how to prevent outside pressures from interfering with the capacity to listen to the child's story. Many of the defence mechanisms were familiar companions; workers were often distressed in discussion, when reflecting on children's pain which they felt forced either to deny or avoid.

# Chapter III: A Theoretical Reservoir: Working with Children in "The space beneath, between" – relief duty at the broken end of the arch

Your children are not your children.
They are the sons and daughters of life's longing for itself.
They come through you but not from you,
And though they are with you they belong not to you.
You may give them your love but not your thoughts,
For they have their own thoughts....
You may strive to be like them, but seek not to make them like you.

Kahlil Gibran: The Prophet

Children of divorce, contrary to Kahlil Gibran's dictum, are frequently viewed as belongings, pawns in a complex grown up game, with puzzling and ever changing rules. They are often given other people's thoughts in abundance, experiencing a strong pressure to think and feel the same way as one parent or another – sometimes even both. As a consequence, one of the problems they encounter is how to express feelings that are their own, in a way that, firstly, someone else will recognise and secondly, that will be treated as valid, irrespective of how different or unusual they may be.

As a social worker involved with children experiencing divorce, I became increasingly preoccupied with ways of enabling children to be freed to have their own thoughts, and with helping them to separate these from those of their parents. This involved the construction of a knowledge base to enable me to understand, and interpret their communication, in the context of their overall development. The theoretical framework which informed my understanding of children's functioning was drawn from a number of interrelated disciplines.

Despite differences of opinion among social workers about their roles, what is not in dispute is that the welfare of the child is the paramount consideration – as indeed the law dictates it must be. The problem is that life for the average social worker is beset by many demands, and constrained by deadlines. These get in the way, when it comes to giving a child time and attention. That the child's voice

31

might not be heard presents an obvious potential danger.

My research findings and my practice experience convinced me that it was time to offer children the same quality of service as that extended to adults. A framework, an approach, and a theoretical perspective had to be devised.

## Getting Started

In terms of a basic philosophy, it seemed useful to consider Dryden's observation that "men are but children of a larger growth" and that children should be seen as very small, inexperienced grown-ups – not in the Victorian sense, in terms of expectations of maturity, and constraints on behaviour – but in the sense that they are people in their own right, with minds, intelligence, sensitivities, opinions, perceptions and feelings of their own. As individuals, they are entitled to the same quality of professional service as grown-up clients.

> "The first guiding principle is that work with children is no different from work with adults, and must be set within the context of a professional relationship." (Aldgate 1988)

The delivery of this service might take longer, due to the different ways it may be provided, but this seemed no argument for not attempting to do it.

Embarking on short-term therapeutic work with children – or indeed any therapeutic work with children – requires a delicate approach. This, for me, involved being a child and an adult simultaneously, so that I was able to enter a child's world sufficiently to be able to get a sense and a feel of what was going on, but not to get so lost in this world, and identified with the child, that the adult, worker self ceased to function. This implies that the pores must be sufficiently opened to allow the child's communication to be experienced, but not to the extent that the worker is so paralysed by the feelings engendered that no work is possible. A belief in magic and a comfortable sense of oneself as an adult are also useful. Axline (1964) offers eight guiding principles for therapeutic work with children which include the development of good rapport as soon as possible, acceptance, respect and the ability to recognise feelings and reflect them back in such a way that insight may be gained. These seemed to me particularly relevant to the work I was attempting to do.

On both a practical and an emotional level, then, I wanted to create an atmosphere in which this communication between worker and child could take place, by providing an office and a playroom equipped with appropriate toys, a dolls' house and a play house. It seemed particularly important to create a safe environment, where children could feel able to express powerful feelings, where there was privacy and a sense of safety and where children could move backwards and forwards in time, if they chose to, and simply 'be' when things became unbearable. This safe place, then, was somewhere offering what Winnicott (1960) called a "holding" environment, where needs could be noticed and responded to and what Bion (1959; 1962) refers to as "containment", where an additional element could be provided – a dynamic process in which feelings and reactions could be grappled with and diffused in some useful way. In my work with the children I attempted to provide both these experiences.

Providing a range of toys and play materials was also important, as children did not necessarily want to play with age-appropriate things. Cushions and shawls helped not only to soften the room, but also provided useful things to hide behind and throw, enabling strong feelings to be directed at harmless objects. Office equipment often proved useful as well, particularly telephones and tape machines, so that discussions could take place in the third person and, as a consequence, made to feel less threatening. Preparing the room in advance – getting ready for the child, so that he or she felt thought about – and ensuring that toys which were particularly favoured on the first occasion were also present on the second and third was also a way of conveying to the child that they were remembered. By the same token, taking something that was significant to the child on a visit to the home was a way of sending the same message.

Equally important was finding both a voice and a comfortable way of being with a child. Achieving this was inevitably governed by what I felt comfortable with – the important thing was to find a way of being that felt right, in which I could work. For me this often meant sitting on the floor, or climbing into the play house. It also meant learning to talk to a child as a person, rather than in the tone so often reserved for children by grown-ups – a voice several octaves higher than usual. Finally it meant working hard to adapt language – and often develop language – in a way that made sense to children whose unique ways of looking at the world could so easily be missed, and often struggling hard to ensure that something that had been said had been correctly heard – reflecting it back to them, using the childs words and terminology.

The central elements of my approach were psychodynamic concepts rooted mainly in a Kleinian framework, with a particular emphasis on mourning theory, and the skills associated with infant observation and its wider application. Informing this approach were core skills derived from social work theory and practice.

As a backdrop to this was knowledge of child development – physical, psychological, social, and cognitive. It could be argued that there is some conflict involved in combining frameworks which imply a sequential progression through 'stages', with psychoanalytic approaches that suggest 'positions', and the oscillation between them. However, I found that at certain points, they were helpful in assisting me to identify where a child might be in terms of overall development. I should stress, therefore, that they acted as a form of background knowledge, rather than occupying a central role in my analysis, since my main interest was in the effects of parental separation and conflict on states of feeling rather than on psychosocial or cognitive development.

## Theories of Child Development: Knowing How Children Work

### i.  Physical

With this in mind, then, as a foundation, it was clearly important to have a working knowledge of child development so that an assessment of physical progress could be made. It was often relevant to look at developmental milestones, and note instances when they had not been reached, since this could provide an indication of developmental delay or regression – a possible response to emotional stress. In addition, it assisted in the assessment of both age-appropriate play, likely concentration span, and the range of ideas and concepts that a child might be able to understand – notions of time, for example, and ideas about past, present and future.

### ii.  Cognitive: Piaget's Stages of Development

From thinking about a child's physical development, I tried to bear in mind what might be likely to be happening in a child's psychological life. Three of Piaget's four stages of development – those which span the years between birth and eleven years old – were particularly relevant to the children with whom I worked. In the first of Piaget's stages, which takes place between birth and two years, he traces a process which begins with learning through activity, exploration and manipulation of the environment, moving on to an ability to differentiate between the self and the world outside, and heralding the beginning of a sense of identity. During this stage, a child also learns that one action produces a certain result – shaking a rattle produces noise, sucking produces milk – and ultimately achieves 'object permanency' – an awareness that things continue to exist even when not visible. This was particularly germane in terms of thinking about children's tendencies to blame themselves when a parent left – assuming it was something they had done which caused the departure, that action x had caused reaction z. It also helped in looking at the ability of a small child to hang on to a sense of the departed parent, and enabling children to get hold of an awareness that a Mummy or Daddy remains a Mummy or Daddy even when they are no longer in the same household.

During Piaget's second stage, between the ages of two and seven years, the child becomes capable of symbolic representation of the world, using play, launguage and imitation, and representing one thing with something else. Language and drawing are increasingly used as a way of representing experiences, although the capacity for sustained systematic thought has yet to be achieved. This has implications for the interpretation of drawings and play during sessions, and underlines the importance of an awareness that such communication had symbolic meaning. The other interesting development during this period is a decline in the child's egocentricity – there are, in fact, other people in the world and the child perceives that s/he is not the only important person. Hence an increased ability in many children of this age to express concern and anxiety about parents, brothers and sisters, often assuming an adult, parental role in relation to others.

In the third stage, between the ages of six and eleven years, the child becomes capable of limited, logical thought and is increasingly able to classify, ordering things in sequence and grouping or collecting objects on the basis of common features. More relevant to children of divorce was the fact that, during this period, the child develops the capacity to distinguish one relationship from another, making assessments about their relative importance, and can focus on more than one aspect of a situation at a time. There is also an awareness that certain aspects of things remain the same despite changes in appearance. During this stage there is little room for ambiguity, things must be one thing or another, and the child takes what is said very literally – euphemisms, for example, are taken at face value. Once again, an awareness that children tend to think in this way at this stage is useful in assessing how they are dealing with what is happening to them. It also helps in the process of untangling good and bad, right and wrong, since, while acknowledging the need for things to be one way or another, it is also important to help children gain a sense that situations and people can be a mixture of things. This dilemma is often characterised by children's belief that if one parent no longer loves the other, then they no longer love the child, or that if they do love the child, they should surely do what the child wants and remain in the home. This is an age of clear solutions to the complexity of separation, and a great preoccupation with fairness, very much reflected in suggestions for access arrangements – one week with each parent, one month with each parent, and so on.

### iii.   Psychosocial: Erikson's Stages of Development

It was useful to think about Erikson's stages of psychological and

psychosocial development regarding both developmental assessment, and prediction concerning understanding and possible reactions in children (Erikson 1965). Erikson's first four stages were
particularly relevant to 'my' children, spanning as they do the years
between birth and puberty. It is useful to consider the basic task
with which the child would normally be struggling, assess the degree
to which they are resolving the inherent conflict, and think about the
effect that change, loss or trauma might be having on that process.
By the same token, the stages relating to adolescence and young
adulthood often appeared relevant when thinking about parents'
responses to the trauma of separation, in terms of identity and role
confusion.

Erikson's framework lays emphasis on the tasks that have to be
mastered during each period of growth, and addresses the possible
consequences for the child if these stages are not resolved successfully. The task is viewed in terms of conflict resolution between two
opposing states in each phase – basic trust-v-mistrust, autonomy-v-
shame and doubt, initiative-v-guilt, industry-v-inferiority.

In the first stage, from birth to eighteen months, the baby is
grappling with the development of basic trust-v-basic mistrust,
experiencing the world either as dependable and satisfying, or as
frustrating, and filled with pain and uncertainty. If this stage is
resolved satisfactorily, the infant will develop a reliance on the
caregiver; if not, fear, anxiety, and suspicion will become prevailing
feelings. From eighteen months to three years, the child's task is the
resolution of autonomy-v-shame and doubt. During this stage, self
awareness is developing and there is a strong need to do things for
oneself, and to exercise choice. There is an urge to discriminate and
manipulate, but there is a need to retain confidence in these powers,
even when they do not work. The experience of autonomy must be
well guided and gradual, otherwise, argues Erikson, the child will
turn these powers against himself, becoming obsessed by repetition,
as a way of gaining mastery over his environment. Shame is one
consequence of this – or as Erikson puts it "one is visible and not
ready to be visible", in a state where rage is turned upon the self.
Doubt 'the brother of shame' follows close behind, with the fear of
what one has done. The negative outcome of this stage is loss of self
esteem; the positive is a balance between conflicting forces, and a
sense of the self as worthy.

Between the ages of three and six, the child struggles with
initiative-v-guilt. Conscience and imagination begin to develop, as
does an awareness of what is expected by adults. The growth of
initiative is an important step during this period, dependent on
encouragement to make plans and express fantasies safely. In the
ideal world, the desire to try new things is supported; excessive
control or punishment by adults in this period can constrain and

suppress this urge to discover. The positive resolution of this stage is the ability to learn, and enjoy mastery. If this stage is not completed successfully, there is a danger that the child will be unable to control the newly felt power, and the realisation of possible failure will lead to guilt, and the fear of punishment.

The fourth stage, occurring between six years and puberty, revolves around the conflict between industry and inferiority. This is a socially decisive period where a child becomes aware of competitive impulses at school, and that recognition can be won by mastering tools and skills and producing things. The child begins to put problem solving skills and ability with language to work, and derives pleasure from completing tasks through diligence and concentration. If this stage goes well, the child will develop self confidence, and experience the pleasure of competence and the value of work. However, if a child begins to despair of his/her skills, and of his/her status among others, there will be a failure to identify with peers and with the world of work and skills. This, argues Erikson, may lead to a sense of inferiority and inadequacy.

During the fifth stage, which I found to be applicable to the adults with whom I worked, the major preoccupation is the individual's place in the wider scheme of things, and finding an answer to the question "Who am I?" The positive resolution of this stage should take place during adolescence, but this process is often reactivated by crises in later life.

## Social Work Theory in General and Crisis Intervention In Particular....

The involvement of a social worker – particularly a court welfare officer or a guardian ad litem – in the life of a family is, by definition, of short duration. There is a task to be performed, an assessment to be made, and an end product to be produced in the form of a report to the court. Clearly there is no one social work model which is exactly right for working with children experiencing separation and loss but task centred crisis intervention seems an obvious way forward. This combination of theories based on psychodynamic ego psychology, in the context of brief, focused involvement, with a clear purpose, and a definite end point can concentrate both the energies of the worker and those of the client. This seemed to fit the bill.

As far as therapeutic work with children was concerned, any approach had to combat the arguments of many social workers and welfare officers to whom I spoke, who maintained that unless you were prepared to be available on a long term, open-ended basis, short term, crisis intervention should not be attempted, unless you were a qualified child psychotherapist – indeed this apporoach was actually described as "dangerous" by one of the welfare officers I interviewed. This attitude seemed particularly ironic in view of the fact that much child care work is born of crisis, and staff turnover militates strongly against long term involvement, but some workers were able to acknowledge that a far more compelling reason for avoiding such work was the fear of children's pain. Hopkirk (1988) candidly admits that she was

"....running away from the pain of children, and that if I could not face that, I would never be able to help a child to do so....the pain of children is so distressing that it is very much easier to devote our energies to working around them than to work directly with them."

What gave Hopkirk courage to experiment with this work was Winnicott's strong belief that crisis intervention with children could forestall emotional disabilities in adult life. Indeed Winnicott goes as far as to assert

"if we could only learn to respond effectively to children at the crisis point in their lives which brings them to us, and at subsequent crisis points which are a part of growth, we may save many of them from becoming clients, in one capacity or other for the rest of their lives." (Winnicott 1986)

In this context, the duration of the contact does not appear as relevant as the professional approach taken to the work – in fact it almost seems as though she argues against encouraging a child to believe you will always be there, as she goes on to say

"if we side-step the professional nature of our work and mislead children into thinking that we are available indefinitely as their best friend, we are badly letting them down." (Ibid)

These seemed to me to be powerful and persuasive arguments for short term work with children and it was this that encouraged me to believe that short term therapeutic work, at a point of crisis could be beneficial to children of divorce.

The fundamental principles of social casework underpin any professional involvement in human interaction, and these seemed as appropriate when applied to child centred practice as to that involving adults. The ability to listen and observe, move at the client's pace, and enter into the feelings of people were particularly pertinent to work with children, as was enabling the client to feel recognised as a particular individual through a demonstration of attentiveness to detail and practicalities when making appointments, ensuring privacy for interviews, keeping appointments, and pre-paring for meetings thoroughly. In this context it was important, as I indicated earlier, to make children feel expected, prepared for, and to show them their space in my diary, where their name was written. These guidelines, together with the worker's capacity for the purposeful expression of feelings, provide the basis for sensitive client centred practice, with wide application (Biestek 1961).

By the same token, the belief that one must "think with wisdom but speak the client's language" and the need for a balance between scientific thinking and "staying where the client is" were of obvious relevance (Garrett 1942; Hutten 1977). As I have already indicated, an essential part of my approach was to create and maintain an atmosphere within an interview which generated a feeling of safety and security so that children could express, and play out their thoughts and feelings. For this to have been achieved, the presence of "breathing and thinking space around the worker and the client" – which in real terms meant trying to clear one's mind of other concerns, particularly the deadline for the court report – and an awareness of the influence of the unconscious on both participants were both important (Hutten op.cit.).

## Transference and Counter-Transference

Inevitably, it is here that social work concepts, and ideas drawn from psycho-analytic literature began to converge, although it was important to be aware of the crucial differences between the two disciplines which affected the way in which transference and counter-transference were viewed – of particular relevance to my approach, since much of the interpretation of children's material was based on this process. In view of this, I consider it important to pay some attention to the definitions upon which I will be relying, since this has a significant bearing on the understanding of interpretations I made of the case material which is to follow.

Transference and counter-transference are complex phenomena with a range of different interpretations. The idea of transference originated in the work of Freud and its understanding was developed by Klein (Freud 1895; Klein 1952). Klein's construction of it, synthesised by Salzberger-Wittenberg, refers to the "transference" by the client to the worker of a range of feelings which

> "....include not only repressed conflicts but the whole range of earlier emotions which enter into a relationship....what is transferred are both more grown up elements and all the infantile feeling states which persist right through life." (Salzberger-Wittenberg 1970)

The term 'counter-transference' was originally used to identify feelings which the worker transferred inappropriately from his or her past onto the relationship with the client. It subsequently came to mean the reaction experienced by the worker as a response to the client's transferred feelings (Salzberger-Wittenberg Ibid). I used these definitions of the terms to inform my interpretation of children's communications, exploring the way children made me feel and using this as a possible source of clues about their inner world.

It was, however, the practice of social work in which I was involved and not that of psychoanalysis. In practice, then, this meant that an understanding of an unconscious process, whether in the child or the adults, was important in the context of tackling the task of helping all parties come to terms with and, hopefully, resolve the consequences of separation, but pointing this out or interpreting it directly was not always either necessary or desirable. This did not, however, prevent an appropriate response, borne of that understanding. The difficulty that inevitably presented itself was how to separate out what belonged to whom – were depressed feelings coming from the child, were they in the worker, or did child and worker each have a little of their own? The untangling of these strands required a willingness in the worker for self examination, the provision of effective supervision, and the checking out of feelings and impressions both on the basis of more than one contact, and with reference to the observations of parents, teachers, health visitors or nursery staff.

## Infant Observation: 'Being' not 'Doing'

Particularly relevant, in the context of understanding and working with transference and counter-transference, was my experience of infant observation, undertaken as part of a post-qualifying training course. Infant observation is a well known element in child psychotherapy training, and is increasingly becoming a part of social work education, too. The aim is to learn about early emotional development through watching an actual baby make sense of its world, without taking any active part in what is happening. Thus, as an observer, one is exposed to the powerful primitive communications of infants, and, as a result must also grapple with their impact upon oneself (Rustin et al 1989). The process raises issues about how to allow oneself close enough to feel, without becoming actually involved, how to resist the urge to 'do', and how to use what is felt, seen and experienced, as a road to understanding. Bick sums up the complexities of the process in this way:

> "In order to observe at all he [the observer] must attain detachment from what is going on. Yet he must....find a position from which to make his observations, a position that will introduce as little distortion as possible into what is going on in the family. He has to allow some things to happen and resist others....". (Bick 1964)

The practice of infant observation, then, and the rationale which informs it, was the most important influence on my approach to child-centred work. As a divorce court welfare officer, preparing court reports in custody and access disputes, there was a tremendous pressure to make it all better, sort it out, and 'do' something, in a climate where powerful feelings were experienced by everyone concerned, often to an unbearable degree. The baby observation, in contrast, was a place where you were not allowed to 'do' but simply had to 'be'. I use the term 'simply' advisedly, since there was nothing simple about it. However, the experience of 'being' rather than 'doing', seeing, in the first instance, rather than assessing, brought with it such freedom that other senses were allowed to predominate – rather like the emotional equivalent of a sauna where all the pores open and allow sensations and feelings to get in.

## Transitional Objects, Loss and Change

Working with children of divorcing parents is about coping with loss, managing separation, and dealing with transition and change, whilst, at the same time trying to hold on to something good that might provide support and sustenance while all this is going on. During the course of my observation period I was able to watch and experience the way a baby learns to deal with these things, both in terms of brief separations when mother has to leave the room, and more intensely, when weaning takes place, and the baby attempts to gain some control over what is happening to him or her. To watch a baby holding on to either a part of themselves, or to an object as a way of coping with loss, managing change or a move from one place or state to another, while trying to avoid going to pieces, taught me to notice this in other children, as well as understand it, and to some degree experience part of the emotional strain involved. It also enabled me to gain a sense of the significance and use of these transitional objects (Winnicott 1971) – relevant to work with parents and children experiencing loss.

Watching the baby taking charge of the comings and goings, gains and losses in his or her life was also a revelation, as increasingly the baby extended this sense of control by learning to take charge of loss and recapture through playing hide and seek with mother, as if to say "I can play this game too – see how you like it!" Suddenly the fact that many of my child clients spent part of interviews playing hide and seek, wanting to be found, and deciding when they would be seen and when not, began to make sense – it was all about trying to exercise some control over chaos. Equally telling were the ways in which many of the children managed the comings and goings connected with contact.

Three elements that sprang from this – the significance of transitional objects, enabling a child to cope with change, the

symbolic importance of hide and seek games, and the experience of
the observer in the counter transference – all became central to the
knowledge/skills base I was developing. This framework enabled me
to make connections, guess at and explore what was happening in a
child's external world and what was going on inside. It became
increasingly important to make space for my child clients, and to
take their play and their conversation seriously, as well as respecting
the quality of their communications. A simple example of this was
the idea that a child's most precious possession, or their transitional
object – the 'comforter' object they carried around with them to
make them feel safe – had significance as an important part of the
self. To be given such an object to look after seemed to me to be a
serious statement to the worker about confidence and trust, and the
response to this could have important implications. Once again, I
found a pattern emerging among many of my child clients who felt
particularly torn between their parents. I would often be given a
favourite toy or something the child would call their "baby" to take
care of, and in executing this responsibility, I felt I was taking care of
a part of the child that was in particular need at that time.

Becoming more available to children's feelings in the counter
transference had a number of benefits. Firstly it enabled me to gain
some sense of how the child might be feeling about what was
happening in his or her life. This was particularly helpful when a
child was unable or unwilling to communicate in a direct way, and
when I was having trouble understanding the meaning of their play.
A vivid example comes to mind of a very silent four year old –
Tanya, who will feature in Chapter VI – who was not exhibiting any
outward sign of distress about her parents' separation. The quality of
her play, however, and the atmosphere surrounding it filled me with
an intense sense of despair, which I was unable to attribute to any
other source than the child. I was able to help her parents realise the
extent of her feelings and she became more able to express them in
ways which could generate the comfort she so desperately needed.

## The Psychodynamic Framework

### i.  The Relevance of Freudian Theory

Since my subject matter was young children and their states of
feeling, demonstrated and expressed in ways which were often
unconscious, harnessing aspects of a psychodynamic framework,
drawn principally from the theories of Freud and Klein, was
particularly pertinent.

Freudian theory proved relevant in two ways, although I did not
apply it rigidly. Firstly, in terms of looking at a child's preoccupations at different developmental stages – oral, anal, phallic and

latency – it was useful to consider whether children had successfully passed through each stage and if not, where they seemed stuck and how this manifested itself in their behaviour (Freud 1901). It was of course often difficult to distinguish between a child's 'stuckness' and a child's regression to an earlier stage as a defence against the trauma of separation, and parents' accounts of 'before' and 'after' behaviour were often illuminating in this context.

Like Erikson's theories, the Freudian framework offered a sense of possible hurdles to be overcome, states of mind to be resolved, at points of growth, heralding a move onto the next stage, and its subsequent resolution. From this perspective, then, it enabled a sense of progression, or the absence of it, to be assessed. Issues of trust, levels of security, dependence, control, or lack of it, a child's sense of autonomy and ability to share were often reflected and demonstrated during sessions; this was a useful additional framework in which to consider how to understand such behaviour.

The second aspect of Freudian theory which had particular relevance to some of the children in the sample related to the Oedipal conflict, characteristic of the 4-6 year age group. The implications for a child of the loss of a parent at this stage seemed particularly complex, and made assessing reactons to this loss more than usually difficult. In theory, a child at this stage has fantasies about destroying the same sex parent, in order to possess the opposite sex parent. However the child also fears retaliation for these forbidden desires, which in boys takes the form of fear of castration. Alongside this is the more primitive fear related to the same sex, rival parent – the child fears both loss of protection and object loss. The oedipus complex has now been almost universally used to highlight the triangular relationship that exists between parents and child, irrespective of gender (Moore and Fine 1990), with the associated realisation that adults have a relationship with one another in which the child cannot share.

It was useful to use Freud's perspective in situations where parents had separated when children were in this age band. It also had implications for the ways in which children needed to be helped, since, although many children at every age, believe that they might have been responsible for a parent's departure, these feelings were even more profound during the phallic stage, causing intense reactions, and confusion, both in terms of behaviour and of parent/child boundaries.

## ii.   The Importance of Kleinian Theory

The elements of psychodynamic theory which most influenced my theoretical model, however, were derived from the work of Klein, linking closely, as it does, with the thinking associated with infant observation, emphasising the connection between what is experienced in the child's internal world and how this is manifested in external reality, through behaviour, play, fantasy, and relationships with others. In addition, I relied heavily on Klein's model of child development and the mechanisms she describes which enable the infant to deal with the conflicting feelings of love and hate, related to the two innate instincts that the new born baby brings into the world with him or her (Klein 1926; 1955; 1956). Unlike other developmental theories, Klein suggests that the reactions and responses she describes are not stages, in the sense that a baby moves from one to the other, with resolution taking place in between, but are states of being, or mechanisms for being – positions – which remain with us throughout our lives, operating on an unconscious level, and recurring. Equally importantly are the anxieties and defences that accompany these 'positions'.

Klein argues that in the first few months of life, the baby splits everything into good and bad. The bad, having been split off, is then projected onto the outside world, and thereby got rid of, and disowned. The baby experiences both the good breast – available and satisfying – and the bad breast, which goes away periodically, or is not instantly available. The baby's destructive feelings – emanations of the death drive – make the baby very anxious, and it fears that the object on which it vents its rage will retaliate. Then,

> "In self protection it (the baby) splits itself and the object into a good part and a bad part and projects all its badness into the outside world so that the hated breast becomes the hateful and hating breast." (Klein in Mitchell 1986)

This Klein calls the "paranoid – schizoid position".

The next state of being is the "depressive position". This is characterised by the infant's awareness of feelings of love and hate for the same person, which leads to intense feelings of guilt and anxiety. There is intense fear that the powerful destructive feelings experienced in fantasy will destroy the loved object – leading to "depressive anxiety" – and, as a way of coping with this, the infant employs what Klein calls "manic defences", which include denial of feelings, disparagement and the conviction of his/her own power and omnipotence (Klein 1935).

This theoretical framework proved particularly helpful when looking at children of divorce, when both splitting mechanisms, and the reactivation of the depressive position and depressive anxiety often became apparent. Many of the children in the sample, reflecting the paranoid-schizoid position, 'split' parents into the good and the bad, either idealising the departed parent and blaming the one that remained for the loss, or vice versa. Equally, many demonstrated the clear struggle to come to terms with the mixture of love and hate that they were feeling towards either or both, perhaps most graphically acted out by Robert in Chapter VIII. In some families where there was more than one child it was possible to project these split off feelings onto a brother or sister, so that the hate and anger could be safely acted out by someone else. Many of the 'despairing' children who will feature in Chapter VI adopted manic defences to deal with their fears about their own potential to destroy a loved person. I will be both discussing and illustrating these interrelated states in more detail in the context of the case material.

A central idea, already referred to, and used extensively, is that outward expressions are often manifestations of something important which may be happening inside a child and that, because small children are rarely able to answer a direct question about a sensitive subject, an understanding of this link, and its variations, and an ability to respond appropriately to what a child offers is particularly crucial.

## Attachment and Mourning Theory

Because all the children with whom I worked were experiencing parental conflict, issues related to attachment, and the effects of separation and loss were important. As a consequence, mourning theory provided a central component of the theoretical model I used. It was, however, important to set this against the wider landscape which has attachment theory as its background since, as Aldgate observes:

> "It is difficult to comprehend the impact of separation on any child without a knowledge of child development and attachment theory." (1988)

Attachment theory originated in the work of Bowlby who initially argued that maternal deprivation had long term effects on the psychic well being of the individual (1969; 1973; 1980). He went on to develop a more general theory about the importance of attachment, particularly to the mother, and the significance of the effects of loss of attachment (Bowlby 1979). This debate was widened by Rutter who argued that it was the loss of any significant attachment figure that caused problems in later life and that the effects of separation from such a figure could be counteracted by good substitute care (Rutter 1981b). Subsequent work focused on the effects of paternal deprivation, paternal relations, masculine identification, and social adjustment (Biller 1974). The assessment of attachment is clearly an important aspect of a social worker's role, and includes the ability to identify negative attachment – a bond based more on a child's hope that love and care will be forthcoming, rather than on the sure knowledge that this will be the case. Paternal attachment often proved difficult to argue. For this reason, a sound knowledge base, underpinned by detailed observation frequently proved crucial.

Attachment, separation and loss, then, are inextricably intertwined. Mourning is a response to all kinds of loss, rather than being solely associated with the death of a loved one. Freud was unequivocal about the importance of the process of mourning and highlighted the presence of anger and guilt in reactions to loss, particularly when an ambivalent relationship was involved (Freud 1917). Klein (1940) identified a tendency to defend the self against what she called the "triumph" over the dead, by turning the anger inwards or directing it at someone else close to hand. All these reactions were relevant to children experiencing divorce.

## Stages of Mourning in Children

As far as working with children experiencing loss was concerned, I found the most useful framework for thinking about children's grief, its manifestations and ways of understanding, responding and working with it was provided by Jewett (1984). She identified three phases of reaction, each encompassing certain kinds of responses, and often including aspects of behaviour that might be easily misinterpreted.

The first phase tended to feature shock, numbness, denial, disbelief and alarm – just as the first phase of adult mourning tends to. Often children were anxious, cut off, self-mutilating. Denial could include literally covering ears so as not to hear, denial that the person has really gone, or rejection of the lost person as being of no importance. Busyness, hyperactivity, and the need for constant noise, argued Jewett, could all be indications of denial – examples of behaviour that are not only easy to misinterpret, but likely to receive an unsympathetic reaction, particularly from an equally bereaved adult. Many of the children in the sample whose principal adaptation to separation was what I describe as 'parental' exhibited behaviour which fell into the category of early grief – anxious, restless, busy, controlled children assuming a role which constituted a denial that one parent had disappeared, exhibiting a false maturity which effectively constituted a state which cut them off from what was really happening.

The second phase, which Jewett described as acute grief, is similar to what Bowlby describes as "yearning and protest" and Parkes describes as "searching" (Bowlby 1973; Parkes 1972). In children this phase is often accompanied by periods of regression, and a preoccupation with happy endings, and is a constellation of emotions often reactivated by contact with the 'lost' parent. In this period, too, strong and powerful emotions tend to come into play – sadness, anger, guilt – as well as a sense of disorganisation, inability to concentrate, weariness and despair, often accompanied by a helpless, dependent bleakness. The children whose principal state was described as either angry, despairing or retreating exhibited a range of reactions which were characteristic of this stage.

Jewett argues that the resolution of these stages is important, since remaining in either phase for too long can have severe consequences. Ultimately, if such resolution can be achieved, the child is able to integrate the loss and grief, reorganise internal resources, come to terms with what has happened and derive reassurance from the capacity to have survived the ordeal. Clearly, this was the desired outcome of the work I undertook. Very few children, however, had reached this stage by the end of our period of contact, and it would have been unrealistic to have expected them to have done so. A considerable number, though, had been able to shed some of the pain, anger and muddle with which they were burdened, and embark on the mourning process, having had their feelings of anxiety, loss, anger, despair and sorrow validated.

## Conclusion

Understanding how children work, on all kinds of levels, is an essential foundation for thoughtful intervention. In Chapters V to VIII, I hope to demonstrate the way in which I brought theories and concepts together in order to experiment, adapt, develop and apply a model of work with children experiencing parental separation. I will be drawing attention to constellations of children's behaviour which may give important clues to a child's state of mind. What this means for professional practice and for parents will be explored in Chapter IX.

First, however, I want to describe the techniques I used, so that the accounts of the work I did with children can be set against a backdrop which incorporates all the strands of my approach.

# Chapter IV: Communicating with Children: Playing in "the space beneath, between"

Small children have many more perceptions than they have terms to translate them; their vision is at any moment much richer, their apprehension even constantly stronger than their prompt, their at all producible vocabulary.... Maisie's terms accordingly play their part – since her simpler conclusions quite depend on them; but our own commentary constantly attends and amplifies.

Henry James: What Maisie Knew

For me, these words sum up some of the fundamental issues that arise when doing direct work with children – how perceptions and understanding get communicated to adults by children, what adults make of them and how to find ways of entering a child's frame of reference, a child's inner world sufficiently to gain a sense of what may be going on there. In this Chapter, I will be describing the final strand of my approach – some of the games and techniques I have used with children in the course of my work and the ways in which I have attempted to interpret and understood children's communication, with reference to the theoretical framework described in Chapter III. I will also be examining the ways in which I have added data obtained in this way to information and knowledge gained from other sources, to enable a full assessment to be made, and how I have translated this into what I call 'courtspeak' – the language of the court report.

Although essentially applied to children experiencing parental conflict as a result of actual or impending separation, I will also be looking at the ways in which I have adapted some of the ideas to work with children undergoing other kinds of difficulties – notably in the context of adoption and guardian ad litem work, and wardship – in situations where children must cope with the loss of a parent either through death or because, for whatever reason, a parent is unable to continue to be part of a child's life.

Communicating with children has ceased to be simply a desirable skill in a social worker, but has now become an obligation, with the arrival of the 1989 Children Act. The child's voice must now be

49

heard more loudly and clearly than before, and assessment of a child's needs has to include attempts to obtain both the child's point of view, and to observe and analyse their relationship with others. Good practice now demands that evidence be presented to courts in such a way that it demonstrates that this work has been done. As a result there are far reaching implications for the way in which assessments are carried out, and the means by which a child's feelings and behaviour are described. This leads on to the whole area of interpretation – what you make of what a child says and does, and how play, drawing, enactment games and other techniques can be understood and responded to both usefully and appropriately. Finally, there is the problem of explaining and conveying the quality and significance of children's behaviour in a language that a magistrate or judge can accept in a court report.

During the course of my work I have been exploring and developing techniques that can be used in the context of short term, crisis intervention with children in order to address these significant areas of practice – interpreting and responding purposefully to the young client, using these processes to formulate an assessment, and translating this to a court.

This work has, of course, been undertaken in a very specific setting, where a statutory task has to be accomplished. As a consequence, although it represents a therapeutic approach to the task of assessing children's views, feelings and states of mind, in the context of their parents' divorce, it does not presume a level of 'purity' in terms of practice, that would be expected in the fields of child psychotherapy, art therapy or play therapy – all the preserves of highly trained professionals. My approach has, therefore, borrowed and adapted ideas from these other disciplines, incorporating them into the theoretical framework discussed in Chapter III.

The degree of directiveness or otherwise is also an issue worth clarifying here. In more classical fields of child therapy, the therapist creates an atmosphere and physical conditions which are conducive to enabling a child to express him or herself, develop trust, and reveal elements of themselves. Of central importance is the therapist's non-directive stance, working with the child without making assumptions about what the child might be concerned about, although clearly in possession of information from which to develop hypotheses. Harris (1968) encapsulates this approach in this way:

> "By providing a setting where the child is encouraged to freely associate in play, behaviour and in words, without as far as possible, any direction from the therapist through implied reassurance or criticism, we encourage him to convey to us in the course of this treatment the emotional fluctuations and conflicts in his relationships, both internal and external."

The child's communication, then, can be linked to what may already be known, if appropriate, but the process moves forward at the child's pace, rather than the therapist's, during contact which may be for up to five times a week, over a considerable period (Klein 1961; Axline 1964; Winnicott 1977).

Many professionals working therapeutically with children – and I am thinking here mainly of psychiatric social workers in child and family consultation centres, play therapists and child psycho-therapists – are generally slightly less constrained by time boundaries, or by external pressures, than welfare officers, although, having said that, I am of course aware of the time constraints imposed upon them due to requests for assessments, and the sense experienced by most professionals in these fields of never having as much time as they would ideally like to do a piece of work. Another major difference is that their clientele are brought to them by parents anxious for assistance with and help for their children, where, on the whole, no statutory obligations come into play. The sense of compulsion experienced by many of 'my' children and parents would therefore be absent, or at least far less evident.

My setting, then, clearly had an influence on my general approach and in particular on the degree of directiveness involved. With the order for a court report hanging, like the sword of Damocles, over my head, time was crucial – the Judiciary was already wringing its hands over the length of time it took to prepare welfare reports. It was important, therefore, to establish a focus for my work with the children, and yet, within that, to provide freedom for them to express themselves. I would argue that the same dilemmas apply for anyone working with children in a statutory context.

The families with whom I worked came to me because they were ordered to by the court. They were preceded by a wealth of legal paperwork indicating the disputed issues, or hinting at the areas of conflict, and, usually, they made their children aware that 'someone' was going to see them to decide either where they should live, or whether and/or how often they should see one of their parents. As a consequence, my introduction reflected this awareness, and I made certain assumptions about what the problems might be likely to be, as far as they were concerned.

## Making Contact

My first contact with the children was extremely important. I am discussing this in some detail, since I considered it a crucial stage in forming a link with the children and reflects the complexity of the task, and the degree to which the children were made aware of the focus for my involvement. It was against this backdrop that subsequent play sessions took place, involving the techniques that I shall be describing.

Although the explanation sounds rather long and laborious, it should be borne in mind that it was presented in what I hoped were bite sized, easily digestible chunks, interspersed with various meanderings from the subject, over the course of conversations that lasted between twenty minutes and an hour.

The first meeting almost always took place at the child's home, unless this was unavoidable, since there the child was more likely to feel safe and reassured about meeting a stranger. Language and detail had to be adapted to the age of the children concerned, and the degree to which their parents had explained the situation also had to be established. From there, what I aimed to do was to explain that I had been asked to help their parents to reach a decision about what would happen when they divorced/separated. I emphasised that parents were the best people to do this, as they knew their children better than anyone, but that the children's views about what was happening were also important. It was important at this stage to reinforce the idea that grown-ups made the decisions, since many children were already feeling some responsibility to assume this task themselves. I knew, I said, that this was a difficult time, because I had met and spoken to lots of people in similar positions to themselves, and often they had various worries at such a time – worries that were hard to tell a parent about, because they often seemed so worried themselves. I also said that I knew that sometimes it helped to talk to someone who was separate from family or friends, although some people preferred not to talk about it at all, and that was fine, too.

I then explained that, on this occasion, I had come so they could have a good look at me, and decide whether I might be someone they could talk to. We would meet again, at my office, and if they felt like talking, we would, and if they wanted to play instead/as well, that was fine. The emphasis was on providing a private time where difficult feelings could be talked about. At this stage, I avoided asking questions, but willingly answered them – including questions about myself, what I did, where I worked. As Fraiberg (1972:62) observes:

> "Children hate being questioned. Furthermore not one of these questions can be answered honestly unless our youngster knows just what sort of person we are. If we give him time, he will find out what he wants to know about us....this junior interviewer can find out more about us in fifteen or twenty minutes than we can find out about him in the same amount of time."

## Confidentiality

The issue of confidentiality inevitably became relevant, once conversations began to take place. I found it useful, prior to this stage, to explain what would or would not happen, if children decided to trust me with their confidence. In a sense this introductory process took the form of a stream of consciousness – thoughts expressed out loud about things that could be issues or worries, kite tails which could be caught hold of, or simply considered as the children saw fit. I was offering possibilities, options to be pondered but not necessarily responded to at that moment. Confidentiality is always difficult, in my view. I took the course which seemed to make the most sense to me, and which offered the child the most protection – that is, that our conversations were private. However I made it clear to the child at this stage that, if I thought there were things that should be told to other people, I would say so and we would talk about how best to do this. If there were very difficult things to say, and the child did not feel able to say them to the relevant person, I undertook to find ways of conveying the child's view without incriminating them. I was aware that this was a dangerous path to tread. One consequence of it, though, was that generally children were prepared to do their own talking, provided they felt confident about the support and help – as well as preparation – they would receive. The only exception was information that indicated that the child might be in some physical danger, or that suggested there might be other child protection issues extant. Although the same philosophy applied, whatever the child's view about disclosure, disclosure would have to be made. Invariably, however, children were prepared to allow this to happen, in the rare instances where it applied.

What follows is an account of the games and techniques I used.

## Drawing

I often used drawing as an obvious, simple starting point, when attempting to make an initial contact with a child, as it is a familiar activity that generally feels safe, without threat. Klein (1955) saw play as a means of gaining access to unconscious thought, fears, and fantasies. Rather than make suggestions about drawings, therefore, I tended to encourage the child to draw whatever came to mind, thus leaving the child free to choose, and connect ideas, objects and figures in any way they chose. I would then use this as a basis for discussion.

Increasingly, I found that responding to a drawing constituted an important test of the worker by the child.... We can all probably remember from our own childhood spending ages on a drawing, concentrating on all kinds of detail and trying to reflect important aspects of something in the best way that we could. Then the crucial moment arrives. The drawing is finished and we are going to honour an adult with a viewing. "What's that supposed to be?" says the favoured grown up ("supposed to be" indeed!) "A spaceship landing on the moon/Croydon by moonlight/Three tigers and a bear going round Sainsburys," we reply, proudly. "No, no," says the grown-up "a spaceship/Croydon/a tiger doesn't look like that, let me show you...." and off they go, imposing their view of the world on your imagination.

It seemed to me that the important thing about a child's drawing was that it was theirs, a subjective vision of something or someone – the accuracy was really not important. I also found it useful to bear in mind that things were often going on in a child's drawing, even though, obviously, no movement was visible, and that these events often had nothing to do with the real world. As a consequence, I generally found it more instructive to respond either by saying "Tell me about your drawing" or to ask "What is happening in your drawing?" When I asked Ben, aged 4, who appears in Chapter VIII, about his drawing, which, to the untutored eye, appeared to be a series of wiggly lines with the occasional dash of colour, I discovered that he had drawn the sea, and at the bottom lay my bicycle. Furthermore, I was drowning and there was no escape.... This provided us with a way into discussing Ben's destructive feelings both towards me and towards his parents.

In the same way that figures in dreams can sometimes represent a part of the self, I began to discover that characters in drawings could also reflect a difficult aspect of a child, in a safe form. Children often gave me clues, by drawing an animal or a monster who, by coincidence, had the same colour hair, eyes or trousers as the artist. Joshua, who was the same age as Ben, was fond of drawing tigers. All his tigers were feeling sick – a feeling he himself had experienced that very day. Tigers are fierce, and all Joshua's beasts found themselves trapped by fences or surrounded by forests. The fierce part of himself was difficult to contain but he was making valiant efforts to do so, despite the nausea it was causing. By the end of that particular session, Joshua was able to report that the tiger was feeling much better.

The choice of subject was interesting. Cara, aged six, whose parents were in the throes of a fierce marital conflict, leaving all the children in the family feeling lost and confused, drew me an elaborate maze, brought it to me and said "find me". Her nine year old sister, Isabel, meanwhile, was building a castle with a huge moat, occupied by herself and the other children. Beyond the castle walls were her parents, fighting.

Idyllic drawings of beautiful gardens, happy families, wars, death and destruction often provided useful doorways through which to explore fantasies about happiness, feelings of anger. Colour in drawings can also have significance – pictures drawn in predominantly dark colours, full of night time gloom, helped to talk about fears, and bad feelings.

Jim, whose parents had lived apart for some time, had been left in the care of his severely mentally disturbed mother, and as a result, at the age of eight, had had to take on considerable responsibility both for her care and his own. When it became apparent that this situation was untenable, Jim's father was forced to take on responsibility for his son, albeit reluctantly. He found it very difficult to contemplate the idea of depriving his wife of her child, and therefore found it impossible to make a clear decision about Jim's future, giving him vague, unclear messages, whilst demonstrating his practical and domestic ineptitude. Jim's drawings consistently featured superman, rescuing people, doing brave things, making things happen, being strong and getting things done. We were able to discuss Jim's sense of helplessness, and a wish for rescue, and his fantasy of having a strong decisive parent who could care for and protect him.

Clearly there were times – as in Jim's case – when I was fairly confident about the meaning of a drawing because Jim had made it easy for me and because I was aware of the character and behaviour of both his parents. There were times however when I could only guess, although I often found this equally useful – if you are right, you can embark on what may be an interesting journey; if you are wrong you will be told in no uncertain terms.

Drawings, of course, are not definitive. They do not provide hard evidence that will stand up in court, but they can provide triggers for discussion, as well as pointers and clues to what may be going on in a child's inner world. These can then be compared with information and observations from other sources, so that pieces of the puzzle can gradually be put together, or not as the case may be – after all, it is often the bits that don't fit that tell us more than the bits that do. Finally, as DiLeo (1979) reminds us:

"....the interpretation of drawings must take into account the changes that occur normatively in the development of graphic expression.... It is therefore essential to know as much as possible about what is usual or normative in the graphic activity of children at successive stages of their maturation."

Thus, if a five year old chooses to draw dots, squiggles, and circles in a random, uncontrolled way, this could be construed as a statement, since this type of drawing is much more reminiscent of the graphic expression of a two year old. In this context, I found Sheridan (1986) provided a very useful check list of likely age appropriate accomplishments, which include the ability to draw certain figures or shapes at certain stages. This provided me with a useful baseline from which to assess what a child might be likely to be able to do, as opposed to what they chose to do.

Equally significant were the children who could not draw at all – those children too sad to be able to express themselves imaginatively, often either on paper or in play. By the same token, some children felt only able to produce tiny drawings, carefully clinging to one tiny corner of the page. Peter's brother had to encourage him to draw at all. When he did, in response to my request for a picture of how he was feeling at that moment, he drew a tiny picture of a tiny man drawing a picture of a tiny man (see Chapter VI). This somehow conveyed to me the dangerousness of the question, which could only be taken literally, and the extent to which he might be feeling pushed into a corner by it.

## Drawing People in General and the Family in Particular....

Encouraging a child to draw their family or, more generally, all their favourite people, was another useful way I found of making contact, as well as a means of learning about the characters who inhabit the child's world. DiLeo (Ibid.) makes a very clear distinction between asking a child to draw an isolated, anonymous figure – a test which is used to establish knowledge and intelligence – and the request to draw the family, which, he argues, evokes an emotional response, rather than an intellectual one. The child engaging in the latter activity, says DiLeo (Ibid), is telling us "more how he feels about himself and his family and less about what he knows".

I discovered how valuable it was to *watch* a child drawing the family; some people appeared easier to draw than others, and some evoked interesting facial expressions, or other non verbal signs. Again, DiLeo (Ibid) draws attention to a number of interesting features that I tried to bear in mind:

> "size of individual figures (like the ancient Egyptians, the child uses size to express importance, power), order in which the figures are drawn (those that most impress him are drawn first), his position in the family group (as an expression of his status), is he present at all? (feelings of not belonging), has anyone been excluded? (desire to eliminate), who is he next to? or between? is the sex of family members distinguishable? whom has he embellished by addition of extra clothing or ornamentation? who has accentuated arms and hands (symbols of force, aggression) what has he added other than persons? (pets, trees, houses, sun)."

Oaklander (1978) will use a family drawing to encourage a child to talk to each figure, or to identify something they like and something they don't like about each one. She will also encourage a dialogue between two figures in a picture – a process she often finds overwhelming in its impact. Keeping family drawings enables new and different dialogues to take place from time to time, with the opportunity for additional or new feelings to be expressed. Several children were able to talk to absent parents by communicating with their drawings, or to enact discussions and arguments between various members.

Often pictures will reveal huge, all pervading babies, perceived by the child as getting all the attention, figures without eyes, ears, mouths – can they see or hear how the child is feeling? Can they talk about what is happening? Huge Mummies can be either comforting or suffocating; huge Daddies can be frightening or protective. By the same token, little Mummies can be perceived as too small to cope with worry and powerful feelings, in need of protection themselves; tiny Daddies can be perceived in the same way. Sometimes the largest, most carefully drawn figure is the cat or the next door neighbour. Ben's sister Claire drew a picture of me with a huge red mouth and tiny, tiny ears. I realised that I had been talking too much and not hearing enough, and when I speculated about this, she confirmed my suspicions.

I was often told by one parent that a child either had no recollection of a departed parent, or very bad memories about the person concerned. Asking a child to draw that person often told me a rather different story, as the child would painstakingly and clearly lovingly recreate an image that conveyed that the person was kept in mind in some form – albeit idealised at times – but nonetheless remaining a significant and precious figure. Such drawings would often usefully lead to a discussion about the real and the imagined, the things you are told about a person, and what you yourself remember, as well as the way they were and the way a child would like them to be.

Brian, aged six, had been very firmly told by his mother that his father was bad, that he was not interested in Brian, had never been kind to him, and that seeing him would not be a good idea, particularly as he could hardly remember him. In discussion with Brian, the bad memories did not emerge – whether suppressed or non existent was never apparent – but he responded enthusiastically to my suggestion that he draw me a picture of his father, so that I would be able to recognise him when I saw him the following week.

This drawing was not easy, however. Brian looked worried as he carefully created an image of a smiling, solid looking man with his arms outstretched, as if in welcome. The figure had no distinguishing features and Brian would respond to questions about beards,

moustache, glasses and so on with a firm answer and a look of
uncertainty. What we agreed in the end was that it was very hard to
remember some one you had not seen for two years, particularly
when your memories got muddled up with other people's, and when
you wanted to remember that person in a particular way. Brian was
very unsure about whether or not he wanted to see his father; what
he was sure about was that he wanted me to show his father the
picture – a first, tentative communication.

Following on from using drawings of whole people as a means of
opening up discussion, I decided to experiment. I wondered whether
it was possible to use it to explore mixed feelings, by asking a child to
draw bits of the self – or others – that wanted or thought one thing,
and bits that wanted or thought another. Asking a child to draw
parts of themselves, when trying to explore confused mixed up
feelings, seemed to me a safer and more vivid way of tackling a
complex problem.

Beatrice, aged five, who features in Chapter VII, was grappling
with the problem of whether or not she wanted access to her father,
particularly as she was aware of her mother's strong reservations
about this. Sometimes, Beatrice told me, she felt she did want to go,
and sometimes not – "I do want to stay with daddy, but I also
don't". I suggested that she drew the bits of her that wanted to go,
and the bits that wanted to stay, and although she thought this was
an extremely funny idea, it seemed to catch her imagination.
Interestingly, the bit that wanted to go was very large and included
her legs; the bit that wanted to stay was much smaller and included
her head – the bit of her that was worried about what her mother
would say, if she expressed how she really felt. Beatrice's drawing
gave us an opportunity to talk about what it felt like when bits of you
were pulling in different directions, and Beatrice's decision to show
it to her mother revealed to the latter, in a very graphic and
compelling way, the tension that Beatrice was experiencing.

## The Squiggle Game

This game was originally pioneered by Winnicott (1971) and is
described in 'Therapeutic Consultation in Child Psychiatry'. Using
the squiggle game as a method of making contact with a child,
Winnicott would sit with a child, each would have a pencil and a
piece of paper, and they would take turns in making a squiggle
which the other had to turn into something. As the game continues,
child and therapist talk about the pictures and any other associations
that arise. Winnicott's detailed studies reveal the potential for
illuminating communication, through what, on the surface, appears
to be a simple exercise in sharing imaginative ideas.

I found that the most helpful element about the squiggle game was that it could be as simple or as complicated as one liked. At its simplest, it was an easy way for me to begin a relationship, particularly with smaller children who like to scribble, and the turn taking and sharing element seemed helpful in conveying something important to the child. At a more complicated level I felt it provided a safe vehicle for the discussion of difficult or frightening feelings, and revealed some of a child's anxieties and needs in quite a graphic way.

Sally, who first appears in Chapter V repeatedly drew me the same squiggle every time we played this game. Each time she announced that it was a worm, and give it to me with the request that I turn it into a snail. A very parental child, constantly anxious about, and protective of her mother, I believed that she was telling me, with her squiggle, about the vulnerable, unprotected part of herself, and asking me to do something about it.

## The Faces Game

The faces game provided me with another safe and interesting way of looking at both a child's feelings, and the imagined or real feelings of other people. The game involved drawing a number of circles, to represent faces. They could either be provided with a range of ready made expressions (see Fig. 1)

**Fig. 1.**

or I would suggest that the child drew in expressions as they went along, depending on age and drawing ability. Again, it's a game which I often shared with the child, perhaps beginning by saying "when I am worried, I make a face like this....what face do you make?" The child could then either choose a ready drawn face with an expression on it, or create one. I moved on to expand this game to provide a way of encouraging the child to speculate about possible feelings as well as actual feelings, both in relation to themselves and to other significant people in their lives: "How do you feel when....?" questions, speculative "How do you think you would feel if....?" questions, and ruminations about the feelings or reactions of others – "How do you think your sister/brother/mother/father would feel if....?" In terms of exploring fears and anxieties connected with parental reactions to contact, or to positive feelings about a departed parent, this approach was often very effective, particularly for children too sad and anxious to say very much. Peter, for example, found this the only avenue through which he could begin to explore his sorrow about what was happening to his family.

Again, mixed feelings can be reflected, with half a face feeling one way, and the other half another (see Fig. 2).

**Fig. 2**

## Attachment Games

I use the term 'attachment games' to refer to the ways in which I have tried to explore issues of closeness, distance, trust and loyalty with the children with whom I worked. Such issues were of crucial importance both in the context of parental separation, and in terms of the child's wider world – even though the family appeared to be shattered, it was often reassuring for the child to be enabled to recall and count all the other significant people in their lives, so that they felt less alone and more secure. Issues of reliability and safety could also be explored – who can I rely on most? who makes me feel most safe or least safe? I also discovered that the two games which I used most proved to be invaluable tools when working with loss of any kind, whether to bring a lost person back into consciousness, or to assess the significance of people from a child's past, and the clarity of their memories.

## Genograms

The genogram – or family tree – is a tool traditionally associated with family work and it was in this context, while developing skills in systemic family work that I first learned to use it. From this basis, I began to explore its potential for use with some of the older children in the sample. Using the generally accepted range of symbols (Burnham 1976) and adding some of my own, and others specifically chosen by the children, it was possible to create a picture of the inhabitants of the children's world – all their important figures, whether animal, vegetable or mineral – in order to encourage the child to explore feelings, experiment with relative distances, include, exclude and generally view the way things were and the way they might be. (See Fig. 4)

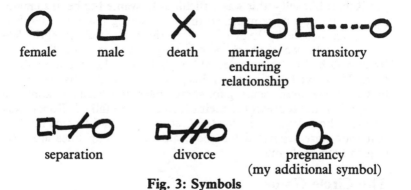

**Fig. 3: Symbols**

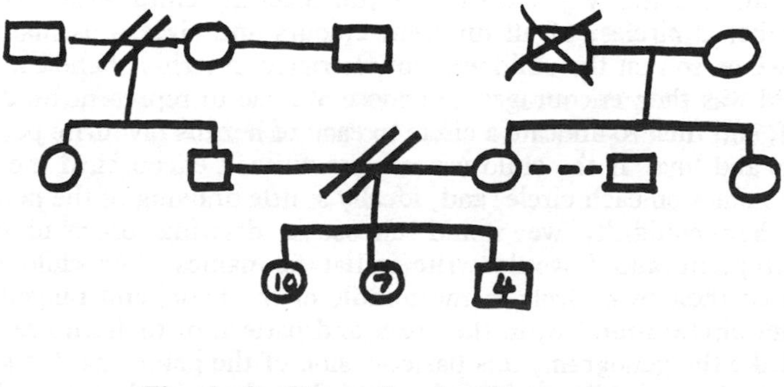

**Fig. 4: An Example of a Genogram**

Robert was particularly enthusiastic about the idea of a genogram, when I first suggested it to him. At the age of eight he had initially become his mother's new partner, had struggled to cope with ways of maintaining a relationship with his father, and then observed both parents forming new relationships – all rather confusing. In the process, he had experienced a range of very powerful feelings, and cried tears both of sorrow and of rage. There were times when he wanted to maim or destroy each of his parents, as well as his father's girlfriend and her child, whom he perceived as replacing him in his father's affections.

Robert and I did his genogram together, although he chose the structure, which was something of a departure from the traditional model. We included grandparents, pets, school friends, various friends of his mothers of whom he was particularly fond, as well as his immediate family. We spent a long time working out where to put Robert himself – this was difficult as he wanted to be in so many places at once, but we managed this by ensuring that he was linked to various people by lines of varying thickness and strength. We looked at who went where, who belonged with whom, discussing some who had to be included although Robert did not want them there. We looked particularly at his parents – how they had been and how they now were, pausing for some time as we discussed applying the symbol that represented their divorce. As we talked, Robert was able to acknowledge that, for the first time, he had to face the fact that they were separated for good, although strong lines attached him to both of them.

## The Circle Game

The circle game, first introduced to me by Jean Moore, in 1986, was the logical extension of working with genograms, being, as it is, rather like a genogram or family tree that has been taken off the page – a moving, dynamic structure, capable of change.

This was the way I used it. I provided the child with a set of cardboard circles, of all different colours and sizes – as many as possible, so that the child was not restricted in terms of choice. The child was then encouraged to choose a circle to represent him/her-self, and then to allocate a circle to each of her/his favourite people, pets and toys. If the child was able to write, I encouraged them to put names on each circle, and, ideally a little drawing of the person. If they couldn't, we would choose a drawing or symbol as appropriate and I would write initials or names. The child then placed their own circle in the middle of the floor, and ranged the other circles round it, in the order and pattern of their choice.

Like the genogram, this basic version of the game enabled some sense of the child's world and its people to be gained, and to allow the process of choosing and balancing to be observed. The child and I would then move on to the next stage – removing the 'child' circle, imagining that he or she has been flown to some magical place, gone off in a space ship, or been zoomed through time to another planet. I would then encourage the child to think about a range of options – who would they want to take with them? if they were in trouble, who would they choose as rescuer? to whom would they send postcards and why? who do they think would worry most about them if they disappeared?

I found this game useful not only with the children experiencing divorce, but also when working with children who had lost family through care proceedings, and who were having difficulty in hanging on to important memories. It can also be a valuable way of helping a child bring a dead person back into consciousness.

Martin was twelve when he discovered his mother's dead body. She had been murdered by her boyfriend, with whom she had had a heated argument the night before. Various members of Martin's family offered to care for him, and he soon found himself the centre of a fierce custody dispute, ultimately being made a ward of court. A welfare report was duly ordered. Martin's family were shocked and horrified by what had happened and were unable to talk about it. The funeral was delayed for many months as a result of autopsies, criminal proceedings and technicalities.

When I met Martin, he had not talked about his mother for six months. She seemed to be a taboo topic of conversation, and no one wanted to distress Martin by mentioning her name. One day, I decided to play the circle game, to get her back into the present. Initially Martin completely omitted her from the cast of characters he had created, until I gently reminded him. He was then able to demonstrate how close they had been, and for the first time was able to mention her name and talk about what had happened.

When a child had created his/her own set of circles, I would keep them safe, and have them available at each meeting, in case additions or subtractions became necessary. Using such symbolic representation, a child can be freed to enact powerful feelings, for example screwing up a circle standing for a parent, brother or sister. It then becomes important to keep the 'damaged' family member safe, as the child may subsequently request its return, and some attempt at resolving the destructive feelings can take place. This reclamation, as Klein (in Mitchell) observes:

> "....suggests that by then we have been able to analyse some important defences, thus....making it possible for the sense of guilt and the urge to make reparation to be experienced."

## The Holiday Game

The holiday game is another game about making choices, and ordering the people in your world. It is also about relationships between people, all of whom you may like, but who may not necessarily like one another. The game addresses issues about who likes whom, who could happily coexist with whom, and what might happen if x and z are placed too close together....

Ask the child to imagine he/she is going on holiday, and spend some time deciding what sort of holiday this will be and where they would like to stay – a tent, a treehouse, a castle, a house boat, and so on. The child is allowed to take all his/her favourite people on holiday too, so the next task is to take a large sheet of paper and make a list of all the invitees, down the centre of the page.

Off they all go. However, when they all arrive they discover that instead of there being one large tent, treehouse, or castle, there are two small ones, neither large enough for the whole group to stay together. The child's task is to decide how to divide the group, using lines or arrows to indicate who should go where. Rather like this....

**Fig. 5**

In the course of this game, the child can experiment with various combinations. In my experience, children of divorce frequently place their parents together. This provides an opportunity to help the child look at the way things used to be, the way they would like them to be, and why they cannot be the way they were. This exercise often frees anger, feelings of unfairness, and evidence of conflicting loyalties.

During one of my meetings with Peter and Paul, I suggested the holiday game, as a way of bringing into consciousness what was too painful to talk about. Peter elected to actually draw up the list of holidaymakers, but Paul watched very intently throughout. Peter listed all his favourite people, beginning with Mum, Dad and Paul, although forgot to include himself, until reminded. He put his parents, Paul, himself and his best friend in one of the houses, and we considered how this might work, and what might happen if Mum and Dad started to argue. Peter was unable to decide which of his parents would move out – "I can't decide, I can't do it," he said, very sadly. This seemed to sum up the enormous sense of conflicting loyalties he was experiencing.

On a more general level, this game can generate information about closeness, principal attachments, and security. Jilly, when playing this game for the first time, placed herself, her father and her best friend in one house, and her mother and everyone else in the other. This seemed to reflect what appeared to me, from my direct observations of Jilly with each of her parents, to be a closer, more relaxed relationship with her father, and a slightly more distant, anxiety provoking relationship with her mother. Jilly insisted on showing her father this holiday game, when I saw them together. On this occasion, mother was omitted completely.

Put alongside observations of parent/child interaction, and tested out through discussion or other games, a picture can evolve which usefully informs a family assessment. Again, it has a wide application, since it has relevance for any child coping with loss or change, or making the transition from one family to another. It also enables the child to choose freely from all the people she/he knows, and as a result can yield surprising information about the way a child perceives the people in his/her world.

## Enactment Games

I use the term 'enactment' to refer to any kind of activity that enables a child to either play out any kind of feeling they may be experiencing, or to actually recreate and enact scenes from their lives – whether real life or fantasy life. Children chose to show me their perceptions of what was happening in many different ways, using bricks, stuffed toys, families or animals and people, cushions, furniture and sometimes even role play, where I would play them, and they would play the significant other part in the scenario.

In addition to a range of toys I had already collected, referred to in Chapter III, I was particularly fortunate in having been lent a dolls' house for my office, where the families of both people and animals could reside. Equally useful was a large play house which had been supplied for the office play room, big enough to accommodate both children and, on occasion, welfare officers.

Children were free to choose any of the materials available. Bricks were used for building followed by angry destruction; puzzles were used as a way of imposing outward order on inner chaos; Liam, Jay and Carrie, who were being fiercely fought over by their parents, used a game of Monopoly to convey their feeling of being caught up in a game of chance. Rachel, aged three and a half, who appears in Chapter V, chose to play with a large, wooden elephant puzzle which had, as an integral piece, a baby elephant that fitted underneath its body (see Fig. 6).

**Fig. 6**

Separated from her mother herself, she attempted to put this puzzle together, but found herself unable to do so – a predicament which seemed to me to speak volumes. She chose, instead to build what she described as a house, using bits of this puzzle and others. Having created her house, she placed a small animal in it, referring to it as a baby with the same name as herself. This baby apparently lived all alone, although she had numerous material things for company rather than people (a real reflection of her family's tendency to replace her lost mother with goodies). Unfortunately, however, this baby was periodically menaced by a large blue stuffed dolphin, and admitted that she was frightened. This seemed to suggest that there was some nameless anxiety threatening her, and that she felt she had been left alone to deal with it.

A favourite toy for enactment games was a set of anteaters – small, medium and large, that fitted into one another (see Fig. 7).

**Fig. 7**

Camilla was very graphically able to enact scenes from her family life in which the two bigger anteaters – identified by her as a Mummy and a Daddy – were so involved in one another that they did not notice that the baby was walking behind them and could easily be lost or forgotten about. At one stage, in fact, the baby disappeared and neither of the parents noticed. This enabled us to talk about Camilla's feelings of insecurity, and fears of being lost.

Many children used the dolls' house to re-enact scenes from their lives, or to recreate more ideal scenarios. Oliver's house contained a Mummy and a Daddy who slept together "unless they argued". They had a very self possessed baby of Oliver's age, who was always on the lookout for an enemy threatening this peaceful scene. At one stage the enemy managed to get the baby, and we looked at the parents' reaction to this. "The Mummy can't handle it at all," said Oliver, "but the Daddy can handle it – he's big and strong." This very much reflected Oliver's perception of his mother's fragility – he knew she had been ill – and his fear of what would happen if she lost him. He was telling me both about her fragility and his sense of being unsafe in her care, rather than in the care of someone who could cope – his father.

Jilly recreated the family as it had been before the separation, although included an extra Jilly, so that there were two of her – a reflection, perhaps, of her sense of being two different people now, depending on the household she was in. She then demonstrated how the Mummy had left home, removing her from the house and hiding her behind a chair. Although Mother had in reality taken Jilly with her, both Jillys remained in the house with Father. Suddenly however, Jilly swept all the contents of the house onto the floor. This enabled us to talk about the way it had been, the way it now felt spoilt, and that everything had been destroyed.

In the play house, many children were also able to act out a parent's departure, the sense of threat from something sinister outside, and their sense of isolation and loneliness. Ben and Claire eventually acted out arguments between their parents about who should have what, in terms of house contents, although, interestingly, this culminated in a role reversal, with father emerging triumphant rather than mother, as was the real case. Claire made herself a house out of floor cushions, but Ben then stole them all and took them into the play house. She stood at the door plaintively asking for them back, but he was implacable. Both were adamant that they could not possibly live together.

Enactment games also took the form of "Show me what happens when...." particularly in relation to access visits, involving the creation of houses using armchairs, with children moving backwards and forwards between them. This also helped, when things were too difficult to explain or describe.

## Techniques for Indirect Communication

For many children, attempts at addressing issues directly proved, understandably, very difficult. For this reason, I tried to ensure that indirect means of communicating were available, in the form of telephones, tape recorders, and puppets. In fact, what I discovered was that, if so desired, anything can talk to anything, so, in the absence of any of these materials, it was possible to suggest conversations between staplers and hole punchers, wooden animals, pieces of puzzles, and so on, such games could sometimes be suggested – "If x were here what do you think you might say to them?" – but more often would be initiated by the children themselves, who would use my telephone to ring absent parents, or use puppets to have angry fights with someone. One particular puppet had a pouch which held a baby puppet, enabling many conversations to take place between parent and child. These often gave some insight into the concerns of both – very concerned parental babies, and anxious parents, very affectionate cuddles between the two, great panics if the baby went missing.

Andrew and Kathy chose to use alternative means of communication at a stage when they seemed ready to express some of the anger they were feeling towards both their parents. Both children decided to tape their voices, initially saying light hearted things and then playing them back, but subsequently using the machine to shout into, as though listening to the shouting confirmed for them some sense of their own power. Kathy also taped herself saying "No! No! No!" a litany that became a theme for that particular session, in which she appeared to be determined to drown out the sound of any discussion about the reality of what was happening in her family.

Andrew also used the telephone, constantly trying to dial his home number, but each time finding that something had gone wrong. This seemed to me a way of conveying how difficult he was finding it to get through to his parents at this stage, as well as conveying, perhaps, some wish to make contact with the home life he used to know. Several other children in the sample used the telephone in this way – an attempt to get in touch with something lost forever, perhaps. Equally, Megan and Philip, subjects of a Guardian ad Litem report in adoption proceedings, chose to talk to me via the telephone as a safer way of expressing views, and particularly of asking questions about the future.

Sophie chose to use a doll as an indirect way of telling me something about her life at home and some of her preoccupations. Sophie was not only a child of divorcing parents but had also been sexually abused, allegedly by her father. Sophie initiated a game in which her doll became her little girl. This little girl was feeling very sick, but this was not due to something she had eaten – "seeing her daddy makes her feel sick," she said, adding that her daddy didn't like her. At our next meeting, Sophie gave me her little girl doll to hold, adding that she was still feeling sick – she did not know what was wrong with her, but she still felt sick when her daddy looked at her. Further discussion revealed that the doll had no friends at school, and that she caused her mother a lot of worry because she felt so sad. This gave us the opportunity to talk about some of these feelings, since they were safely in the possession of the doll, rather than Sophie herself.

Animals, whether toy or real, also provided a useful vehicle for presenting or introducing powerful feelings that were too dangerous to own. As Lieberman (1979) observes

"Because displacement is a common defence among children, it is easy to understand them, if one is willing to listen to what they actually say. When they talk about an animal, another child or a story book character, the character will be speaking for them and for the important events in their lives. The character's feelings will be their feelings."

I found this a very useful idea to keep in mind. In an early interview, Tanya, a four year old caught in a puzzling situation between her parents that no-one had explained to her, devised a tableau in which a lamb was very angry with both a womble and a bear. On a subsequent visit to her father's home, during a period of access, she took me to see her tank of tropical fish (all incidentally called Emily, her middle name) and informed me that some of the fish were very angry, although she could not say why. Tanya was one of the saddest, most depressed children I met. This seemed to be the only way that she could convey how angry she was feeling.

Puppets proved particularly useful as a means to enable difficult questions to be asked without appearing to cross examine or persecute. The most effective method (and least demanding in terms of thespian ability) was to make the puppet whisper in my ear, as though asking a question. I could then convey the question to the child – "The lion wonders what you do when you go to stay with your mum"...."the lion says he's a bit confused – can you explain to him why you don't want to see your daddy" and so on. The use of a puppet captures the child's imagination, and the dialogue can take place between the child and a safe third party.

In the absence of actual puppets, dolls or figures, a packet of pipe cleaners can prove an invaluable asset, with the added advantage that it can be taken on home visits very easily. Children can then create their own people, creatures or constructions – monsters, space ships, animals and so on – with whom indirect conversations can be initiated.

## Issues for Practice

One of the crucial issues that confronted me when I began this work
was my lack of experience in the area of direct work with children.
As a probation officer, I had been generically trained, and then
(1975-77) as now (with very few exceptions) although child
development was taught as an academic subject, no one taught us
what to do with or say to a child when we saw one. As a consequence
I had some limited understanding of how children worked, but little
opportunity to put this into practice, in the usual course of probation
practice, other than in the context of the occasional divorce court
welfare report. As I explained in the introduction, my move to a
specialist post gave me the opportunity to develop skills in working
with children; my anxiety about how to understand the outcome of
this communication led me to undertake further training.

There were a number of problematic issues inherent in the work I
was doing with children. If some of the examples I have given
convey the impression that it was easy, that all children co-operated,
and that I always knew what to say and do, and how to interpret
what was going on, then I apologise. This was in fact far from the
case. Some children either could not or would not allow themselves
to let go enough to play, and despite my best efforts, some did not,
as I had hoped, see my room as a safe place in which to explore
feelings. Some of the children had been so primed by their parents
that it was impossible to separate what were their thoughts from
those of others; some had been made so anxious about meeting me,
what I might do, what I could do if they said the wrong thing, that
no amount of reassurance on my part made them feel at ease.
Although such children were a small minority, they still demonstrated that, for some, a welfare officer might not be the best person
to have around when you are going through your parents' separation
or divorce.

I was constantly under pressure from the court to provide a swift
and thorough service. It was difficult to forget this, and hard to free
my mind from any sense of pressure, so that my concentration could
be focused solely on the child. This took considerable practice, and
required mental preparation in advance, so that I could actually be
there for the child rather than writing a court report in my head at
the same time.

Initially the availability of toys was rather ad hoc, before I was able
to get together a range of playthings that I felt would cover all
eventualities. There were issues about whether to suggest things if a
child seemed stuck, and at what stage to try certain techniques or
games. These were children, after all, not guinea pigs, and it was
important to follow their lead. At the same time, however, I was
trying to test and develop a methodology for working with children,

and the twin tasks at times seemed to me to be in conflict.

I had considerable anxieties about when to respond to what a child was saying or communicating, by whatever means, and how this should best be done. Because of what I often already knew about the family and the history, it was often tempting to assume I understood what was going on, rather than considering that the child might be offering me something different, a new insight. There were times when I had absolutely no idea what a child was telling me – a feeling that I did not understand enough of what they were saying to respond usefully, as opposed to empathically. There were times when I was unsure whether what I had managed to say or do had been the right thing or not; at other times I was sure I had said the wrong thing, got the wrong end of the stick altogether. This was one of the ways I discovered how tolerant and forgiving children can be. Finally, there were times when, despite my best efforts, I found what children told me to be so distressing that I felt too helpless and paralysed to respond in the way I would have wished.

A critical part of the work, therefore, was individual supervision, and case discussions. These were essential mechanisms which enabled me to clarify and understand what was happening, allowing me to sort out my own reactions as well as test out and modify my approach and technique. It was easy to get lost in the child's world, to under or over estimate the significance of a certain sequence of behaviour, and to fail to realise how some children might experience my intervention. This is not the kind of work which can or should be done without both support and a regular framework which allows for reflection and analysis. As Aldgate (1988) observes:

> "Because experiences of loss are universal, seeing children in distress may evoke recollections of workers' own experiences. Some of these may not have been resolved; they may get in the way of work with the child unless they are confronted and examined in supervision."

I considered myself to be particularly fortunate to have not only a manager, with a psychodynamic approach, who was particularly interested in the development of this kind of work within the team, but also colleagues who were interested and stimulated by what I was doing.

Another problem was knowing when or whether I had enough information from the children to make a clear assessment. In the main, I saw children on average three times on their own, as well as in the company of each and/or both their parents, usually more than once. As a result, I had information flowing from a number of different sources, some confirmatory, some contradictory. At the end of the day, I had to rely on whether or not I had gained a clear picture in my mind about what the issues were, what everyone thought about them, and how everyone got on with everyone else. It often felt akin to completing a giant jigsaw puzzle. Some people's puzzles, of course, inevitably had bits missing. I tried to reduce the size of those bits to a minimum, but made a point of indicating in the report what these gaps were, as well as any contradictions or uncertainties.

## From Assessment to 'Courtspeak'

Assessment in relation to children comprises a number of inter-related dimensions, including preparation of both the child and the worker, history taking, analysis of attachment and interaction with others and observation. This framework proved particularly relevant in my work with children. An additional part of any social work assessment is anxiety about getting it right, being certain, doing the right thing for the client. When that assessment is also linked to the production of a court report this anxiety is understandably given an additional dimension. There was considerable pressure to be sure, to decide, to make it alright for the children.

Although the initial emphasis was on helping parents make their own decisions about their own children, there were often times when this was not possible. Many courts share the expectation that, under such circumstances, welfare officers, Guardians ad Litem and social workers generally, will recommend a course of action – in short, advise them about which parent would make the most appropriate full time caretaker, or which solution or option would be in the child's best interests. When I felt able to do this, I considered it my responsibility to do so and I did. However, there were many occasions when this was not possible, and under these circumstances, I tended to put forward the views and wishes of each parent, and the pros and cons that I considered might attend the placing of the children in their care. Whichever turned out to be the case, it was rarely possible to tell children what would happen, although it was possible to think about what might happen and how that could be dealt with. It was also often difficult to reassure them about any of the things that worried them most – would Mum and Dad ever be friends? what would happen if either of them met someone else? if they found they didn't want to live with the parent they were told to live with, what could they do? would Mum /Dad be alright on their own?

Having made an assessment, the problem arose as to how to translate this complex process into a brief court report – a process which in many ways mirrors my problems in transferring my research material into a coherent account. Both activities involve a balance of fact, opinion, judgement, observation, professional perspective and objectivity; both involve selecting material that lends itself to a particular point of view so that the conclusion will flow from what has come before.

As I have already indicated, my conversations with, and observation of the children on whom I wrote reports was extensive. It was, however, neither relevant nor appropriate to tell the Judge everything that had taken place, as much for reasons of confidentiality – already referred to – as anything else. What was important was to convey to the Judge several fundamental things – the thoroughness with which the child had been assessed, the quality of the child's experience, and the nature of the child's relationship with both parents concerned, and any other children in the family – so that decisions could be made based on the child's welfare as well as parental competence.

An adjunct to this was to be prepared to respond to, and elaborate on any elements in the report that were questioned or challenged in court, back up professional observation with examples, and refer to, and connect relevant practice theory and research data relating to attachment, separation, and loss and their effects on children. This raised the whole area of pre-court preparation, and the ability to perform on the courtroom stage – what I have called, elsewhere, 'courtcraft' (Jones et. al. 1992).

The quality of the assessment seemed to me to be the cornerstone, since I considered that it lent both weight and credence to the other two areas. If you state you have only observed a child once in the company of a parent, it does not qualify you to make assessments about how the child feels, responds, and copes with a difficult situation. Given the fact that welfare officers are still considered 'the eyes and ears of the court', and that their contact with a child obviates the necessity for the Judge to see that child in person (an explanation of the role that I have heard many times from Judges) this part of the process is clearly of some significance. Equally, a child needs to know that their views and wishes have been heard, while at the same time being freed from the pressure to choose between two parents, although this, as Phillips (1993) attests, is a responsibility sometimes forgotten, which can have disastrous consequences. A full assessment, then, enables the child to become three dimensional, since it draws together aspects of family life, school life, and inner life, for want of a better term, so that the child comes alive as a person in their own right – a person who, after all, is the paramount consideration in law.

Conveying the quality of the child's experience was very much related to this first aspect. A sense of the child's social and physical world had been created – what was going on in it in relation to the family crisis of divorce? Often the most powerful way of communicating this was to use the child's own words – "I wish this was a video so you could wind it back to the time when it was good",...."my heart doesn't know how it feels inside" – or to offer a brief explanation of a piece of interaction which vividly conveyed how the child was feeling – the way, for example, in which Tanya cried and keened during interview when her father's absence was mentioned, or the fact that Liam, Jay and Carrie chose to play Monopoly during discussion of their future, caught up as they felt they were, in a game of chance.

Clearly, however, you have to be rather careful in offering an interpretation of such interaction in any definitive way, although it is possible to speculate on its meaning. Some of the children's comments will of course stand on their own, but care must be taken with descriptions of play or of drawings, so that they are placed in context and so that a possible interpretation, rather than a definitive one is offered, and then preferably connected up to information from other sources. In the case of Liam, Jay and Carrie, for example, they clearly stated that they were all very uncertain about what would happen, where they would be living and with whom, and felt that they had no control over this. The game of Monopoly confirmed this sense of helplessness, in my view, and could be used to support my hypothesis that beneath generally calm exteriors, the conflict between their parents was causing them all profound anxiety. A school report would often serve to confirm my sense of a child's isolation and depression; conversely it would be reassuring to know that a report contradicted that sense, suggesting perhaps that there was somewhere where the child could feel relaxed and secure.

An evaluation of a child's relationships also needs to be drawn from a number of different sources, and conveyed as such, incorporating what the adult says about it, what you yourself see when you watch it, what the child conveys about it when alone in interview, and even perhaps what other children in the family say about it. These different perspectives can often be offered without commentary, although it is useful to highlight incongruence or congruence between them.

My approach was to make observations based on what I had seen, incorporating aspects of play or drawing, without being specific. I would then use these as supplementary sources of information, when cross examined, rather than dwell in detail on them in the body of the report. I would, however, quote the child's words, when relevant. What I did go to great pains to avoid was the use of social work jargon, including terms associated with psychodynamic theory. In my experience, Judges dislike such language, and I can only assume that this is because it is over-used, abused and often totally meaningless as a result. Any interpretations, therefore, were put as simply as possibly, as were descriptions of family dynamics (which I did not, of course, describe as 'family dynamics'), the child's state of mind, and so on. By this means I felt that I was finding a language that could be precise, simple and clear.

In this Chapter, I have described the way in which techniques and games combined with the other elements of my approach in practice, and how I maintained my statutory role and function, while providing a short term, therapeutic service to children, as an aid to assessment and decision making in the court process. With this context in mind, I now move on to the detailed accounts of the work undertaken with the children, who are grouped according to the typology of adaptation described in the introduction – parental, despairing, retreating and angry.

# Chapter V: The Parental Child:
## Upholding the Broken End of the Arch

If we were like sisters to the world, it was because we were both children, and it seemed to me, more and more, that I was going to have to be the one to grow up, if we were to survive....the more I observed, the more I could see that we were one mother short and that it was going to have to be me that looked for the breadcrumbs and led us both from the forest.

Janet Hobhouse: The Furies

Who is it that can tell me who I am?

William Shakespeare: King Lear

For parents and children going through the experience of divorce, Lear's question is often an extremely relevant one. In the adult's case, the loss of a partner, a marriage, a social status, frequently re-activates past losses. Powerful feelings come into play – rage, despair, fear, murderous anger – as well as a sense of shame, failure, and intense rejection. The mature, responsible part of the self often becomes paralysed, and the parent is often catapulted back in time to a much earlier stage of development, where boundaries become confused and identity shifts and blurs, depending on mood or circumstance.

Parents frequently express their sense of being lost, confused and afraid, their need to be looked after, protected and cared for, and their child-like vulnerability in the face of what feels like an onslaught on every level. As one mother said to me, "All I ever hear is: what about the father? what about the child? Well, what about ME? I'm a thirty-five year old child – when is anyone going to listen to me?" She then marched out of the room. After a pause her eight year old son, Will, appeared. He gave me a knowing look, and said, in a long-suffering, matter-of-fact voice: "Well, you know what she's like now. She often goes off like that." He was speaking with resignation about the vagaries of a wayward child; the child happened to be his mother.

For the child, changes in parents' behaviour can be confusing, frightening and worrying. Grown-ups, after all, are supposed to have a grip on things, to know what they are doing and to behave in a certain way – otherwise what is the point in having them in the first place? Their job is to provide a safe, secure place to be a child – to provide what Winnicott (1971) describes as a "holding" environment and to keep their worries and their problems to themselves. Dressing like teenagers, crying into the washing up, getting drunk, staring into space, asking you to sleep with them in their bed tonight, and discussing problems – even consulting you about decisions – just doesn't seem right. It's flattering, of course, but it's also muddling, especially when at any second the parent may suddenly revert to 'adult' mode, remember that *you* are the child and start treating you like one.

The children who will be encountered in this chapter are those I have chosen to call 'parental' children. By 'parental' I mean that their principal response to what was happening in their lives was to become more adult than usual or more adult than the adults – watchful, anxious, concerned, responsible, protective, and censorious – so that effectively they could be seen as either taking over the role left vacant by the departed parent or standing in for the remaining parent, who had abnegated responsibility in response to their loss. This also seemed to suggest a denial that anyone or anything had in fact been lost. Such children were characterised by their preoccupation with adult concerns and anxieties, and in their play, frequently took on the role of the adult, a tendency observed by Klein (1955) who opined that the child did so to "not only express his wish to reverse the roles, but also demonstrating how he feels that his parents or other people in authority behave towards him – or *should* behave" (Klein in Mitchell 1986).

Parental children are not 'created' simply by experiencing their parents' separation and I do not intend to suggest this. What did seem significant, however, was the degree of adult maturity assumed by some of the children – particularly the very young – which may have had its roots in pre-separation behaviour, but appeared to take on a more serious tone, especially in inverse proportion to the loss of adult functioning in the parent. It must also be said that all the children who feature in this Chapter are either only children or the older/eldest in the family. Research indicates that such children, by virtue of their position, are more likely to adopt a mature veneer, as a matter of course, although it also suggests that the picture is inevitably over simplified and is considerably more complex (Dunn 1990). I will be arguing, however, that despite this, the level of grown-up behaviour still appeared to be unusual, by general standards, and that this was due to the experience of loss, separation and parental conflict to which they were exposed. What I hope to show is the ways in which theoretical concepts were applied to working with children, and how I attempted to explore, experiment with and clarify existing models, in order to put together a workable typology of my own. I also hope to demonstrate the constellation of kinds of behaviour that are common to these children, so that questions related to what this might mean, under what circumstances might this occur and what should be done about it can be considered (see Chapter IX).

Children who feel obliged to take on a parental role in relation to their parent or parents can tread a dangerous and uncertain path. Their parents often have mixed feelings about this, which can mean that assistance given and concerns expressed can be appreciated one moment but resented the next, and help with the other children can be seen both as a valuable source of support but also as an implicit criticism. As the child's sense of responsibility increases, so do its worries, which often extend to boyfriends/girlfriends, working hours, and brothers and sisters. Once entrenched in this adult persona, it becomes harder and harder to go back to being a child, to play, to ask for affection. The child gets lost and lonely and it gets harder to remember who you are supposed to be.

Wallerstein and Kelly (1980) found that such children fell into two categories – those they describe as "Empathetic" and those who have become victims of what they call "Role reversal". In the former category, they argued that the children gained something valuable from being able to support and care for a parent during a difficult time, provided it was only for a limited period. In the latter category, however, it seemed clear that assuming responsibility for a parent over a long period of time could have serious consequences in later life, where children's own needs had been unmet due to the overwhelming nature of those of the parent, and the fact that the child had not been able to be freed from the burden they represented – a conclusion that seemed to be borne out, at least in part, by follow-up studies (Wallerstein 1989).

Although I found these two categories useful in thinking about this particular issue, my own exerience suggests that at the time that the worker becomes involved, one is frequently faced with children in a category that falls somewhere in between, and where it is too soon to tell how long the dynamic is likely to last, and therefore what the likely consequences might be if nothing is done to address it. I therefore chose to make the assumption that what both children and parents trapped in this dynamic most needed at such a point was help to enable them to be clear about their respective roles and identities, so they could resume their appropriate places. What follows will be an attempt to both illustrate this dynamic and look at ways of working with it.

## Sophie

Sophie was nearly five when I met her for the first time. Poised, articulate, and sharing Will's matter-of-fact manner, and exasperated yet resigned attitude to her mother, she was none the less clearly worried about her and maintained a vigilant oversight which would have exhausted a lesser child. Sophie and her brother Sean, aged two, were the children of a very young mother and a violent, abusive father who drank to excess and even after the separation, despite injunctions, would come to the home and cause scenes. Sophie was witness to many of these and had seen her mother's distress and anger graphically expressed. She could see that her mother was vulnerable and upset and did her best to look after her – was she alright? Wasn't her skirt a bit too short? "Pull it down a bit, Mum!" Had she noticed that Sean needed his nappy changing? She would often put her hands on her hips, looking quite disapproving, while alternating between mothering Sean and competing with him. Sophie's mother would, in her turn, alternate between expecting Sophie to look after Sean, criticising her if she failed to do so, and suddenly becoming angry at the implicit suggestion that she could not manage her son herself.

When Sophie came to the office for our second individual meeting she brought her baby, Emma, with her and gave her to me to look after, once we were settled in the play house. This seemed to me to be an indication that there was a baby part of herself which needed attention, and that this was a safe way of asking for it. She told me that her "little girl" still wasn't quite right but could not say what was wrong. Bustling anxiously about the house, she seemed to all intents and purposes the epitome of the harassed parent with too much on her mind. A lengthy game ensued, in which Sophie became the devoted mother of four children – including me – whom she tended with great dedication. Although she denied it was hard work, she made it clear that she got no help at all from the children's father – "he's useless" she told me, with contempt, adding that he was always drunk and never did anything round the house. Sophie's play consistently reflected adult concerns – tidying the house, meticulously folding the children's clothes, making sure the children were being good, and worrying about burglars. Ceaseless activity accompanied this play, and a sense of overwhelming responsibility which often seemed unbearable both to her, and to me – there seemed no end to her tasks and anxieties, and no solutions to her problems.

In contrast to this game, which so closely reflected what I had come to learn about the real life of her mother, Sophie's 'play' period with her mother and Sean struck me as artificial. She became falsely cheerful, very manic and seemed to find it difficult to play in any way for more than a few minutes at a time. The similarity, however, was the constant need for activity. This seemed to suggest a denial that something had happened, something was wrong. As Jewett (1984) observes "by keeping very busy, a child can avoid thinking about what has happened". Her mother, by comparison, was teasing and provocative, encouraging Sean to react jealously to the fact that she was giving Sophie a cuddle. The overall effect was of two people confused about who they were and which was supposed to be which. Unfortunately this situation deteriorated so dramatically that Sophie was eventually taken into care and placed with foster parents. I was struck by the fact, that once Sophie had settled, both her foster parents and her social worker reported that she was able to shed her adult persona to some degree and had started to behave in a more child-like manner.

## Camilla

Camilla's predicament was slightly different. She had taken on the task of watching over two parents who had abnegated their roles almost completely, to the extent that it seemed as though they had forgotten they had a dependent child at all, unless or until it seemed expedient to use her in their marital battle. Although in the middle of divorce proceedings, Camilla's parents continued to live in the same house in which the tension was often palpable. Camilla's mother had become increasingly timid, depressed and dependent; her father's behaviour had become increasingly adolescent and he persistently and openly abused drugs. Camilla, aged eight, felt duty bound to share herself equally between her charges, and ensure that they were looked after. Although eventually she was able to express her anger about this (see Chapter VIII), in general she maintained a poised, mature, calm and controlled attitude to the entire affair, on one occasion describing aspects of their behaviour as "a game they were playing". My overall impression was of a child who was dealing with the intensely painful experience of being torn in two by imposing control on chaos, exhibiting a false maturity which constituted a denial that anything was amiss, and yet conveying an intense level of anxiety – both very much features of the early stages of grief (Jewitt op. cit.).

On Camilla's first visit to my office – our second actual meeting, the first having taken place at her home – she displayed a considerable understanding of the reasons behind her parents' decision to divorce. "Before I was born," she said, in a very grown up, matter of fact way, hands neatly folded in her lap, "Daddy had all Mummy's attention and all her love and when I was born, Mummy gave me all her attention and Daddy was jealous." It emerged that Camilla had been burdened by both parents with a wealth of detail about their relationship, although she had also had personal experience of their arguments to enable her to draw her own conclusions. Despite her apparent sophistication, however, Camilla used our sessions together to play – and generally to play with toys more suited to younger children, suggesting a degree of regression common to the acute stage of grief. Her favourites were a set of wooden anteaters – large, medium and small – that fitted inside one another rather like a nest of tables (see Chapter IV Fig. 6). On her first visit, she made them into mother, father and baby, placing them in a row, nose to tail, with the baby at the back. However she soon became concerned about the baby's position, commenting that this wasn't a very safe place for it to be as anyone could snatch it away and neither of the parents would notice. She then tried to rearrange the anteaters in a variety of ways, in the hope that the baby might feel safer if the parents had a better view of it and could see it more clearly. This seemed to me an eloquent expression of Camilla's own predicament and her sense of being overlooked. At one point in the game, while the mother and father were preparing supper one evening, the baby simply wandered away. No-one noticed.

Like many of the most troubled children in the sample, Camilla seemed reluctant to leave a safe place where she had the room to be a child, and where her anxieties could be expressed and accepted. I reminded her that she would be coming to see me soon when she would be able to play once again and it was Camilla who added "And come and talk." On her second visit, Camilla resumed her play with the anteaters, and we recalled the previous game in which the baby's safety had been such a preoccupation. I suggested to Camilla that the baby's predicament was very much like her own and she was able to acknowledge that this was true. Her increasing absorption with finding a place for the baby seemed to reflect her anxiety about her future, as she tried to fit it into some comfortable relation to the other figures.

Several important worries then seemed to emerge. Firstly, there was an issue about whether babies fitted better with mummies or daddies. Having experimented with the anteaters in various permutations, Camilla said she felt that the baby fitted best in the hollow of the mother's body – "after all, babies come out of mummies' tummies", she said, sagely, connecting this with something she had seen on television about divorce, and adding "Other people I know are with their mummies because they came out of their tummies", confirming findings from McGurk and Glachan's research (1987). To make absolutely sure that she had come to the right conclusion, she then struggled to fit the baby and the Daddy together but sadly concluded "There's just no way the baby will fit, there's just no way." We talked about how bad this felt and how distant she and her father seemed to have become.

The second issue seemed to be connected with Camilla's struggle to come to terms with the loss of the 'ideal' family that had once existed, and the reality of divorce. Still calm and composed, Camilla fitted the anteaters together, with the Daddy protecting the mother and the baby. We talked about how good it would be if things could be that way for her, but, unfortunately, Mummy and Daddy could no longer fit together, and Camilla was able to acknowledge that this was true. "When they're divorced, they'll be more like this" she said, separating the three figures so there were spaces in between. "It'll all be looser". I agreed with this, and helped her to experiment with different ways to place the Daddy anteater so that he was still accessible, in view. This proved difficult, and we talked about the fact that, although Camilla was pretty fed up with Daddy, and often angry with him, she still wanted to hang on to him very much and was afraid he would drift away and that she would lose him. Once again, this seemed to reflect a parental concern for a wayward offspring who might not manage too well on his own, as well as a considerable attachment to a father, who, despite his shortcomings, was an important figure.

The third preoccupation seemed, once more, to be connected with Camilla's uncertainty about both her parents' capacity to look after themselves, and more specifically, her mother's ability to cope alone. Still absorbed with the family she had created, Camilla persistently placed the baby on top of the parent – "Watching over them" as she put it. I commented that I thought this was too difficult a job for a baby to do, and that Camilla must often feel in a similar position. I added that, although her parents were lucky to have her to look after them, this was not her job, and that I was going to try to help them sort out the best way to separate so that she could remain friends with both of them, and they could resume looking after her, instead of the other way round. I felt it was important to acknowledge that when grown-ups were upset they often behaved in odd ways which didn't seem grown up at all, but that, usually, when the upset was over, they went back to being the way they used to. This enabled Camilla to talk about some of her parents' behaviour, and also seemed to reassure her that at least she had someone with whom she could share her task, even if she did not feel quite ready to give it up altogether. Her particular worry seemed to be related to the size of the Mummy anteater, who seemed rather small. She raised this several times, and it seemed to be her way of expressing her concern about her mother's capacity to cope alone, meet her needs – was she big enough for the job? Like Oliver (see Chapter VIII) who was so convinced of his mother's "smallness" and fragility, Camilla had seen a frightening vulnerability in the parent who would, in all probability, be taking sole care of her, emphasising the point by referring, periodically, to "Poor Mummy" waiting downstairs. I let her know that I was aware of what was worrying her and would continue to see both her and her mother until things felt safer. While continuing to prepare the welfare report, I was able to encourage Camilla's mother to transfer some of her dependence from her child on to me, helping her to cope with her feelings of helplessness, loss and despair, and make some room in her world for the needs of her eight year old. As a result she became more able to see Camilla as a child, rather than a confidante, and during some sessions which included Camilla, I was able to help her tell her mother about what she needed and the help she wanted, whilst Camilla in her turn was encouraged to see her mother as someone who had been incapacitated for a while, but who was now beginning to take charge once more.

## Robert

Clearly, for the only child, in such circumstances, the parental responsibility was particularly burdensome. Robert (see Chapter VIII), very conscious that, now he had been left alone with his mother, he was "the man of the house – all she has left", had a special anxiety about her, due to her suicide attempt after his parents separated, causing him to become prematurely adult to an alarming degree. This, coupled with his difficult relationship with his father resulted in a strange sense of isolation from both his parents, and his response to this was to become so self-sufficient that he was effectively parenting himself for a period of almost two years.

## Rachel

Rachel responded in a similar way, although for different reasons. Rachel's parents had been teenage sweethearts, marrying young and giving birth to her within a year. According to the accounts they had given me, neither had really been ready for either the responsibility of one another or of a child, and arguments began, often involving the smashing of objects, verbal abuse and considerable violence, on both sides. Rachel's mother freely admitted that she had had some understandable difficulty bonding with her, particularly as she felt she had to compete with her for her husband's attention. Effectively, two young children were trying to parent an infant. Ultimately, Rachel's mother felt she had no alternative but to leave. Since she had nowhere to go she decided to leave Rachel with her father. Access took place in an atmosphere of intense acrimony, often punctuated by further arguments. It was against this backdrop that I became involved; Rachel's mother had accepted that, at this point, Rachel should stay with her father, although she wanted reassurance that the arrangements for her care were appropriate. The task, then, was to resolve the dispute about contact and establish whether or not

Rachel was being properly cared for.

I first met Rachel eight months or so after the separation. She was three and a half, a sturdy, energetic, articulate little girl, with a very independent streak, and a rather sophisticated husky voice. She was extremely suspicious of me when I visited her home, and kept checking to make sure her father was alright, during his discussion with me, obviously anxious about him and needing to keep him in view. It felt rather like courting in the presence of a maiden aunt – generally parents exhibited this kind of watchful behaviour during my discussions with their children; I had never experienced it in reverse before. During the course of a lengthy stay, Rachel assessed me with her wary, sombre gaze, while bustling about doing her 'ironing', and playing with her dolls in a very motherly way. She declined her grandmother's suggestion that she show me her bedroom, and only relented, some time later, when her father agreed to come too. During the time we spent together, her father was not actually in the room, but she was only prepared to see me provided he stayed close by, and she regularly called out to him to ask, in rather imperious tones, what he was doing – on one level, in her parental role, to check he wasn't getting up to any mischief and on another to reassure the abandoned child in her that she had not lost her father too.

Rachel's response to the explanation of who I was and why I had come was minimal, although she did eventually give me a toy to look after for a while, as though to test my ability in this area, in case she should consider entrusting anything really important to my care. I told her that I was going to ask her father to bring her in to see me so that we could have a private talk. "I don't want him to go," said Rachel. On one level this seemed to be a clear anxiety on the part of a little girl who had already 'lost' one parent, about losing the other. However it also had an intensely protective quality about it. What gradually emerged was Rachel's wish that she and Daddy could stay in the house together and not go anywhere. Clearly, in her eyes, they had become a couple and this had to be protected. The obvious interpretation, taking a Freudian model, would be that Rachel's ultimate fantasy had come true – mother had been removed and she was free to 'marry' her father. On another level, however, Rachel had been made aware of her father's distress and fragility and was trying her best to take care of him. During my discussion with Rachel's father, he spoke with pride about the way in which Rachel brought him cups of tea, and asked what he wanted for his dinner. He, in his turn, was now inclined to consult her over decisions – for example which day they should come to the office and at what time. He also made it apparent that, as far as access was concerned, this was Rachel's decision, and that he would simply go along with her wishes. It was equally apparent that he was not keen on any contact taking place, due to his pain over the separation, and his views about Rachel's mother. He made this quite explicit during our conversation; Rachel had been left with no illusions about his attitude, and therefore was not free to express a wish of her own that she knew to be different from his.

When Rachel came to see me at the office, I reminded her of our last meeting, and that I knew that she was a bit confused about where Mummy had gone and whether she should see her or not, because she was aware that Daddy was worried about it. We talked about the possibility that if she said she wanted to see Mummy, this might upset Daddy, and about Rachel's awareness of how upset Daddy had already been, due to Mummy's departure. We also talked about how upset Rachel had been, and she told me she could remember arguments and shouting – "Mummy cut Daddy with a knife." Although initially she said that she had seen this incident, it subsequently emerged that Daddy had in fact told her about it. What was clear, however, was Rachel's concern at the prospect of Mummy and Daddy coming into contact with one another – she felt this would not be a good idea although couldn't say why, but added that she knew they didn't love one another. Once again, a Freudian model would suggest an obvious motive for such a concern, as well as highlighting the tensions in this triangular relationship, and Rachel's mixed feelings towards her mother, who was both wished away and wanted. My view was that Rachel felt a real responsibility to protect her parents from one another, and was expressing a clear anxiety about their capacity to behave in a grown-up way.

During our discussion, Rachel was playing with a wooden boat full of little figures. When I asked her what was happening in her game, she told me that all the wooden figures were little girls and that the boat was their play school too. I was struck by the fact that, in this little world of Rachel's, there were no adult figures – a confirmation, perhaps, of the fact that neither parent felt 'adult' or 'grown-up' to her. After a while, however, she decided that Daddy had to leave play school and go home – even though she identified him as a "little Daddy", implying, perhaps that he was not quite ready to move on, but none the less she felt that he should. I wondered whether this was a way of telling me about what Rachel needed from her father, as well as an enactment of a rapid growing up process that she herself felt she had undergone. The family of anteaters were also drawn into this game, although they were all identified as being Rachels of different sizes. Her sense of responsibility for being her parent's parent seemed graphically illustrated when she placed the baby sized Rachel on top of the largest one, rather as Camilla had done.

Rachel then chose to play with a large wooden elephant puzzle, which had, as an integral piece, a baby elephant that fits under the mother (see Chapter IV). Rachel took the puzzle apart, but found she was unable to put it together again, and as though picking up the symbolic significance of this, I found that I was unable to do so either. At this point I found myself feeling very anxious, and quite impotent – surely at my age I ought to be able to master a simple puzzle? I realised, however, that I was in fact picking up something very powerful in the counter-transference and that Rachel's feelings of acute anxiety and helplessness were overwhelming me, giving me an important clue about her real state of mind, covered over by her grown up façade. Using this feeling, then, we talked about how uncertain and powerless she must be feeling, how hard it is to lose a Mummy and how difficult it was to put the bits of her family together again, so that things would go back to being the way they used to be.

As the pieces would not create the picture she wanted, Rachel chose to use them to build the walls of a castle, adding the anteaters for good measure. She placed all the wooden figures inside the wall and seemed very satisfied with the result. Then she said "I want to build a house," and did so, placing the smallest anteater, whom she referred to as the baby, carefully inside. When I asked her about this baby, Rachel told me that her name was "Rachel", she was three, and lived alone. I said it was unusual for someone of three to live alone, and I wondered whether this baby ever got lonely or frightened and Rachel admitted that she did – in fact a large blue dolphin was attacking the house, making a loud noise, and Rachel said this was very frightening. The outside world had clearly become an unsafe and unpredictable place for this little girl, and her sense of being alone and unprotected was quite acute. As this seemed to reflect my earlier feelings about her true state, I felt more confident to explore it. As we talked about this, Rachel placed some additional toys in the house, but made it apparent that these were things and not people. She then covered the baby up completely, commenting that now she was all covered up she felt better. I thought that perhaps she had gained some sense of protection from the fact that her anxiety, loneliness and fear had been heard and understood, and as I talked to her about this, I also made it clear that I felt that it would be good for her to see Mummy again, so that she could be reassured that she was alright. I told her that I understood her worry about Daddy's reaction to her seeing Mummy again, and asked her whether, if I could persuade Daddy it was a good idea, she would feel better about it. "Yes," said Rachel, emphatically. We then agreed that I would be telling Daddy this, as I did not think it was the sort of decision she should be left to make on her own.

Although Rachel seemed relaxed and happy by this stage, and had turned her attention to playing with the doll's house, I still suspected that her worries were only just below the surface.

Apparently out of the blue – although clearly connected with our discussion about her missing Mummy – Rachel said "Oh, Daddy isn't here any more – he's disappeared!" I said that I knew that it must feel as though he had disappeared, as he was no longer in the room, but he was in fact waiting downstairs. However, I also acknowledged that when one parent disappears, there is always a fear that the other one will, and that perhaps she feels that Mummy has disappeared and will never be seen again. When Rachel confirmed this anxiety, I reminded her that I had seen Mummy, spoken to her, and knew that she missed her and wanted to see her again. We talked about what she looked like, and Rachel could remember their last meeting, when she had gone through her mother's hand bag and tried on her lipstick. It seemed particularly important to bring the lost person back into consciousness, and thus give Rachel permission to talk about her – something that was not allowed at home. By the end of our session Rachel was more content and was able to listen calmly and without anxiety to my conversation with her father, and the arrangements for the first access. I was also able to help him to convince her that he understood that she wanted to see her Mummy and that he would help her to do so, although he admitted he would still be worried about it for a while, until he saw how it went. Regular contact was eventually established, and although there were problems from time to time, Rachel somehow managed to hold on to both her parents, while coping with the periodic battles that still raged between them.

Like Sophie, Rachel demonstrated the tendency in the prematurely adult children that I met to express their concerns through an intermediary – a toy, a doll, a 'baby' figure – so that the baby part of the self could be attended to and heard in a safe way, without relinquishing the adult persona. The sense of isolation experienced by these children was particularly striking, and one might assume that, had they had brothers or sisters, the burden could have been reduced and the worry shared. What I found, however, was that a parental child, rather than gaining support from other children in the family, simply took on responsibility for them as well, replacing or assisting the non functioning parent as caretaker and protector. Anxiety in all the children was often projected onto one; the child subsystem in the family then regulated itself accordingly (Burnham 1986; Preston-Shoot 1990). As a consequence, this often freed other children in the family to respond to the conflict between their parents in a more natural, child-like way, and removed much of the anxiety and worry, since this was effectively being carried by one child. Although on one level the parental child gained a sense of self worth from playing this part, a wistful desire for release was often apparent, as were intermittent bursts of envy and anger towards the other, more carefree children when the burden became too great.

## Liam, Jay and Carrie

Liam, Jay and Carrie were eleven, nine and seven when I met them for the first time. Their parents were still living together, although had been trying to get divorced for the preceding three years. The delay had been caused by a number of factors, including a long wait for a court date. One welfare report had already been prepared but was then found to be so out of date that another was ordered. Liam clearly saw himself as the spokesman for the group and was very conscious of his role as the "eldest" child, aware of the serious predicament the family was in. All the children knew that both parents wanted the children to live with them, and made it clear that they were unable to chose between them. What I found striking was the qualitative difference in their attitudes to the problem and their methods of dealing with it.

For Liam it was evidently a serious and persistent worry, manifested by an almost constant expression of gravity and wariness, and a marked reluctance to discuss the matter more than was absolutely necessary. I also got a clear sense that he listened carefully to comments made by Jay and Carrie, as though acting as judge and censor, in order to maintain the party line. Despite being the least keen to talk to me, he eventually gave me a complicated practical task to do, requiring considerable delicacy (rather like the resolution of his family's situation) which felt to me rather like a test of both my patience and dexterity. He then unashamedly showed me his collection of cuddly toys – again, an indication both of a degree of regression (Jewett op. cit.) and perhaps a wish to provide me with a clue that a softer, smaller, younger, more vulnerable self coexisted with this young adult persona. Liam's position as self appointed watch dog freed Jay to adopt a more flexible role as equivocator, holding the balance of pros and cons of what each parent had to offer, and frequently acting as mediator between them, distributing himself with sensitivity and fairness. Lucky Carrie was freest of all – protected in any event by being the youngest, and rather spoilt as the only girl, she knew that the boys had a grip on the situation and apart from complaining that they were often horrible to her, she did not appear either worried or anxious about the future, but was able to retreat from the fray, as though it was not happening.

On their first visit to the unit, all three children chose to spend the time playing Monopoly. This struck me as a clear symbolic representation of the game of chance in which they must have felt they had become involved. My comment to this effect was met with no reaction at all, however. By their second visit Liam was beginning to express his weariness and anger about having to be so grown up, attacking Jay and eventually retreating in tears of rage. We were able to talk about some of their fears and anxieties and the fact that the anger they began to express to and about one another was in fact to do with what their parents were doing to them, and they were more able to share some of their sadness and confusion, enabling Liam to release some of his grown up hold on the situation, by retreating into boisterous play, and 'beating up' a large stuffed toy with great abandon.

## Paul and Peter

Paul's situation, although similar to Liam's, was even more acute. Paul and his brother Peter were thirteen and nine respectively when their mother decided to divorce their father, and I became involved very soon afterwards. Paul's father was in his sixties, a diminutive but robust man who had married a woman many years younger than himself, with a history of mental difficulties. As the marriage deteriorated, there were increasing arguments between the parents, often culminating in violence on both sides, and Paul's mother became increasingly girlish, abstracted and vague, leaving the gas on and wandering around the house in the early hours of the morning. The strain of the proceedings also told on Paul's father who, during the course of the preparation of the welfare report, had a minor heart attack. The family continued to live under the same roof while a fierce battle raged, both over the children and the house.

This was clearly not a safe place to be. Visiting the home, I was struck by the sense of abandonment and disintegration – wallpaper peeling from the walls, old drawings done by the children years before, clinging forlornly to their drawing pins. Paul was a serious looking boy, with a rather quaint turn of phrase, who exuded anxiety, and who had responded to the spectacle of his parents squabbling like children by adopting the role of the referee cum peacemaker, often coming between them and simply shouting "Shut up!" as loudly as he could. In between, he cared for his brother, cheering him up, helping him with his homework, and giving him affectionate pats and prods, coping with his tears and talking to him about his worries about what would happen to them when their parents separated. After a difficult first meeting in their bleak house, with both Paul and Peter apparently in shock – another characteristic of the acute stage of grief (Jewett op. cit) paralysed by a mixture of suspicion, uncertainty and sorrow, they came to the unit and we began the gentle process of discussion.

"It's always up there," Paul told me, pointing to his head, as we discussed his fears about the future. When it became really bad, he said, he tended to go on a bike ride or have a skirmish with Peter – "It helps to bend the old knees a bit." The real problem was that whichever parent Paul and Peter lived with was likely to continue to cause Paul acute anxiety since they were both fragile and in need of supervision, as far as he could see. The sense of the inescapability of his inappropriate adult responsibility was a massive burden, but one that Paul found too dangerous ro relinquish – too dangerous, because, as we were to discover, it masked a huge and terrible anger that could not be permitted to escape.

Paul was, initially, very concerned at the prospect of Peter seeing me on his own and they agreed, between them, that Paul would be present. Peter sat close to his brother, occasionally touching Paul's foot with his own, as though to gain courage and strength. While Paul held the worry, Peter was free to express all the sadness, pain and desolation that the loss of the family had caused. During the sessions that followed, both children became increasingly able to talk about their feelings, and I was able to gain a clear sense of the extent of Paul's burden. This helped me to convey his predicament to his parents, and I encouraged them to see the urgency of resuming their adult responsibility, to free Paul from carrying it for them. Although they both found this difficult, and it was hard to relinquish the habit of 'using' him in their battle, they were able to free him to a limited extent, releasing him from the role of referee. As a result, he became able to talk about his anger and Peter was able to tell him how much Paul's care and support mattered. Meanwhile I continued to help both parents assume their adult personae once again, so that they could demonstrate to their children that they could cope, and were no longer in need of their son's supervision. By parenting both the children and the parents during a critical time, they reached a stage where they felt able to resume their rightful positions in relation to one another. Both children continued to actively seek sessions with me after the report was prepared and prior to the court hearing. Ultimately the children's mother decided to agree to the children remaining with their father and obtained generous contact, which was fully encouraged by their father.

## Carla

Carla, at four, was encountering similar problems to Paul, although only in relation to one parent – her mother. She was quite clear that her mother needed someone to look after her, and that she and her two year old sister Amy could do with a bit of a break in the care of someone else, until her mother was strong again. "You have a talk with Miss Kroll," she used to say, with a benign and indulgent air, when her mother brought the children to the unit. She was always very reluctant to leave, and when I visited the home she would watch my departure from the window, waving sadly. Once again, using counter-transference reactions, I was frequently left with a sense of desperation and a longing to make things right for her. The sense that Carla was yearning and pining for her father's return, a different end to her story, was clearly communicated by the intensity of her gaze as she stared out from behind the curtains.

Carla and Amy were the children of very young parents, whose marriage had been precipitated by pregnancy. The births of both children caused severe post natal depression, with psychotic symptoms, and this, coupled with the stresses caused by two young children, as well as financial problems, put the marriage under considerable strain. After a protracted period of violence and bitter argument, the children's mother petitioned for divorce, and had her husband removed from the house by court order. Custody was in dispute, the children's father arguing that their mother was not mentally or emotionally fit to look after them.

Carla made her dilemma clear from the outset. On the one hand, she rather enjoyed keeping her eye on her mother, asking after her health and drawing attention to what Amy was doing. On the other, however, she could see from the way that Amy was treated, that being a baby had much to recommend it, so at our first meeting, she climbed onto my lap, drinking from a feeding cup, and making grunting noises, rather like a small animal. Any discussion about her parents' situation, even when not directed at her was unbearable – "Don't talk," she begged her mother, and moved backwards and forwards between us to create a diversion, as though intense activity could mask, block or eradicate what was going on – hyperactivity as denial. A little later she told us about a game she had played when she was at Granny's – "I was Mummy *and* Daddy when I was at Granny's and I'm going to be Mummy and Daddy here." Then she decided that in fact she was just going to be Daddy, Amy was going to be Mummy, and her mother and I were going to be sisters – effectively turning the children into adults and vice versa. This was the first of many attempts, as I saw it, to either fuse Mummy and me into one person, or to get me to take responsibility for her. On a subsequent visit, Carla brought me her mother's shoes to wear, expressing a wish to exchange them so that her mother could wear mine. She then decided to wear them herself, but found that they were too big – a way of telling me the extent to which she was trying to take on her mother's role, but how difficult she was finding it. She also needed me to know about her mother's fragility – "Are you better now?" she asked her, on one occasion. When her mother denied that she had been unwell, Carla ignored her, as you would a wilful child, and simply added, reassuringly "You're better now – the doctor will make you better."

What gradually emerged, in the course of my work, was that Carla's mother had spent her childhood in care, had taken on adult responsibility very young, and was now finding that the breakdown of her marriage had caused such confusion that she had found herself catapulted back to a much earlier stage of development, leaving

Carla to take over from her. Rather than finding this a comfort, she was experiencing Carla's vigilance as intensely persecutory and, as a consequence, their relationship was deteriorating. They were totally muddled up in one another's worlds – two lost, bereft children with a toddler to look after.

Carla's play, like Sophie's, reflected adult preoccupations with the home and the care of babies, although she found it difficult to become involved in anything active or imaginative in relation to this. She would sit in the play house, gazing out of the window and making comments about snow and her fear that there was a wolf outside, but this was all very matter of fact, and she retained a calm and poised composure throughout. Like many of the other children, she saw the unit as a sanctuary, often pretending that it was my home, and being reluctant to leave. During the course of a game with the doll's house, Carla identified the various dolls inside in terms of being mummies and babies. She placed a baby doll in the arms of a mother doll, ensuring that the pipe cleaner arms of the latter were firmly wrapped round the former. We talked about how good it would be if she and Mummy could be that close, but that there was a gap between them that we would have to try to remove. Carla then chose another baby, identifying it as Amy, and placed it in the arms of a doll she named as her Mummy. The third baby was called "Carla" and once again, was placed in the arms of a larger figure. When I asked who was holding Carla, the real Carla replied "Nobody". We talked about how perhaps she felt that no-one was holding on to her at the moment and that although she felt quite grown up sometimes, there was still a baby part of her inside that needed lots of cuddling. I told her that I was going to help both her and Mummy to sort this out and that I could feel how hard and difficult it was at the moment. Soon after this Carla asked to leave the office and go and see Mummy who was waiting downstairs. She immediately rushed up to her and gave her a big hug.

My work with this family centred on giving Carla's mother the time to try and look at her own childhood experiences so that she felt the vulnerable, child-like part of herself was being attended to. This gave us a little room to look at the real children in the family, so that it was possible to see them as they really were – sad, confused little people, coping with the loss of their father, and with the bewilderment of seeing their mother acting in a very different way. Gradually the sense of competition and criticism diminished and I was able to help Carla's mother to reclaim her children, as well as resume her adult role, while working with Carla to try to free her from some of her anxieties and encourage her to remember the baby part of herself which had effectively been wiped out. "I never was a baby," she told me, sadly. "I'm a big girl." Eventually, together, we were able to begin to fill in this gap in her experience.

## Sally

Sally shared Carla's concern about her mother's capacity to cope on her own and to attend to the needs of her little sister Laura, who was only four. She, at least, was a very grown up person of seven, and therefore knew about these things. Sally had seen her mother hit by her father, and was aware that contact with him caused her mother anxiety and distress. Despite her obvious attachment to him, therefore, she judged it politic to accept her mother's decision to terminate contact, with the result that she did not see her father for two years. Although ostensibly she was allowed to express a view about this, she was well aware of what this view was expected to be.

I became involved when Sally's father applied for a residence order, on the grounds that a fit mother would not withhold contact in the way in which she had. Sally, of course, being in her mother's confidence, knew all about this, and, furthermore, had been informed that I was coming to see them to find out who they wanted to live with. As a result, the first thing that had to be done was to make my role a little bit clearer, emphasising my wish to find out what they thought about what was happening, and talk about any worries they might have about it. I also stressed my wish to help their parents make a decision about their future, because I didn't think this was a decision they should be left to make for themselves. Sally's response to this was to declare that "Daddy should be taught a lesson," adding that she thought a grown-up should do this. I said I had a feeling she meant me and she agreed that this was true. Implicit in this seemed to me to be her lack of confidence in her mother to take on this task – perhaps even an indication that she was no longer sure whether her mother was a grown-up or not. This confusion had been intensified for her, I think, by the fact that after the separation, mother and children had moved in with mother's parents, from whom, according to the children's father, she had never really separated. The children had therefore seen their mother in the role of a child again, and it became unclear whose responsibility it was to parent the real children in the family.

Sally obviously enjoyed her grown-up role some of the time, and proudly told me that "Mummy has told me everything about this" – including details of the property dispute that was also raging at the same time. "When we get the money from Daddy, I'll be allowed to do gymnastics!" She confirmed that she knew Daddy wanted her and Laura to live with him, echoing her mother's belief that he was only asking for them to hurt her. However, she spoke of him without any hostility or rancour and although she knew about things that he had done "before I was born" and that "He was a bully – he used to bully Mummy", she also acknowledged that he didn't bully *her*, and conceded that it was possible to be quite good as a Daddy, even though you might not be very good at being a husband. It was apparent that she enjoyed going to see him, although it was difficult to admit this to Mummy, but she made it equally clear that she wanted to live with Mummy and thought that Laura did too, "but I don't want to tell Daddy this because I don't want to make him angry".

Being grown-up and diplomatic, however, as well as keeping an eye on Laura and ensuring that her mother knew when she needed to go to the lavatory, was clearly getting quite exhausting. In addition it was cutting Sally off from her own needs – particularly for affection and physical and emotional 'holding' – and I was struck by how unable she was to ask for affection for herself, but, like many of these grown up children, could only make contact through toys. While Laura – an equally needy child – instantly climbed onto my lap, hugging me, asking to come home with me, and demanding attention, Sally was unable to be so explicit. Her first move was to give me a special toy to look after – a common test of trustworthiness to which I have already referred. She then issued a challenge – "I bet you can't pick me up" – but responded very affectionately when I did so. When I was leaving, Sally informed me that her toy wanted to kiss me goodbye and duly did so.

During visits to the unit, Sally often chose to play the 'squiggle game' (see Chapter IV) which I had taught her. Each time she drew a squiggle which she identified as a worm; each time she gave it to me she asked me to turn it into a snail, by drawing it a shell to "keep it warm and safe". This seemed to me to be an eloquent expression of her desire to have the vulnerable part of herself taken care of – a sign that she was perhaps not as grown up as she would like to have us believe. Other elements of her behaviour bore this out; they will be described in Chapter VII.

As with Carla's family, my work with Sally and her mother centred on helping Sally to relinquish her burdensome adult responsibilities, and regain confidence in her mother's capacity to parent. Meanwhile, I had to drag mother. protesting somewhat, back out of the childhood into which she had retreated, and help her to free her children to be children once again. In this work I was able to use what I had learned about what it was like to be Sally, once again using my feelings in the counter-transference, and to talk to her mother, in her presence, about the difference between decisions children could make and those they could not, divided loyalties, diplomacy and what children needed to know, as opposed to what they could not assimilate. During these discussions, Sally initially looked from her mother to me with some anxiety, moving across us, unsure of where she was in relation to what was happening. However, when she heard her mother accept that worries about access and where children should live were for grown-ups to sort out, and that Sally need not worry about them anymore, she became much calmer, and bestowed a look of great approval on us both. Both parents subsequently reported that she seemed less anxious, and more cheerful.

In subsequent sessions Sally was able to talk about her worries about her mother's loneliness and her fear of upsetting her, and I encouraged them to talk to one another about this. Sally's mother was clearly amazed by the extent of Sally's concern, and this realisation enabled her to resume her role as parent.

## Summary: The Parental Child

These 'parental' children, then, reflected a wide range of responses which spanned both the early and the acute stages of grief. Levels of anxiety were high, often masked by premature sang froid; there was often an air of wariness, watchfulness and a searching, pining quality in their non verbal communication which was intensely painful to experience in the counter-transference. Matter of fact discussions were often followed or accompanied by bursts of play more suited to a younger child; most of the children, given the opportunity to share their anxieties and unload the burden, jumped at the chance. With one exception (Liam) all these children were functioning in a family system in which at least one parent was abnegating their responsibility on a regular basis. This left a 'vacancy' for a parent.

An adult persona effectively provided a carapace, representing what I felt to be a manic defence in the form of both a denial that anything had been lost, as well as a way of demonstrating how powerful and important the child still was. This persona also seemed to protect the child, at least for a time, from knowing about or dealing with some of the more powerful feelings which they were experiencing towards their parents, anger being both the most feared and the most frightening. Robert, Liam and Paul were eventually able to let their angry child selves out and express that anger, as was Camilla; for most of the girls in this Chapter however, this seemed not to happen. Whether this was linked to gender related socialisation was hard to determine; what seemed more relevant was the child's developmental stage. For the older children mentioned above, ambiguity was problematic, and things had to be one thing or another – a feature of Erikson's developmental framework (Erikson 1965). By the same token, what was said to them, particularly by their parents, had literal meaning – "we love you and we don't want to hurt you" type statements made no sense to these children at all in the face of what was actually happening. Much of the anger seemed to be about this dichotomy – saying one thing and doing another – and there was also much emphasis on fairness. One of the tasks was to help such children appreciate that situations could be mixtures of things, as could people, and that their logical, grown up solutions to their complex problems were not always possible.

For the younger children, preoccupations were different. They were at a stage when they were increasingly aware that they were not the only inhabitants of their world, and thus were beginning to develop a concern for others (Piaget op. cit). Clearly this was a tendency which seemed to become intensified in response to loss and change and appeared to be a contributory factor in the development of the 'little parent' characteristics which were being exhibited.

All the children in this group, as I have said, were either only children or first born. Clearly this left them in a particularly difficult position, and it became especially crucial to me to enable them to shed some of their responsibility. Few seemed to gain any real satisfaction from what Wallerstein called this "role reversal" although some, like Robert, clung to their adult role for a considerable length of time.

Experiencing the counter-transference often left me feeling overburdened, hopeless and very anxious, with a desperate desire to 'rescue' children from their adult isolation, and enable them to regain their childhood once more. "Who is it that can tell me who I am?" became a relevant question for me, as well as for the children and the parents. I think there were times when we were all confused, and it was often only expert supervision which enabled me to untangle what was going on – such supervision being a crucial element in any provision of effective child centred work, as Aldgate, Banks and Mumford (1988) point out. The effects on the worker of becoming accessible to children's pain is a theme to which I will constantly return.

# Chapter VI: The Despairing Child:
## Losing the Rainbow

> That the birds of worry and care
> Fly above your head –
> This you cannot change.
> But that they build nests in your hair –
> This you can prevent.
>
> Old Chinese Proverb

It was difficult to find a suitably evocative word to describe the category of children who will be encountered in this Chapter. It was tempting to call them 'depressed' but this fails to convey the sense of yearning, sorrow and loss that communicated itself so vividly to me during my talks with them, and, in addition, had a clinical, somewhat distancing ring to it which threatened to become a defence against confronting the pain inherent in the work we tried to do together. Depression also carries with it connotations of pathology, illness, and a set of symptoms which were often not relevant. Kleinian concepts of depressive anxiety and the depressive positions appeared to me to be a more useful framework for understanding these children, particularly, as Rosenbluth (1965) points out, they relate to "certain constellations of the ego's relation to objects, and the kind of anxieties and defences at work in these different constellations". In addition, these states were not seen as either stages of development or adjustment, occurring at a particular time and then giving way to the next phase. Rather they were seen as a way of being at a particular point – and a way of being that could come and go if allowed to remain unresolved.

As I have described in Chapter III, according to Kleinian theory, the 'depressive position' relates to the central conflict faced by a child when s/he realises that s/he and mother are two separate people, and has to confront the feelings of love and hate s/he has towards her. The child then becomes beset by anxiety that the feelings of hate may destroy or damage mother, since s/he is equally aware of both the love s/he feels and his/her total dependence upon her. Depressive anxiety occurs as a result of the child's fear that the 'good object' will be harmed or lost as a result of the violent attacks that take place in the child's fantasy. Manic defence mechanisms are often brought into play to cope with this anxiety. Thus a child will deny the importance of those on whom s/he depends, becoming convinced of his/her own power and importance, and appearing indifferent when one would expect him/her to be sad. This constellation of related states can be reactivated at any point in relation to loss and mourning. Thus the range of losses I will be addressing will frequently precipitate reactions which could usefully be understood in relation to these concepts.

Equally significantly, I considered that there was a useful distinction to be made between despair, sadness and depression. There was nothing pathological in being distressed and sorrowful in response to the separation of one's parents. Such feelings however could become so if the child became 'stuck' in that particular state. It was therefore important to differentiate between appropriate sorrow, overwhelming despair, and the deeper, more problematic state of depression.

The children I encountered whom I placed in the 'despairing' category seemed forlorn and lost, sad, tearful, distracted and wistful, and often conveyed a sense of bleakness, yearning or pining – all reactions associated with what Jewett identifies as the acute stage of grief. In addition, from my observations, these children often found it hard to concentrate, seemed unable to play and were reluctant to be stimulated.

This category of children distinguished itself from the others in terms of what it was possible to do in the context of short term therapeutic work. Whereas I found it was sometimes possible to help resolve feelings of anger, and untangle inappropriate muddle when children became too parental, as well as persuade regressed children to 'return' to their real positions, these children changed little between the beginning of contact and the end. What I will be arguing, however, is that simply to allow a child to express intense sadness, acknowledge that it is appropriate – accepting and understanding it, at a time when parents find it so unbearable that they prefer not to see it – is valuable in itself. This provision of what Bion (1962) calls "containment" of feelings by the worker, with its integral elements of intuitive understanding of communications and the ability to cope with anxieties, and other strong feelings, seemed both particularly important for these children, and extremely difficult. As a minimum intervention, however, to validate the child's reality, by refusing to say "It'll be all right!" or "Cheer up!", and to provide a receptacle for some of the pain, seemed to me to be a crucial role for the worker to play.

Despair, sadness and grief, like anger, are well documented reactions that occur during the mourning process. The loss of a parent, often for reasons that elude a child's understanding, brings further losses in its wake – the loss of a familiar structure and routine in the family, and the loss of what is still commonly considered to be a 'normal' life, in which children live with two parents, without thought or question. Further loss can be experienced in the form of changes of home and school, often occasioned by shifts in financial circumstances, and children can often find themselves cast adrift from several important touchstones of security all at the same time.

The remaining parent, as I have already suggested, can also become 'lost' to the child at such a time. The parent can become unavailable, on an emotional level, due to personal preoccupations, and the struggle to come to terms with the sense of loss they are experiencing in their own right. On a practical level, the necessity to support the family can mean unaccustomed absence due to the need to work; the need to forget, escape, reclaim a sense of worth and develop a social life can mean equally unaccustomed absences for these reasons as well.

Contact with the departed parent can often contribute to the overwhelming sense of loss and sorrow with which everyone must struggle. This re-enactment of the original parting can cause such pain and difficulty that it is often not pursued for this reason. The assumption is that it will always feel this bad, and the prospect of it continuing is unbearable. The despair and disappointment experienced by children each time the access parent fails to come home to stay, after a visit, is intense. Their efforts to lure a parent through the front door and detain them by any and every means – "Could you just come in for a minute so I can show you something very secret?" – and their abiding belief, even in the face of subsequent remarriage on both sides, that one day they will all live together again as they once did, gives some indication of the profundity of the impact upon them, and their refusal to let that particular rainbow go.

The birds of worry and care do indeed fly above the heads of these sad and bereaved children but can be warded off to some extent during the initial period of loss, when denial that the parent has really gone for good can be maintained. The nest building starts in earnest, when this no longer becomes possible. As a consequence, the child often becomes overwhelmed by sorrow, yearning for the departed parent, and many symptoms of depression can become apparent – disturbance in patterns of eating and sleeping, lack of concentration, tearfulness, moodiness. It is significant to note, in this context, that in previous studies of the effects of divorce on children, the main psychopathological finding was depression (Wallerstein op. cit.; Mitchell op. cit.). This manifested itself in a number of ways, and was frequently masked by intense anger. This seemed to correspond to the Kleinian concepts of the depressive position and depressive anxiety already referred to, with children, initially confused by the mixture of conflicting feelings they have for the loved person, and subsequently fearful of the angry feelings and the damage these might do. This seemed to lead to a tendency to turn these angry, destructive feelings inward, rather than risk the consequences of expressing them. Many of the angry children in my sample would alternate between rage and sorrow, and as a consequence some of the material in this chapter will overlap with that in Chapter VIII.

In the accounts that follow, I hope to demonstrate how very young children, in particular, experience acute despair which needs to be seen and acknowledged, if healthier feelings of anger are to be enabled to be expressed. What will also emerge will be recurring themes in the children's play which I will argue give important clues to their states of mind and to what is happening in their internal world. Death, destruction, fire and flood, impending threat from wolves and burglars are all enacted as the children's fantasies emerge. A preoccupation with order and tidiness, and the need to impose order on chaos was also evident. In addition, I will also examine the link between the experience of loss and the sense of being lost – the fear and despair inherent in being carried along on a wave of events over which you have no control, particularly when you strongly suspect that no one else is in control either. This in turn will be connected to the problems of projected sadness, where the child is not only sorrowing in his or her own right, but is carrying the parents' grief as well, and to the importance of clarifying which feelings belong where.

The powerful feelings engendered in me by the children in this chapter will once again also feature both as a source of information, and as a means of assessment, relying principally on the processes of transference, counter-transference, splitting and projection. Children frequently projected their mixed feelings about either or both parents on to me, since it seemed far safer to split them off in this way than express them directly, often demonstrating fondness and anger within minutes of one another. In response to these feelings, I would often experience certain reactions of my own. It was clearly crucial, therefore, to remain alert to this phenomenon. With particularly sad children who were able to play little and sometimes talk even less, I often relied on the way they made me feel to gain some clue about their emotional state. These accounts will, I hope, highlight the very real issue of management of these difficult feelings for any worker involved in therapeutic contact with children who react to loss in this way, and the problems inherent in simply being there, without being able to 'do' anything to make it better.

## Tanya

Tanya was four when we first met. The court had requested a welfare report on the question of residence which was in fierce dispute. Tanya's mother wished to emigrate with her; Tanya's father maintained that her mother was unfit, and proposed that he and his new partner should care for her instead. Tanya's parents had separated some four months before, after a period of protracted difficulty, when her father had spent increasingly lengthy periods away from home. Even after the 'official' separation, Tanya was encouraged to believe that her father was at work, rather than living elsewhere. By this stage she had begun to wet and soil herself during the day, had started to sleep with her mother every night, and became acutely distressed at parting from her, when she was taken to nursery. Her mother was concerned about all these symptoms of distress, but was feeling so bereft and unhappy herself that she found it very difficult to confront the problem, or to talk to Tanya about the reality of what was happening.

When I went to Tanya's house to meet her for the first time, I was struck by the bleak and abandoned atmosphere that seemed to prevail. Various items had been removed by Tanya's father, leaving gaps and holes everywhere. He had apparently stored the rest of his possessions in one of the bedrooms which was kept locked. The message to Tanya was very clear – the gap and hole left by her father's departure was real, he was no longer available or accessible. Why would no one acknowledge this was the case, and reassure her that she was not to blame?

Like many of the other parents and children in the sample, Tanya and her mother had got rather confused in one another's worlds. Tanya had been described to me as a very protective child, concerned for her mother's welfare, and generally anxious and parental. This, however, was not the child that I encountered. I found her to be sad, withdrawn, and distant, often regressing quite dramatically in her behaviour, and occasionally revealing little flashes of violence. Her mother, meanwhile, had become a child again – a grief-stricken child, mourning the loss of an important parent figure (her husband had been considerably older than herself, and they had had what sounded like a mentor/pupil relationship) and overcome by feelings of insecurity, dependence, anxiety and fear about the future. She constantly stressed Tanya's need for love, security, stability, and protection – "Tanya's only a little child – she shouldn't have to suffer these things....all this pain being inflicted on her....". What was manifest to me was that she was also talking about herself.

Watching Tanya and her mother together was reminiscent of two children playing – two babes in the wood who snuggled up together every night in this bleak and abandoned home. Tanya accepted my presence and explanation for it without reacting but was not prepared at that stage to talk about anything very much. However she regularly turned huge, sad, dark eyes towards me with what I experienced as a look of appeal and when I explained that she would be coming to see me at the office the following week she seemed quite keen. Although she said little on this occasion, she did give me some important clues about where her anxieties lay and these emerged during her play with her mother.

Games revolved round Mummies, babies and snuggling. Tanya would climb into her mother's arms, talking in a baby voice, declare she was a baby lion and ask where her mother was. She and mother – also occasionally talking in a baby voice – then snuggled up together, with Tanya being rocked and cradled. A game then ensued which involved the simulated theft of one another's noses, resulting in some fairly rough play at times on the part of Tanya, and culminating in attempts by Tanya to eat her mother's nose, and by mother to eat Tanya's belly button. Beneath all this clearly lurked Tanya's real uncertainty about where her mother was and the extent of both her power and her resilience – who would eat, and who be eaten? I also saw the beginnings of Tanya's anger, which could only be expressed in the safe persona of a lion. At the end of this visit, just as I was about to leave, Tanya's mother suddenly became very upset, and, amid floods of tears, poured out all her sorrow and distress, about everything that had happened, and her fear of losing her child. Tanya was present throughout, and stood gazing out of the window, completely impassive.

Tanya's first visit to my office took place the following week. She arrived with her mother looking very serious and infinitely sad and plodded up the stairs to my room with an air of weary resignation. I reminded her of our previous meeting, my awareness of the difficulties when a Mummy and Daddy stop living together and my wish to help her to learn to live with this sad development in her life. She smiled suddenly at the mention of her father and mentioned his girlfriend, whom she referred to as "my friend". I explained that I would be coming to see her at Daddy's house the following week and would be able to meet this friend and see what they do when they are together. Tanya accepted this without comment, pulling a chair up to the window, climbing onto it and gazing blankly out onto the street. She then began to make a strange, monotonous sound, reminiscent of keening or some primitive pre-verbal attempt at communication. This lasted for a few minutes, to my considerable alarm, while I stood close beside her to ensure that she did not fall. The sound then stopped as suddenly as it had started, and Tanya began to explore the toys in the room.

Tanya began by arranging a lamb, a womble and a bear on several chairs. This was done with great care and concentration, and in silence. After moving the animals around for a while, Tanya announced that the lamb was angry with the womble and the bear although she could not say why this was. This seemed to me to be connected with her anger towards her parents for not remaining together, but Tanya would not pursue this tableau further and became engrossed with the anteaters instead. In this game, the anteaters were identified as Daddy, Mummy and baby, according to size. The story began with them all on the same chair. The Daddy anteater then jumped off the chair and began to move away. "Daddy don't go!" called the baby, plaintively, but nothing happened, so Mummy and baby set off in pursuit. The baby then got stuck and Daddy returned. However, after a few seconds, Daddy left once more. Once more the baby called him back, and again he changed his mind and came home, only to depart shortly afterwards. This sequence was repeated several times, as Tanya painstakingly re-enacted her father's departures and returns. She also seemed to be exploring the limits of the baby's powers over the Daddy, as well as concerns about whether her depressive anxiety might have destroyed him so that he would disappear forever.

After a while, I gently made the connection between her game and her life, and that I could see how desperately the baby wanted Daddy to come back, and how sad she was every time he went. Tanya listened without comment, continuing her game, while I talked about the fact that her Daddy had gone and was not going to come back to live with Mummy and how difficult that was. In response, it seemed, to this, Tanya effected yet another family reunion. However, this time she gathered together a number of other toys and piled them on top of the anteater family until they had completely disappeared. This seemed to me to have two possible interpretations. One was that Tanya wanted the means to ensure that the family stayed together by trapping them so no-one could escape. The other was that this was a family 'burial' – that something was lost and had died – and that at some deep level, Tanya was able to acknowledge this. It was my conclusion that the latter was the more likely in view of the mood of sorrow in which the play took place. It also seemed to make more sense in the light of our subsequent session. After the 'funeral' I reminded Tanya of our next meeting and asked her if she would like to come to the unit again. Once again, she began to make her strange, monotonous keening sound, and began sucking her thumb. She was very reluctant to end the session, moving among the toys to prolong her stay. Finally, after several reminders about meeting again, she allowed me to take her back to her mother.

When Tanya came for our second session, she was solemn and unsmiling, once again plodding up the stairs with a resigned air. By this time, I had visited her at her father's home, and I referred both to this, and to our previous meeting at the unit, asking if she remembered certain things in my room. Tanya wandered about, disconsolate, and then began putting some little wooden people into a boat. When I asked where they were going, she said she didn't know and they didn't know either. This seemed to me to be connected with her own uncertainty about whether anyone knew where she was going, and her own confusion about this. Tanya remembered the anteaters and spent some time fitting them together and then separating them. Once again, this seemed to me to be a safe way for Tanya to enact what had happened to her family, as well as a way of coming to terms with it, whilst being permitted to be sad and silent. Occasionally the Daddy anteater would climb over the back of the chair, as though looking out to see what was on the other side; at times the baby would take on this role of 'look out', very much as the baby in Camilla's game had done (see Chapter V). Tanya couldn't say what was happening or what the baby could see – an eloquent statement, perhaps, of her own position.

Tanya's attention was then drawn to a rag doll who was sitting in a corner in her underwear, looking rather pathetic. With the same expression of sadness, Tanya began to dress her but found this difficult, and allowed me to help her. She then took the doll and placed her in the flat hollow roof of the doll's house, as though it was a bed, pulling her hat low over her brow, and completely covering her with a piece of material. At this point, I had a strong sense that this was about death, and that this covered body in something reminiscent of a coffin, being tended by a sad and silent little girl, was a graphic manifestation of Tanya's own feelings of her life ending, as well, perhaps, as her wish to escape from the field of combat. When I tried to explore this with Tanya, however, she simply said that the little girl had to get up for play school, then go to play school, then come back and then go again. This served to confirm my sense that the doll was part of Tanya, and that the to-ing and fro-ing in her life was unbearable. I therefore simply acknow- ledged how difficult and tiring this must be for her.

Throughout this play Tanya's eyes were blank and dead looking. She moved round the room collecting animals and dolls, lying them face down, in rows on several of the chairs, in complete silence, and with the same depressed air that I had noted on the previous occasion. Again, I experienced a strong sense of death, and a powerful feeling of despair and helplessness, which was being communicated to me by this grieving child. There was nothing either of us could do about what had happened – all that remained was to attend the funeral, try to take in the fact that something was lost forever, and be permitted to begin the process of mourning. It seemed that only by having this funeral, could Tanya even begin to approach the reality of what had happened between her parents. After a while, Tanya seemed to become less sad, and began playing with the wooden people quite cheerfully as she tried to find them all seats on the bus. It would have been easy – and indeed a great relief and comfort to me – to construe this as some acceptance, and a sign that Tanya was coming to terms with something important. The fact that I continued to feel bleak, and desolate long after her departure, however, gave the lie to this reassuring interpretation, although it did suggest that she had been able to shed some of her burden.

Eventually I suggested that we ask Mummy to join us, and Tanya looked at me quite brightly and agreed. As soon as her mother came into the room, Tanya climbed onto her lap and snuggled up like a baby, sucking both her own finger, and occasionally one of her mother's. Tanya's mother remarked that since her first session with me, Tanya had seemed much happier, she'd settled down at play school and had started to talk much more to a family friend about her parents' separation and her visits to her father. As we went on to discuss the progress of access, however, Tanya began to make little baby noises as though to try and drown out the sound of the discussion and this increased as her mother referred to her father's refusal to talk to her about their child. When she referred to her plan to emigrate, Tanya's noises got louder, and I made a connection between this and the pain of listening to something so confusing and worrying. Finally Tanya began to wail, got off her mother's lap, and tried to pull her towards the door, repeating "I want to go" and becoming increasingly angry. I explained that unless I talked to Mummy and Daddy I could not help them to sort things out for her, and that sadly this situation wouldn't go away, and couldn't be escaped from. Tanya seemed to fall silent at this point, became calmer, and left the unit quite composed.

My work with this family centred on helping Tanya's parents to talk to her about what was happening in her life, and acknowledging the reality of father's departure and the permanence of it. The whole issue of the loss experienced had been so assiduously avoided that it had been difficult for Tanya to ask questions. It was therefore important for a climate to be created where such questioning was possible. My sessions with Tanya had enabled her to face her father's loss for what appeared to be the first time, and the account I gave her parents of her behaviour dispelled their desperately held belief that she was too young to really understand what was happening. As a consequence they were both able to talk to her more openly and became more sensitive to her predicament.

Unfortunately for Tanya, however, the court process took far longer than usual and two years later, the situation remained unresolved. By that stage, my original report was out of date, and the court requested another to be prepared, particularly in view of the fact that Tanya's mother had decided against emigration, and it was hoped that her father might concede care and control as a result. When I met the family again, it became clear that the parents' relationship was still strained and that poor Tanya continued to move between them in an atmosphere of tension, and on father's part, there were occasional outbursts of outright hostility. Tanya had been seeing her father very regularly but he refused to discuss her with her mother, or permit any mention of mother's name or Tanya's life with her. Not surprisingly, perhaps, both parents reported that Tanya often behaved in a babyish, attention seeking manner – and after so many years of living in a war zone, who could blame her for wishing to become a baby again?

However, some significant changes had taken place, not the least of which was the transformation of Tanya's mother from a lost, lonely, bereft child into a more confident happier adult who had come to terms with her loss, and rebuilt her life. She had found a job, established a social life, committed herself to remaining in England, and had gained considerable insight into her earlier desire to return to her parents. As a result, she appeared to be far better able to meet Tanya's needs and no longer relied on her for support and companionship. Despite this, however, Tanya remained a rather sad, wary little girl, still occasionally given to making primitive, animal noises, and clinging fiercely to her mother, but no longer showing the overt signs of despair that had been so evident before. What struck me when we had our first private session together was how weary she was of her parents' conflict, and that she was now feeling intense anger towards them for both creating and maintaining a situation that caused her such discomfort and conflict of loyalties. She seemed relieved to see me again, and to have the opportunity to talk; I felt that we were picking up again, after a gap, and that perhaps, had I not invested time and attention in the earlier work, this would not have been possible. Our subsequent contact was therefore focused on helping her with this next stage of mourning, so that eventually she could be helped to move on to more of an acceptance of what had happened without needing to retreat into babyhood.

In one of our discussions, Tanya seemed to me to outline her position very graphically. While we talked and looked at the various things that were bothering her, she took apart and put together my large wooden elephant puzzle (see Chapter IV), over and over again, while I tried to help her examine and then connect her various worries and fears. We both agreed that putting it all together and making it into a whole was very difficult, and no sooner did things come together, than they appeared to fall apart once more. Tanya was telling me how difficult it was to keep her world in one piece – perhaps the most acute problem for the divorced child.

## Ben

Ben, like Tanya, was also bereft when he 'lost' his father at the same age, and, like her, often seemed preoccupied with death and destruction, although he chose to direct these impulses largely at me, perhaps viewing me as a safe receptacle for them. Despite the fact that I considered that Ben's principal reaction to his parents' separation was anger (see Chapter VIII), it was clear that in between bursts of passionate fury, his sorrow and despair would seep out as he struggled with a range of complicated feelings. It was also difficult for Ben, as it was for many other children in the sample, to hang on to a sense of the departed parent, so that when they were not in view, there was a fear that they were 'lost' for ever and no longer existed. When I explained to Ben that I would be seeing his father at some stage, he looked sad and troubled, expressing uncertainty about whether I would be able to find him. He in turn felt lost and abandoned by him – "I wish I had gone with him!" he said, adding "I hate it here – this house hates me". Ben's play, as I will be demonstrating in Chapter VIII, reflected a powerful belief both in the power of his own feelings to destroy, and his sense of the outside world as a dangerous and persecutory place. His despair about being able to hang onto his father was reinforced by his father's frequent failure to turn up for visits. Ben's anxiety about whether I would be able to find him proved to be well founded – he failed several appointments and when he did finally come to see me he was quite inaccessible, on any level, as he was drunk.

## Laura

Laura's play also reflected concerns about death and the threat from something dangerous outside, whether in the form of fire, nettles growing all around her house, or something nameless but frightening. This concern about an outside threat had featured both in Sophie's play, where burglars were suspected, and in Carla's, where wolves were believed to be prowling around. In each case, such concerns became manifest during a period of quiet play in the play house where attempts were being made to re-create some form of family life, either lost, idealised or hoped for, at a point when each child was confronting the sadness of what had been. The danger seemed to me to spring from a fear that something powerful and unsettling inside the child, which was being projected onto the outside world, would break into consciousness at some point in the near future – whether it be anger, overwhelming grief, or simply the destruction of the fragile situation in which they currently found themselves was hard to determine. What did seem clear, however, was the sense of being both besieged, scared and defenceless.

Laura, at four, was the younger of two children, having a seven year old sister – Sally – who featured in the previous Chapter on parental children. It appeared to me that while Sally could busy herself being grown up, Laura was left free to be sad, both in her own right, and as a reflection of her sister's sadness as well. There was something strangely bleak and distant about Laura, as though she was in a reverie. Despite the fact that she was a demonstrative child, able to ask for affection, there was a hollow quality about this, although her desperate need, and sense of sorrow were palpable.

During Laura's first visit to the unit, it became clear that the play house was the only thing that really interested her and she spent most of the time in it, encouraging both Sally and myself to join her, with an anxious urgency which suggested a need for safety in enclosed surroundings. At one point she became very concerned about fire – "Quick! there's a fire outside – help me to keep the door shut!" She then became confused about whether the fire was on the inside or on the outside, as if uncertain which was the greater threat – mother or father – since both were causing her so much worry and pain as a result of their endless arguments, violent outbursts, and the pressure they were each exerting on the children. Finally, Laura decided that the fire was on the inside so we left the house in something of a hurry, unnerved to find that nowhere appeared safe. This seemed to me to be connected with Laura's own fiery feelings from which there seemed no escape.

Most of Laura's second visit was also spent in the play house, grappling with a range of domestic issues concerning her "baby" – a doll she adopted to play this role. Once again, the house caught fire but this time Laura herself became a fire engine, reacting with tremendous energy in her frenetic attempts to deal with this, and telling me that water was coming out of her mouth. For a few moments, Laura was all powerful, able to deal with both the crisis, and her desperate anxiety about it, by employing a manic defence – triumphant and in total control. Sadly this state was not to last, however. Soon she became worried about nettles growing all round the house, but was unable to rouse herself to do anything about them.

Laura also became absorbed in a game involving two toy dogs – a Mummy and a baby. "The Mummy has hit the baby and she's dead," she told me. After a while it emerged that it was the Mummy who had died rather than the baby – a point clarified by Laura with total unconcern and detachment. This seemed to me to reflect the fear that angry feelings had killed mother off, and indifference was being used as a manic defence against the anxiety this engendered. Once again there was a powerful awareness of the baby's dependence, and the need to defend against the anxiety that provoked, as well as the fear that feelings of hate and destruction were so frightening that they had to be defended against. In addition there also seemed to be the need to enact the baby's murderous anger, and this was further developed when the surviving baby attacked me. Laura and I talked about how when you feel very angry and sad you feel afraid that it might damage someone else. I was also able to demonstrate that I could survive the dog's onslaught.

Laura had a clear need to re-enact some of the aspects of family life that she had both experienced and failed to understand. In this game, I became her husband – "You are my dear husband and you have to go out to work and I stay at home with the baby". There was quite a lot of anxiety when I failed to grasp the time I should be home, particularly as there was also a sense that there was something nasty lurking outside the house, and at one stage I was given the baby to look after and Laura did the leaving. Whether this was a way of trying out the two alternative caretakers in the residence dispute, or whether it was Laura entrusting the baby part of herself to me, was hard to determine. The sorrowful, ponderous, almost ritualistic rehearsal of events, however, seemed to have both a valedictory element – family life that is lost – and an experimental one, relating to the future. When the children's mother joined us, both Sally and Laura became increasingly manic. Then they curled up on a cushion and pretended to go to sleep. Although, as I have said in the previous chapter, work with Sally could be undertaken in terms of helping her relinquish her adult role, work with Laura was more difficult. Ultimately it amounted to being there to receive, accept and validate the sadness of her predicament, and reassure her that her murderous feelings were understandable, but would not in fact cause the damage that she feared.

## Jilly

The opportunity to enact what had happened in the family seemed particularly important for many of the smaller children, appearing to set them free to either talk about what it felt like, or to help to make it more real. Like Tanya and Ben, Jilly had 'lost' her father suddenly when she and her mother left the family home after a violent scene. She was the only child of parents from very different backgrounds, where there was a considerable age difference, and who had both been married before. Although Jilly's mother had had no children, her father had two sons, one of whom – Ned – lived with him. Accounts from both parents indicated that tensions developed in the marriage as a result of all these factors, and Jilly's birth, rather than bringing her parents together, simply provided them with another arena for mutual criticism and competition. Matters were compounded, as far as Jilly's father was concerned, by Jilly's mother's interest in spiritualism, and reached crisis point when she had an affair.

Both parents sought custody of Jilly and a report was ordered. Both were making serious accusations about the other, and Jilly could have been in no doubt about their mutual antipathy, despite the fact that she was only three. Although outwardly, she appeared to be coping with what had happened, she had a poor appetite, and often complained of stomach ache. A tiny, elfin child, with striking tangerine coloured hair, she habitually wore an expression of wary gravity.

After an initial meeting at her mother's home, Jilly paid her first visit to the unit, accompanied by her mother. There was something bereft about Jilly as she sat in my room, and although she took some interest in the toys, she wore a sad little smile and said very little. Her most graphic communication was to shake her head while saying "yes". As I explained to her once again who I was and why I had wanted to see her, she drew brightly coloured abstract designs on pieces of paper with a distant air, verbally admitting she could remember when she, Mummy and Daddy had all lived together, while physically contradicting herself. She then became very interested in my collection of pottery animals, arranging them with care and precision in the dolls' house – a concern with order and tidiness with which I will be dealing in more detail later. This led to a wish to draw them all, and Jilly got very excited about this, although I could not really understand why. What quickly emerged however was her determination that I should do these drawings for her, because, as she told me, she couldn't. It may be too far fetched to connect this with her need for me to do other things for her – reconcile her parents, for example, or decide where she should live – but there was an intense quality to the appeal that seemed to transcend the immediate task in hand. As we continued to draw, extending this to pictures of herself, Mummy and Daddy, her favourite food, and so on, I noticed a marked lack of confidence to try to do any of these things, almost as though she was feeling too low to bother.

When Jilly's mother joined us, and we began to discuss access, Jilly, looking increasingly anxious, moved between us with some uncertainty, often coming physically very close to me. She hid first behind my chair and then behind her mother's, almost as if she was trying out each of our roles, and then decided to deal with the situation by concentrating on the apparently soothing task of handing her mother a series of pottery animals, and little wooden houses, taking them all back, and starting again – both a way of distracting our attention from the discussion, but also perhaps, her way of imposing order on the chaotic problem of Jilly-sharing.

The second time Jilly came to the office, she was brought by her father. Once again, her attention was drawn to the dolls' house, and as we talked a little about what she and Daddy do together at weekends, I wondered whether she could show me by using some of the dolls' house people. Jilly chose a "Daddy" and a "Jilly" and then another little figure who was also a "Jilly" – almost as though there

had to be a Mummy's Jilly and a Daddy's Jilly to deal with the
conflict she was in. A "Mummy" was added to this group, then a
half-brother and they were all placed very carefully in the house. I
commented that this was the way things used to be, that once
everyone had lived together in the same house. After a moment's
reflection, Jilly removed "Mummy", placing her behind my chair,
and leaving both "Jilly" in father's care. Suddenly she swept all the
figures out of the dolls' house onto the floor, as though everything
had been destroyed by what had happened. As I talked to her about
how sad it was to remember what had happened, and how different
things were now, she simply sat in silence, moving the figures
around in a half-hearted way, but unable to enter into any further
play with them. When I suggested visiting her at her father's home
to have another talk, she gave me a very eloquent look, and then
began drawing with some enthusiasm. Although the subsequent visit
was low key and uneventful, my impression was that Jilly had felt
that her situation had been understood, and that this in itself had
served some purpose.

## Kevin

Like Jilly, order, tidiness and repetitive play, as a means of creating
the illusion that control could be had over the external world, was
evident in the play of several other children I encountered,
constituting a recurring theme particularly when they were present
during discussions with either one or both parents. As the grown-
ups grappled with the ramifications of untangling the life of the
family, to enable separate existences to become possible and children
to be shared, their children would become engrossed with the dolls'
house, its occupants and its contents, with a desperate concentration
and attention to detail worthy of the most dedicated houseperson.
The sense, however, that the children were listening to every word,
alert to every nuance, and ready to spring into distracting activity at
the slightest sign of conflict, remained an almost tangible force in the
room.

Kevin was a long suffering, world weary toddler of two when we
first met. Old before his time, he would gaze at me with an air of
tranquil resignation as I attempted to help his parents resolve their
battle over his future. Clearly he knew something I did not, but
unfortunately he was in no position to tell me what it was. Kevin's
parents were both very young, and his conception had been an
accident. The first conflict occurred even before his birth, when
there was a fierce disagreement about whether this should be allowed
to take place or not. During the period that followed, the
battleground simply moved, from time to time, but dedication to the
war remained constant.

Kevin had little enthusiasm for play, preferring to totter between his parents during sessions. Mother eventually 'won' the battle for residence, but before long father returned the matter to court due to his dissatisfaction with contact. This led to a period of prolonged work while various patterns were tried, sabotaged, re-considered, and re-tried. By the time he was three, Kevin was a rather anxious, albeit charming, little boy, with a grave manner, who had trouble sleeping, coping with separations, dealing with his father's new relationship and half sister. Throughout his life, he had been subjected to regular arguments between his parents, contradictory sets of rules in each household, and conflicting standards of behaviour and differences in moral outlook and life-styles.

There was little I could do for this sad child except talk to him about how confusing all this was and allow him to tidy my office to his heart's content. He would spend most of the time re-laying the dolls' house carpet, re-positioning the staircase, and smoothing out pieces of material to act as coverings of different sorts. He would become very anxious when carpets did not fit or he could not find a place for something, but if things were going well, a secret smile would slowly appear, and a sense of calm descended, Kevin said very little to me during our long acquaintance, but his expression spoke volumes. I used what he 'told' me to help his parents to think about what *he* might be going through, as a consequence of the anger and acrimony that both still felt (by their own admission) towards one another and what his world might feel like. Gradually it became more possible for them to remember he was a person too, and that he had feelings about what was happening around him.

## Kathy and Andrew

Kathy, who will also feature briefly in Chapter VIII, was also preoccupied with order, but was able to talk about both her sadness about her parents' separation, and how weary she was of the battle being waged over herself and her elder brother Andrew. When I first met the children they were eight and ten respectively, and their parents had been apart some six years. A battle had arisen, however, as a result of their mother's imprisonment. During her sentence the children's father had assumed their care, but as her release approached, mother made it clear that she expected them to be returned to her, and that she had only ever seen the arrangement as temporary. Meanwhile, their father had discovered what the children's life with their mother had been like, and became increasingly convinced that she was not a suitable caretaking parent.

My initial meeting with the children took place at their father's home. Rather like Tanya's house, there was an abandoned, desolate air about it, and, again, like Tanya's parent, the only grown-up left

for the children to lean on was himself a sad, anxious and fragile
figure. The children's account of what they could remember of their
'story' was even more complex and fraught with loss than I had
realised. When their parents separated, they 'lost' their father,
whose visits had been problematic, and was further complicated by
the children's move to the north, while he remained in the south.
Four years later, they 'lost' their mother very suddenly, when she
went to prison – an outcome not anticipated, and therefore not
prepared for. The children were then returned to their father, and
were now, two years later, facing regaining one parent at the expense
of the other. The problems of coping with separation and attachment
were further compounded by prison visits, where the loss of their
mother was re-enacted, over and over again.

It was Andrew who highlighted the fundamental dilemma of the
divorced child – never again being able to have both parents at once
or, as he put it "It's being with one and then leaving and being with
the other and then leaving that's hard." Both children talked very
sadly about their wish for their parents to be together while
acknowledging that this was impossible in view of the arguing, both
past and present. They were equally aware that they themselves were
now a source of conflict and that there had been discussion about
splitting them – or the 'Children as Three Piece Suite' approach to
custody resolution. The prospect of losing one another was clearly
unbearable – vividly reflected in the look of horror and pain in
Andrew's face, when Kathy told him that one solution she had heard
discussed was for their parents to have a child each.

The prospect of visits to my office produced very different
responses in both Kathy and Andrew. Kathy thought this was
unnecessary – "Let's get it over with," she said, frequently
reprimanding Andrew, if he changed the subject – "We're supposed
to be talking about things about Mum, Andrew". Andrew, however,
was resigned to the fact that it could not be 'got over with' and,
despite occasional distractions, was clearly desperate to be able to
talk about the situation, away from the sorrowing gaze of his father.

The first visit to the unit served to acclimatise the children to my
office and its contents, while hopefully laying the foundation for
some degree of trust, enabling either discussion, or enactment about
their predicament to take place. By the second visit, both children
were discernibly more relaxed and talkative. The significant
difference, however, was in Kathy, who dashed about, making a
great deal of noise, frantically tidying my office, the dolls' house, and
my desk, while struggling to talk about the range of feelings she was
experiencing towards her mother and betraying a level of hyperactivity consistent with Jewett's acute stage of grief. Although
clearly uncomfortable and unhappy with the warfare taking place
between her parents, she was beginning to articulate her anger as

well. When I said she seemed very cross about something, she readily agreed – "It should be what's best for us, not them!" She told me she had told her father she was angry, but had not had the chance to tell her mother yet. We discussed the fact that I was due to see them with their mother in due course – "Boo Hoo! I don't want to see her....I don't like her!" said Kathy, adding that this was because she was trying to take them away from their father and "it's his turn". Kathy's reactions seemed to me to reflect many of the preoccupations highlighted by Piaget (1969) – things had to be one way or the other, clear; ambiguity was problematic as was the struggle to cope with the fact that things could be a mixture of things. Fairness, taking turns was a central coda. Indeed there were times when Kathy said she did not like her mother, but she also said she loved her and missed her, too.

Kathy became increasingly energetic, flying an imaginary plane round the room, and chanting "No! No! No!" Once again, this seemed to me to be a manic defence against the anxiety and despair she felt about the likelihood of the issues ever being resolved, and as her noise level increased, after her father joined us, it seemed a clear device to block out any possibility of discussion. At the end of the session, Kathy was extremely reluctant to leave, once again frantically tidying my room, re-arranging things on my desk, moving furniture, and at one stage locking us all in the building together. The office, once again appeared to have become a safe place where difficult things could be addressed and acknowledged.

While Kathy, in my view was carrying much of the struggle, anxiety, and anger for both Andrew and possibly her father as well, Andrew was free to allow his sorrow to surface, while also coping with his fears about his father's vulnerability. There was a real sense, for him, that he and Kathy and what they needed were being totally overlooked, while his parents engaged in a vicious battle that was related to something entirely different. For Andrew, the dilemma was not only to do with losing a parent, or a way of life, but also being lost, and in a muddle, adrift in a dangerous place with unknown perils in store.

Andrew drew my attention to his plight very graphically during my first visit to his home. He suddenly began, a propos of nothing, or so it seemed, to tell me about a computer game he plays, when the weather is bad. Sitting very close to me, he explained that this was a pirate game, showed me the treasure map, the route taken by the ship, emphasising that there were a number of blue pirates who had to be destroyed along the way, and innumerable dangers and obstacles in the hero's path. As Andrew continued with his lengthy explanation, I felt an intense sense of pity and sadness for this lost child, alone in such a dangerous environment. I felt certain that he was telling me something important about how the world felt to him, and that this game was an important metaphor for his life at that point. Andrew went on to tell me that he had never reached the end of this game, as every time anything went wrong, you had to go back to the beginning. He was clearly frustrated by this problem, and anxious to resolve it. We talked about how difficult it was not knowing what would happen next, being frightened by unexpected events, and desperately wanting to get to the end in one piece. Without being explicit, I felt that we both understood that this conversation was operating on more than one level, and I simply allowed Andrew to talk about it for as long as he wanted to.

Interestingly, when he came to my office for the second time, he talked with unusual enthusiasm about a new computer game he had been given. Once again this featured people overcoming obstacles, and being beamed up into space ships before disaster struck. This seemed to suggest that Andrew was developing both better dexterity at the game, and perhaps more resilient resources with which to tackle what was happening in his life. He was also able to express some optimism that things would get sorted out, as I was now there to help them.

## Cara, Isabel and Beatrice

The sense of being lost and in need of rescue, or of feeling torn in two, or beset by mixed feelings, was often demonstrated equally graphically through children's drawings. As I have described in Chapter IV, on one occasion, I was presented with a complicated maze by Cara, aged six – "Find me," she said. Her sister, Isabel, meanwhile, was busy drawing a castle with high walls. Outside the walls, her parents were fighting, and, at the same time, the castle was being besieged by a rather aggressive looking chap on a horse – would this person rescue them or make things even worse? Responding to and attempting to interpret drawings became a regular feature of my approach and the squiggle game proved a rich source of such material – some children were quite unable to do anything in the face of something so uncertain, others needed me to tell them what the shape was, and some, like Sally made their predicament quite clear.

Beatrice, aged five, was beset by uncertainty about whether or not she wanted to see her father, particularly in view of her awareness of her mother's feelings about this. Ultimately she told me that "a bit of me wants to and a bit of me doesn't". It was interesting to see that, when I suggested she drew the two bits, the bit that wanted to go not only included the legs that would get her there, but was also much larger than the bit that did not.

## Livia and Peter

The last group of children I wish to highlight in this chapter are those who are so sad, despairing and anxious that they are incapable of really playing at all, and whose imagination and escape mechanisms appear to have deserted them. These children were particularly difficult, because they transmitted their feelings in such a raw form, as to be at times almost unbearable. Once again, analysing my reactions in terms of counter-transference, I often relied on the way these children made me feel, to gain some fraction of a sense of what their world must be like. This often involved just being there, and doing little, apart from gently conveying that I had some understanding of how awful it must be, the fears and anxieties that can be experienced, and generally throwing out possibilities, or thoughts spoken aloud which could either be ignored or taken up.

## Livia

Both Livia and Peter were vivid representatives of the children in this group. Livia, who was nine, was caught in the middle of a custody dispute, which seemed to me to be a reflection of unresolved issues to do with her mother's departure some two years before. At that stage both parents agreed that Livia should be left in the care of her father. Subsequently, however, her mother became dissatisfied with contact and concerned about her ex-husband's plans to move away from the area. She therefore returned the matter to court, whereupon I became involved. Livia, after two years of moving between her parents in an uneasy atmosphere, was well aware of the issues and tensions inherent in the situation. According to accounts from both parents, it was openly discussed both with her, and in her presence, and she frequently witnessed terse and angry exchanges both in person and on the telephone, which both parents confessed to me they felt unable to control. Livia, at our first meeting at her home, was watchful, quiet but not unfriendly. We finally made what felt like a firm initial contact via her cat, Fifi, who was an important figure in her life and served as a receptacle for many of her important feelings. While Livia remained apparently cut off, numb, immobilised, Fifi experienced danger, injury, and a sense of loss, during Livia's periods away from home. During her first visit to my office she sat almost motionless in her chair, responding with a polite smile or a monosyllabic response, except in relation to any mention of Fifi. She was, however, able to describe the very complicated visiting arrangements, which involved biweekly comings and goings, elaborate practical arrangements and much chopping and changing. I found myself feeling both confused and exhausted by these details and was able to reflect this back to her.

All attempts to encourage further exploration of the issues, through games of three wishes, guessing or fantasy were met with total incomprehension and a definite statement that she "couldn't do it – I can't do things like that". She showed no interest in the things in my room, and I experienced an increasing sense of anxiety and tension, feeling a desperate need to offer her an immediate solution, but feeling very stuck. I realised afterwards that this stuck feeling very much reflected Livia's position, caught in the middle, unable to move or speak freely amid all these complex arrangements and all the shouting. I was then able to tell her about these feelings and convey the reality of her world to her parents more effectively.

## Peter

Peter, like Livia, was also nine. First encountered very briefly in Chapter V, he was the younger of two children, very much dependent on his brother Paul for all that his parents were unable to provide. While Paul took all the worry and grown up responsibility upon his thirteen year old shoulders, Peter was free to express all the sadness, pain and desolation that the loss of the family had caused. At our first meeting, at his home, Peter could say very little. His eyes were constantly brimming with tears, and he confined himself to echoing anything that Paul said, hardly trusting himself to speak. A rather shy, quietly spoken, gentle looking child, his air of vulnerability was intensified by his thick pebble glasses – although these also proved a useful protection against his feelings being perceived at too close range.

Both Paul and Peter had been drawn into their parents' battle to a most inappropriate degree. The sight of another grown-up coming to discuss this matter, when grown-ups, in their eyes, had become unpredictable, extremely un-grown up people, caused considerable anxiety. It was clearly much too soon to engage in any real discussion about their feelings, fears and fantasies about the future. As a result, I spent the time explaining who and what I was, what I was trying to do, and how I had learned about what it was like when parents split up. I also acknowledged that, as I was a complete stranger, they needed time to make an assessment of me and decide whether or not they wanted to talk to me about what was happening, or not – an approach I often used at a first meeting which very much conformed to Fraiberg's (1952) approach to a first encounter with a child client.

Peter listened to this in silence, while waves of sadness lapped around his bleak and desolate bedroom. The only matter on which he was prepared to express a view related to our next meeting, which was due to take place in the office – he was adamant that he wanted to be seen with Paul, although accepted Paul's wish to have a private discussion with me as well.

At the first meeting at the unit, Peter, as agreed, joined Paul and myself after we had had our part of the time. He immediately sat very close to his brother, touching his foot with his shoe, as though gaining strength from this very slight, almost imperceptible contact with him. Occasionally he would glance at him, with a faint little smile, and Paul would look fondly and anxiously back. Although Peter could remember our first discussion, putting words round the feelings was unbearable for him, almost as though by naming the pain, fear, loss and sorrow they would become too real to manage. Instead, we decided to try drawing them, using a series of faces (see Chapter IV), to which expressions could be added depending on what was happening – whether getting up in the morning, going to school, coming to the unit, getting home from school, thinking about the future, and so on.

After a tentative beginning, Peter became quite enchanted with this game. His early morning face wore a wry expression, which turned to something close to cheerfulness when it went to school, as he said this gave him "something else" to think about. The 'coming to the office' face was surprisingly bright, though a little wary, but the coming home from school face became very sad at the prospect of hearing more arguments, and having to confront what was happening around him. "How I feel now" was interpreted quite literally – Peter drew a picture of a little figure drawing a picture of a little figure. He then confessed that he was confused by this question – a statement that perhaps said all that was needed – so he had decided to draw me a picture of how he feels when something good happens. The picture that emerged was of a little figure with a huge smile holding up a sheet of paper on which he had done a good drawing. I had a curious sense, at the time, of Peter's wish to lose himself quite literally in the drawing, rather like Alice through the looking glass. It seemed to be connected to a wish to live in a different place where you could control what was happening, rather than be subjected to the whims of others.

Despite the fact that Peter could enter into this sort of game, he was quite unable to deal with anything that had a more imaginative, speculative element. When I attempted to involve him in "if you had three wishes...." he appeared not to understand what I meant and had no sense of how on earth he could grapple with this. Other very sad children in the sample appeared to share this difficulty, or were unable to sustain a 'pretend' game for very long. It felt very much as though these children had become so preoccupied with worry that they had forgotten some of the lovelier aspects of being children.

By Peter's second visit to the office, he was able to say he wanted to see me on his own, and did not need Paul to be there too. He was also able to talk a little about his worries for the future and was also keen to establish whether, if he thought he might feel slightly better

with one parent or the other – even though he loved them the same –
he could say so and this would be all right. He was equally anxious to
establish whether he would be able to see me again, if he wanted to,
once the prearranged sessions were over. Somehow contact had been
made with this sad little soul, which then had to be taken at his pace.
Both he and Paul continued to request sessions with me, and
although Peter never said very much, he seemed to derive something
from the experience of sitting in my office, knowing I had some
understanding of what he had to cope with, and listening to my
gentle speculations about what his worries were, and how he and
Paul could try to deal with them. Perhaps I absorbed some of the
pain for him – it certainly felt like it – or perhaps my office became a
safe place to be, a quiet refuge from the battleground at home.

## Summary: The Despairing Child

These 'despairing' children exhibited many of the signs characteristic of the acute stage of grief described by Jewett. The sense of loss
and being lost often seemed to me a significant aspect of their
predicament, and the frequently demonstrated need to impose order
on the chaos – often external, but equally internal – that they were
experiencing felt like a clear message about what they might be
needing at such a point. As a consequence, the creation of a
'containing', 'holding' therapeutic environment seemed like a good
way to manage some of these feelings; sometimes it seemed to work,
sometimes not.

Despair spanned a considerable age range, and affected both girls
and boys. Often it was mixed with anger, and the anxiety that such
anger brings, and the struggle to resolve mixed feelings was also
evident, as were the use of a range of defence mechanisms to deal
with this depressive anxiety. Death, destruction and danger were
often in evidence, as was the splitting off of difficult feelings on to
outside objects or figures.

High levels of parental conflict were evident in most of these
children's families, and for almost half the children, battles were of
long standing, involving protracted court wrangles and lengthier
than usual involvement on my part. It may be that for many of these
children, despair stemmed from the sheer exhaustion of managing
the situation, and the strain of occupying the middle ground, as well
as being the source (at least ostensibly) of the conflict.

As I have already suggested, working with these children caused
particular problems. I found it very painful to witness some of their
behaviour, and there was often very little I could do either to enable
them to explore their feelings more fully, or to help them with their
pain. Simply being there was often very difficult, but I became
increasingly aware of the importance of doing this. It also seemed

useful to acknowledge both the children's sadness, and what an appropriate and reasonable feeling this was, under the circumstances. Respecting it and accepting it was often all that could be done.

Once again, my experiences in the counter-transference helped me to communicate to children that I had sensed something of their plight and enabled me to convey something of the children's feelings to their parents. The despair, however, was often contagious and left me feeling hopeless, stuck and lost. The birds of worry and care, it seemed, did not appear to discriminate between worker and child.

# Chapter VII: The Retreating Child: In Search of the Lost Rainbow

So now it is in vain for the singer to burst into clamour
With the great black piano appassionato. The glamour
Of childish days is upon me, my manhood is cast
Down in a flood of remembrance, I weep like a child
For the past.

D. H. Lawrence: Piano

Retreating into an earlier stage of development, as a response to crisis, is a well recognised phenomenon (Bowlby 1961; Parkes 1972; Pincus 1976; Jewett 1984). Many of the divorcing parents I encountered had been catapulted back in time by the loss of so much that defined them as adults, often behaving more like their children than their children. Some recaptured their adolescence in bursts of excesses of different kinds, often accompanied by changes in dress, and sudden switches in mood. Some retreated to even earlier stages in childhood, and like Tanya's mother, encountered in Chapter VI, became, on an emotional level, vulnerable, fragile toddlers – babes in the wood who were so lost and frightened that they could provide the actual children in the family with little or no support.

Periods of regression are generally accepted as a natural feature of a child's normal development as well as being a common response to stress, emotional strain and significant crises in adult life. As we lurk in the doorway that leads from one stage of life to the next, filled with a mixture of terror and excitement, it is both tempting and natural to dash back for one last suck at the bottle, rock in the cradle, or go on the potty, before going forward, clutching whatever transitional object seems best suited to the occasion – be it a scrap of material, teddy, or filofax, depending on age and inclination. Temporary regression is to be expected, under circumstances where there is stress and anxiety. Such behaviour sounds the alarm that all is not well, and that there is a need for special care and understanding until the child feels confident enough to approach the doorway once again. The divorced child however, often finds that parents are so worried and distressed themselves that they cannot bear to see the child's needs, feeling there is no more they can give. Under these circumstances the child has to increase the volume on the alarm, in the hope that someone may eventually hear.

Regression, then, like anger and depression, is a recognised stage in the mourning process, and an accepted, normal means of dealing with a severe shock or upset. Jewett (1984) locates this particular reaction in the second stage of mourning – what she calls the phase of acute grief. Together with the yearning, pining and searching behaviour also identified and described by Parkes (op. cit.), in relation to adult mourning, Jewett (Ibid) describes regression as "a common companion to the conflict and fatigue that results from the yearning and pining stage". Accompanying this period of internal work and adaptation to a new situation is a desperate desire for happy endings, a fondness and fascination for fairy stories with magical resolutions, and a see-sawing between anxiety and despair, in which hope recurs as the moving force between these two states.

What Jewett describes as "magical thinking" as a way of managing this difficult time is not uncommon – "If I'm good for three days....if that cloud has not moved by the time I count six....if I manage not to step on the cracks between the paving stones on the way home from school....then everything will be all right again". All this can be accompanied by what could be called 'searching' behaviour – preoccupation with the 'lost' person, aimlessness, a sense of tense anticipation, as though anxiously waiting for something to happen. Wishing and hoping are compounded by the often intensely mixed feelings towards the lost person, and a sense of fury and impotence in the face of these strong conflicting pressures on the emotions. For children of divorce, this complex set of feelings is constantly reactivated by contact. If visits are irregular, or the child is let down, the caretaking parent may often conclude that the price being paid by the child for uncertain contact is too high. However, as Jewett (Ibid) observes:

> "visiting also allows the child, through trial and error, to work not only towards accepting the situation, but making the best of it.... Through repeatedly being frustrated and letting go, the child gradually understands the reality of the separation".

There is also an additional dimension. Because the lost person is still in the world, in existence, the mixture of hope, magical thinking, and yearning impels many children to seek that person's return. Searching, dreaming and magic are all to do with disbelief and refusal to accept what has happened.

Under what one would call normal circumstances, when parents are able to function at an appropriate level, and are having their own needs met sufficiently, this will enable them to cope with regressed behaviour in their children in a sensitive, tolerant way. Their perceptions of such behaviour will also take a particular form, since they will see it in a certain context, with some understanding of, and sensitivity to both the child's developmental stage, and the 'task' or problem to which the child is responding. However, as has been apparent in many of the families I have discussed so far, parents who are in the throes of separation and divorce not only often behave atypically, but react differently to the same set of circumstances. For many of the children in this chapter therefore, regressed behaviour was not seen by their parents as a normal reaction to what was happening, but in a variety of different ways that were often not only less than helpful, but served to exacerbate the reaction as well.

Randall (1990) points out that parents in the process of coping with separation can mistake normal adaptive behaviour for evidence of emotional or behavioural problems. On a more complex level, however, he also identifies a parental reaction in which natural adaptive behaviour can be seen by the parent as a deliberate act of aggression towards them – a way of annoying them, blaming them, antagonising them. Randall argues that only when the parent is reassured that this behaviour is part of the child's way of coping, can the parent react in a less threatened, less hostile, and more understanding way.

When parents themselves are feeling thrown back into a very much earlier stage of development, it becomes particularly difficult for them to cope with regressed behaviour in their children. Firstly, such behaviour makes increased demands on a parent's time and attention, both of which are often in short supply, not only by virtue of practical circumstances, but as a result of the parent's own emotional state. Secondly, such behaviour underlines children's dependency, vulnerability, and distress – all of which touch the parent in tender places, whether they be bereft, angry, guilt ridden, or relieved about what has happened. Perspective changes, communication becomes more difficult, and the potential for misunderstanding and over reaction is considerable. For many of the children in this chapter, therefore, one of my tasks was to translate a child's 'regressed' behaviour to a parent – and sometimes vice-versa – and enable it to be perceived in a less threatening way, so that it could become more of a request and less of an accusation.

Once again, as with the notion of depression in the children I encountered, I will be using the term 'regression' advisedly. Many of the children who will be encountered here show symptoms of regression – lapses in development, behaviour more appropriate to a younger child, increased attachment to babyhood toys, intense separation anxiety that had, according to parents, been previously overcome, primitive wailing, searching behaviour and so on. To some degree, these characteristics overlap with some of those exhibited by the 'despairing' children – yearning, pining and primitive wailing all feature in both groups. However what defines them for me as 'retreating' rather than 'regressed' is an additional quality. What I will be describing here is something akin to Proust's

'Remembrance of Things Past' – a yearning to retreat or return to what is often perceived as an ideal state, when the family was together, everything was perfect, and the world was a safe, predictable place. Part of this ideal state is actually starting anew with the hope of a different ending – or as Naomi, who will be encountered in Chapter VIII, put it: "It's a pity it (life) isn't like a video that you can put back in the machine and wind back to the place when it was last good".

The children in this chapter were all trying to deal with a frightening and distressing period in their lives, by dipping back into the past in the hope of finding a way of operating that either enabled their needs to be perceived and met more effectively, or removed them from the conflict. It was often convenient to pretend you could neither speak nor understand, as a way of denying what was happening. Denial is the earliest defence to come into play in the human repertoire of self protective mechanisms, often to be observed in very young infants (Jewett op. cit.; Miller et. al. 1989). By the same token, when adult conversations about residence and contact became unbearable, a series of baby-like wails and cries, accompanied by exaggerated thumb sucking and demands for cuddles, could all prove useful means of distraction, as well as providing both an outlet for the dreadful feelings inside, and a source of comfort. This behaviour often seemed linked with the searching impulses common in the mourning process. These children were not only searching for the 'lost' parent, and for the life that was, but also for a comfortable, bearable way of coping – rather like finding a restful position in which to lie, when in pain.

Many of the children were enabled to retreat into babyhood by virtue of the fact that they had older brothers and sisters who could carry the worry, anxiety and adult responsibility, thus freeing them to escape from having to confront what was happening. Some children were able to move back and forth from one state to another – parental children had periods when they retreated to an earlier stage; apparently mature and poised children would suddenly need to let go and dash backwards in quite a dramatic way. Many identified strongly with babies in their discussions, yearning to return to that state as an escape from reality.

In many ways, being a baby is often seen as the most ideal state of all, evoking nostalgic memories of being a central figure, much cared for and protected from harm. Babies get enormous amounts of fuss and attention, everything is done for them, they have no responsibilities, their needs are simple and all they have to do is cry or smile and lo! – these needs are met. Best of all, babies cannot answer questions, take sides, express views about contact, or tell tales. As a result they are largely excluded from the parental battleground. Often forgotten, or unconsciously blocked out are the less acceptable emotions accompanying this state – helplessness, dependency, strong conflicting impulses of love and hate towards the same person or people, and the acute sense of chaos that can so easily ensue as a result of separations, or needs not being met quickly enough. Control can be exerted over circumstances – through feeding, crying, excreting, and play – but on the whole this is a time of powerlessness and total reliance on others. Although this clearly has its advantages, it can have disadvantages too, depending, to some degree, upon those exercising the control at the time.

## Anjit

Despite the pitfalls and the negative aspects, Anjit, at the age of seven, had decided that being a baby was definitely the thing to be. Two factors appeared to me to have influenced this view – the story he told me about a significant and beautiful memory of the time when he was little, and the arrival of his half sister, who seemed blissfully relieved of the kind of problems with which he was contending. Anjit was the only child of Indian parents, born some four years after they had married in accordance with their cultural tradition. By this stage, according to both parents' accounts, difficulties had already arisen, and Anjit's mother petitioned for divorce on the grounds of unreasonable behaviour, maintaining that his father had a drink problem, was frequently violent, and took little interest in either herself or their child. Anjit's father denied all the allegations against him, but the damage had been done. Anjit's parents ultimately parted very acrimoniously when he was almost three, by which time an injunction had been necessary to remove his father from the home, and secure his mother's protection.

After the separation, contact was established, albeit with considerable difficulty, although each parent alleged that the other regularly failed to keep to arrangements made, and the pattern, as described to me, sounded erratic and unpredictable. In addition, it seems that there were frequent scenes between the parents, invariably witnessed by their child. Respective families also became involved, and Anjit frequently heard perjorative remarks being made by each parents' relatives, about the other.

Against this atmospheric backdrop, it was surprising that contact took place at all; it was not surprising, however, that, after just over two years, contact broke down completely, with each parent blaming the other. Anjit was taken to India for a period, and by the time he returned he had had no contact with his father for eighteen months. By this time, his mother had established a relationship with someone else, and this appeared to galvanise his father into taking the matter to court, so that contact could be defined, and thereby, as he saw it, guaranteed. A welfare report was duly ordered. Although, from what he said in discussion with me, it was apparent that Anjit's father found contact very hard to cope with, he made it clear that his son was very important to him, and, in the context of what he saw as his failure as a husband, he wanted to at least attempt to develop an identity as a father, as well as preserving Anjit's links with his extended paternal family. A diffident, uncertain man, who found feelings difficult to talk about, he none the less conveyed that, apart from his need for the role of father, he had interest in and affection for his son, despite equally obvious mixed feelings about the wisdom of reopening old wounds. His account suggested that, during the time contact took place, Anjit's visits to his home were a source of mutual enjoyment for all the family, and he had clear memories of the things they did together.

Anjit's mother was furious about the contact application, and made no secret of the fact that she was totally opposed to it – she made it clear to me that Anjit had a new Daddy now, and the family should be left alone, in her opinion. She left Anjit in no doubt about her view of his father, and resented my involvement as the welfare officer investigating the situation, particularly when I did not automatically agree with her.

By the time I met Anjit, he had not seen his father for two years. Our first meeting took place at his home. A slender, striking child, with big, dark eyes, he was initially reluctant to have a private talk to me in his bedroom. However, his mother insisted and, there, he relaxed and chatted enthusiastically. I explained to Anjit that I had come to see him because I had been told that, once, he, Mummy and Daddy had all lived together, but then Daddy had moved away, had visited Anjit for a while and had then stopped. I told him that I did not know why this was – perhaps he did not know either – but I had come to see what he thought about it, in case I could do anything to help. Anjit admitted that his mother and his aunt had told him I was coming to see him to talk about his "old Daddy" – his name for his father. His mother's new husband was referred to as the "new Daddy" or, more significantly, the "good Daddy". This seemed to represent a process of splitting by which the child was managing these two kinds of Daddy, who were clearly being presented to him as a good one and a bad one.

Anjit said he could not remember when his parents had lived together, and did not know why his father had gone away. He did however, remember, visiting his father at his paternal grandparents' house, but told me this stopped because "he drank and smoked too much" – a rather quaint observation from one so young. What became rapidly evident, was the degree to which Anjit's mother had convinced him that his father was simply a smoking, drinking menace – a bad person who was easily replaced by a "new Daddy". This left Anjit in some confusion, since there was clearly no room for him to express the fond feelings that he had managed to retain for him. matters were not helped by the fact that "Mummy and auntie said that my old Daddy is going to fight Mummy, and auntie, and baby and me", although he had no idea why this should be. He was unable to tell me what his mother thought about him seeing his father, simply changing the subject.

Later on, when I saw Anjit and his mother together, she left him in no doubt of her views about this, and it was obviously not the first time he had heard them.

Anjit's preoccupation with babies ran like a thread through our discussion. He was very anxious to know whether I had a baby, whether I was going to have a baby, and – almost implicitly perhaps – whether I might be interested in taking on a baby of, say, about seven years old. He then told me about his mother's new baby, who was only a few weeks old, and didn't have a name yet – he said he just calls her "baby", adding that she was not allowed out in the sun yet, and asking me when she would be able to do this. He then said "I wish I was a baby – can you remember when I was a baby? How old were you when I was a baby?", almost as though he had lost this part of himself somewhere and needed to establish some kind of context for it. It also felt to me as though he yearned for the kind of care the baby had been getting, and had been unable to hold onto a sense of being loved and looked after, because of all the change and upheaval he had sustained. Listening to him, I experienced, in the counter-transference, a sense of loss, envy and desolation.

Within this part of our discussion, there emerged a recurring wish to "live high up" – sometimes on his own, and sometimes with the baby down below. I wondered whether his uncertainty about whether or not he wanted the baby was both to do with his envy and mixed feelings, but also reflected an identification with the baby. I also wondered about the desire to be up high and whether this was connected to a wish to become both more powerful than the apparently all powerful baby, and to remove himself from the conflicting loyalties presented by his father's wish to see him, and his mother's desire to prevent this. This wish was graphically acted out later on, when Anjit came to the office, where he spent his first supervised meeting with his father sitting on the roof of the play house, but for the time being we simply explored it in terms of escaping from something. I commented that seeing Daddy was a difficult thing to talk about, particularly when he knew Mummy was not happy about it, and that it would be good if he did not have to think about it, by living "high up" and out of the way, but that I hoped, when we met again we could work out some way of helping to sort this out.

Anjit appeared to have no memory of what he did with his old Daddy. Instead, my attempts to explore this brought back an experience he had had with his mother. All of a sudden Anjit said "Mummy took me to Brighton when I was three and we picked flowers". His account of this day had a beautiful, idyllic quality, which seemed to me to be a way of invoking a time when life was full of flowers, when he was a baby. The detail was scant, however – rather like a mirage that goes as suddenly as it appears.

When Anjit and I joined his mother, after quite an animated discussion lasting almost an hour, he suddenly became rather subdued, particularly when his mother made her views about contact clear. He brightened, however, at the thought of coming to the office, and wanted to know how he would get there, what my car was like, and so on. In the event, subsequent sessions proved very difficult. My first attempt to take Anjit to the office was blocked by his mother's fear that I was taking him to see his father in secret, and she insisted that I saw him at her home instead. She then appeared to short circuit what I had assumed was to be a long and difficult process, by suggesting that I saw Anjit with his father so I could see that they did not really have a relationship at all. Equally amazingly, she agreed to a joint meeting with him, to discuss the contact situation.

When Anjit did eventually come to the office, it was for a family meeting, followed by a period of supervised contact. During my discussion with his parents, he absorbed himself in a series of jigsaw puzzles, meticulously sorting out pieces, and carrying them over to the other side of the room, where he then arranged them in a series of neat rows. This seemed to me to be a graphic representation of his attempt to put the pieces of his life together, impose order on chaos, gain some mastery over the muddle. He refused to either acknowledge his father's presence or to speak to him, and the only way he was prepared to be alone with him, was if I stayed in the room too. Once again, he seemed preoccupied with babies, being a baby, and my apparent lack of them. He expressed a strong wish to come home with me, wanting to know every personal detail, from my age, to my address. During the contact, which was quite difficult at first, Anjit was initially insistent that all remarks went through me, although eventually he was able to relax and begin to ask his father various questions. However, he chose to conduct most of his discussion with his father from the roof of the play house. I reminded Anjit of our discussion about his wish to "live high up". He just smiled.

Although Anjit showed curiosity about his father and was able to begin to dredge up memories of their time together, the real issue for him, as far as I could see, was rather more complex than simply grappling with the loss of a parent. In my view, Anjit was struggling with the loss of someone called a "father" that he had had as a baby but had somehow lost. The memories about him were taking shape, sometimes in quite an idealised form, rather like his memory of his day in Brighton with his mother, but the more important bit seemed to do with the fact that he needed a father of his own, as his baby sister had. This seemed to me the basis of the fragile connection that I saw developing between them.

Anjit was able to acknowledge his wish to see his father, and his father appeared relieved and gratified by this. However, having got what he thought he wanted, it soon became apparent that his father lacked the initiative to maintain contact over time, and that this lent grist to his mother's mill. Anjit's father soon began missing appointments for contact, while continuing to emphasise his wish to see his son. No wonder Anjit chose to remain "high up" out of range of these contrary folk who made his life so complicated. No wonder that he yearned for the idyllic world of babyhood, in which I had become the good parent, the ideal mother. I felt that Anjit badly needed someone to recognise his predicament, and help him accept the kind of father he had, while enabling him to hang on to some sense of him, for later on, perhaps. This duly formed the business of our time together. I subsequently discovered that Anjit and his father did begin seeing one another again, and that his mother was accepting this, albeit in a rather long suffering spirit.

## Angela and Patrick

Angela shared many of Anjit's preoccupations, for similar reasons. At nine, she was old enough to have some memories of life when her parents were together, which she insisted were all wonderful, despite the best efforts of her brother Patrick, to convince her otherwise – after all, he was fifteen, and there was nothing he didn't know.

Angela's parents had separated some five years before I met the family, and, like Anjit's, there was a history of violence. Contact had been established, had broken down, been re-established and broken down again so many times that all the participants had the air of punch drunk boxers. I became involved when Angela's father made his third – or fourth? – even he could not remember – application for contact. By this stage, the children had not seen their father for about a year. This was, in part, due to misunderstandings, geographical problems – Father had moved some distance away for professional reasons – and the fact that, on one occasion, he had promised to come and visit but had ultimately been unable to do so. This was something that both Angela and Patrick found very hard to accept or forgive. By this stage, Angela's mother had remarried and there was a baby of this relationship, a little girl of a few months old.

It was made very apparent to me that Angela's parents had never resolved their differences, and the antipathy they felt for one another was almost palpable. Her father, rather like Anjit's, was a man who felt uneasy in the world of emotions, and tended to discuss his children with me in terms that suggested that he viewed them primarily as his property. He saw contact as a practical issue, which simply had to be organised and managed and he was really not interested in any of my attempts to explain or interpret some of his children's attitudes and behaviour. Alongside this approach, however, was a clear wish to get to know his children again, share their interests and their lives, and play some part, exert some influence, as they grew up. His son had particular significance for him, perhaps as a reflection of himself, and there was a suspicion in both the mind of Angela's mother and in Angela's own head, that he exerted pressure on his daughter to see him mainly to gain access to his son, who at that stage was refusing to have anything to do with him at all. An additional factor, never admitted, was the fact that he felt understandably threatened by the children's step-father, to whom they were deeply attached.

Angela's mother, meanwhile, viewed her new husband as the children's real father, in all but blood, since he was playing this role with all the love, commitment and gusto that her first husband had failed to exhibit. She saw contact applications as selfish shows of strength whose aim was sabotage; he saw his applications as demonstrations of his power and rights.

Amid the jigs and reels executed by the adults involved, the children remained troubled and bemused. Their own views about contact tended to change according to who was applying pressure to whom, and, when I became involved, both were saying that they did not wish to see their father, as he had been violent to their mother and had, more recently, been "horrible" to both of them, in ways that were rather hard to fathom. It became clear that the central problem was the discomfort – at times closer to real pain – of being caught between all the adults they loved. It was obviously much easier to reject one side altogether, thus ensuring one's safe position with the other, than to manage the tension of being somewhere in between.

Angela was the more troubled child of the two. One reason was, perhaps, that, from a Freudian perspective, she had first lost her father at a crucial stage in her development, and was now having to compete with a baby sister for the love of her new parent – or so it seemed to her. In addition, unlike her brother, she had good, strong feelings for her father, and a desperate wish to maintain contact with him. However, she was fully aware that this desire not only set her apart from her brother, but roused the antagonism of the parents on whom she was totally dependent for her security. In short, she was making waves, she was fighting the party line, and she was risking eventual rejection. She was also confused and in conflict, feeling pulled in several directions, with what Jewitt identifies as "the need to relinquish what has been lost and the wish to hold on to it – the

pull between the past and the future" (Jewett 1984:33). This aspect
of the stage of what Jewett identifies as acute grief requires the
recognition of mixed feelings, and the identification of conflicting
impulses, so that the feelings can be mastered. This, then, became
the focus of my work with Angela.

Angela's response to this conflict was almost in the nature of a pre-
emptive strike – to all intents and purposes, she went on the attack,
or so it seemed. She became very difficult, alternating between
aggression and regression, – tearful, angry, and deliberately provocative. Problems developed at school, her work suffered and she
stole some chocolate from another child – an action that could be
seen as both a fairly classic cry for attention, and a need for love.
Angela, according to her mother, was becoming increasingly unable
to follow simple instructions, do things for herself, or concentrate.
She got slower and slower at getting ready for school, and insisted
that people did things for her of which she herself was quite capable.
Once again, Angela could be seen to be demonstrating not only the
signs of regression that accompany the acute stage of grief but also
the disorganisation which can also be a feature. At the same time – at
a point when she was driving her parents to distraction, since all they
could see was irritating and infuriating behaviour for no apparent
reason – she was also desperately demanding cuddles, hugs, and
attention. The overriding sense I had was that this little girl was out
of control, thrown back into the terrifying chaos of the helpless baby
who cannot communicate its needs and fears in a way that grown-ups
could understand. Needless to say, the adults concerned were rather
disinclined to respond to her, while she acted in a way that was both
incomprehensible and very annoying. During one discussion with
Angela and her mother, focusing on linking behaviour to issues of
conflict and confusion, Angela dissolved into tears, and went to her
mother to be cuddled and held. The latter found it impossible to
respond to this, and the second time Angela tried to throw herself
into her arms, she said, rather irritably "Not another cuddle,
Angela! Two in one day!" She then pushed her away, in what felt to
me like a very rejecting way, although it was disguised as
playfulness.

As we struggled with the problem of hanging on to the people you
love, when they don't love one another, letting go of the life that
was, coming to terms with how things were now, Angela talked
longingly about her wish to be a baby – to be like her sister Susie,
with one mum and one dad who would never have this problem. She
said she thought it would be lovely to be a baby – "to start from the
beginning again" and not have any worries. This was something we
were then able to talk to her mother and step-father about, and
Angela was able to climb onto her step-father's lap and be cuddled –
something he had found difficult to do until he was able to appreciate

the meaning of her behaviour.

The turning point came in an apparently very simple way. During a period of contact, Angela's father took her to the place where they had all lived as a family. "Everything was different – everything had changed," she said to me, afterwards. This seemed to have had the effect of enabling Angela to relive the fantasy of the old life, and finding it far from the imagined ideal. This, in turn, helped her to put certain things behind her and begin to come to terms with the way things really were – her father was not the man she had pretended he was, she could not recapture the past, she could not go back, and this was the way things were now. Soon afterwards she said that she no longer wished to see her father on a regular basis, but expressed enthusiasm for ad hoc arrangements to be made when she felt ready, rather than when her father demanded contact. It seemed to me that an important period of mourning had taken place – the integration of loss and grief, a degree of acceptance. For Angela, this seemed to be a reorganisation of what she had wanted to believe, and what was now true. She now appeared ready to begin to let go of the past and move forward, dealing with the way things were in the present. It seemed that Angela was now able to start to think about becoming nine once more.

## Beatrice

Beatrice, like Angela, also wanted to recapture the past, and frequently dipped back into babyhood, to deal with her feelings of loss. Beatrice, first encountered very briefly in the previous chapter, was the only child of a very young couple who had had a brief relationship, which they thought had ended until Beatrice's impending existence became apparent. As a consequence, they decided to live together once more, in an increasing state of tension, violence and unhappiness, until Beatrice was two. By this time, Beatrice's mother had decided that, for both their sakes, the couple should separate. Unfortunately, Beatrice's father did not agree, and there was a very difficult period of anger and bitterness, punctuated by threats on his part, leading to the granting of a non-molestation injunction, to protect Beatrice and her mother. When this was breached, the latter concluded that the only solution was to move well away from the area, and duly did so.

Between the separation and this move, contact had taken place on a regular basis. Tempers then cooled sufficiently to enable an agreement to be reached whereby Beatrice's mother would take her to stay with her father for the weekend, every two months or so. This proved, however, to be a confused and confusing period for all concerned. Beatrice's parents resumed an intermittent sexual relationship, sharing a bed during periods of weekend contact.

Beatrice was aware of this, and, as far as she was concerned, things appeared much as they had been before the separation. Had she been able to add at the time, she would clearly have put two and two together and made at least five. Meanwhile father's hopes had been raised, while mother was simply opting for a quiet life, and taking the line of least resistance – or so she said.

After two years of this arrangement, Beatrice's mother realised that she had to be firmer, give clearer messages, and conduct contact in a different way. Beatrice's father was considerably angered by her withdrawal and there was another violent scene. As a consequence contact broke down, and I became involved. By this time, Beatrice and her father had not seen one another for eight months.

Poor Beatrice was understandably confused by all that had happened. She had a memory of her parents being together, then apart, then together from time to time, and then apart once more. When I met her for the first time, at her mother's home, she viewed me with great suspicion, glaring at me with huge blue eyes, set in a sea of freckles. When her mother suggested she talk to me alone, she shook her mass of orange curls in violent refusal. Although only five, Beatrice had considerable style and charm. The contrast between this aspect of her behaviour – poised, mature, sophisticated and articulate as she was – was in stark contrast to a desperately infantile part of herself that erupted quite regularly in our early meetings.

The initial hour of my first visit was spent talking to Beatrice's mother. Throughout this time, Beatrice could be heard outside the door making loud crying noises, giving me the uncomfortable impression that she was quite distraught. Her mother was so upset herself that she paid little attention to this, and when Beatrice was at last invited into the room, I expected to see a deeply distressed, tear-stained child in need of considerable comfort. Not a bit of it. She was bright-eyed and cheerful, and patently hadn't been crying at all, although she was clutching a large comfort blanket. "I don't want to see you and I don't want to talk to you," she said, in a clear and dignified tone. I said that that was fine, and suggested instead that I talk to her, explain who I was and why I was there, and then she could think about what I had said in case it changed her mind. Beatrice began to head for a chair near me in readiness for this address, before being encouraged by her mother to sit on her lap. She duly curled up there and put her blanket over her head.

As I explained who I was, why I had come to see her, my knowledge of what had happened to her, and my awareness of some of the confusion and worry this could cause, Beatrice gave me what on one level I felt to be a clear symbolic representation of the central issue for her. She regularly reappeared, then disappeared behind her protective cover, effectively reflecting the loss and reclamation of her father, and the life she had known when her parents were together.

However, this time, it was she, and not some adult, who was controlling the comings and goings – a game very reminiscent of the 'peep-boo' play of babies and toddlers who are coming to terms with separations and reunions with important figures, and need to feel that they have some control over these. This was behaviour I had frequently witnessed in the course of infant observations and fitted exactly with the symbolic implications described by both Winnicott (1964) and Lieberman (1979), who observes that a hide and seek game

> "represents a reversal of the anxious child who searches for its parents and turns a passive experience into an active one....It enables children to test the permanence of objects" (Lieberman 1979)

After a while, Beatrice came out from behind her cover, fixed me with a very shrewd gaze and listened intently, sizing me up, as though I was being interviewed for a job – as I suppose I was. By the end of the visit she was sitting beside me, checking that I had spelt her name correctly in my diary, and asking whether she could come and see me tomorrow. She then became increasingly exuberant, over-excited and rather out of control, as though the anxiety of it all had penetrated her consciousness once again and had to be driven away.

When Beatrice and her mother came to the office for the first time, the latter had evidently thought about contact a great deal, and was in a rather hostile mood. Beatrice played in the play house, while her mother made it clear that she felt contact should not take place, due to the personality and conduct of Beatrice's father, and her abiding belief that his motives for seeing his child were born of revenge, as well as a wish to see her in an attempt to resume their relationship. She was also very doubtful that the father would maintain contact, once it was apparent that mother was not part of the package.

Interestingly, however, it appeared that since my first visit, Beatrice and her mother had talked a lot about contact, memories, both good and bad, revealing a recollection of details and events that her mother had not realised Beatrice had had. Beatrice told me she could recall "tickling Daddy's feet and that was nice". Although my original intention had been to see Beatrice alone, as is my practice, I decided that in view of the level of Beatrice's mother's hostility, she would be unlikely to accept any account I gave her of what Beatrice said, and that it would therefore be better if she heard it directly.

Beatrice needed little encouragement to begin to untangle the threads of thought in her mind. "I do want to see Daddy....sometimes I think of him when I am quiet and on my own....sometimes when I am resting. Sometimes when I think of him I call him "Brian" in my mind but when I see him I call him Daddy.... I don't

know why I don't see him anymore, except he's a long way away."
She then described how she and Mummy used to go and see him,
but that when Mummy wanted to leave he did not want her to go.
  Beatrice told me she had been to stay at Daddy's house and at
granny's. I encouraged her to draw these houses for me, and
although she only drew the occupants of granny's house, she drew
Daddy's house in some detail – a cosy looking place, with smoke
curling from the chimney, lots of windows and a large, welcoming
front door. As we went through the house, Beatrice identified the
rooms, allocating a bedroom to Mummy. Her mother, clearly struck
by this, was able to explain very gently that she had never been to
stay at this house. "But that's where Daddy says you will stay when
you come to visit," Beatrice explained. I said I thought it was really
difficult when you want a Mummy and Daddy to be together and
they're not, and how good it would be if you could make them get
together again. I also said I thought that Beatrice had probably
worked very hard to make this happen, and that there were times
when it looked as though it had worked. Sadly, though, this was not
going to happen. Beatrice agreed that Daddy wanted to get back
together again, but Mummy didn't. We looked at the problems this
caused for her, and the fact that she might worry that if she said she
wanted to see Daddy, Mummy would be upset. Throughout this
discussion, I noticed that, although Beatrice could maintain a
thoughtful, mature tone for much of the time, she would occasionally retreat from the gravity of it all by saying "I've forgotten" in
quite a babyish tone of voice.
  It then emerged that Beatrice had been very reluctant to come to
see me. She was unable to tell me why this was, so I asked for her
permission to have a guess about this, and suggested that it could be
because we were going to be talking about Daddy, and the
possibility of seeing him, and that she wasn't sure how Mummy
might feel about this. Beatrice simply beamed at me, and told me I
was completely wrong. During the remainder of the session she
made increasingly close physical contact with me, and when it was
time to leave, became more and more manic, speaking in a squeaky
voice, and pretending she had forgotten how to put her shoes on,
because she was only a baby. After trying to hide her mother's car
keys, and then refusing several times to say goodbye, she suddenly
resumed her former poise, and calmly left the building after we had
made another appointment.
  Two weeks later, Beatrice and her mother came to the office again.
This time Beatrice was once again the poised sophisticate, applying
herself to her drawing with mature concentration. Her first picture
was of herself and a cousin in a garden containing one glorious
flower, beneath an ominously stormy sky. In the picture Beatrice
was about to go down the slide, while her cousin stood nearby. This

seemed to sum up Beatrice's predicament rather neatly – about to go down a slippery slope, not knowing whether anyone would be there to catch you. There was the promise that all would be well, however, in the form of the flower. Atmospherically, however, a storm could be brewing.... We discussed the picture, and Beatrice told me that her cousin's parents did not live together either. Her cousin never saw her Daddy, but she – Beatrice – had decided that she wanted to see hers. There she was, then, at the top of the slide, ready to take the plunge.

Beatrice had decided, she said, that she wanted to go and see her Daddy at his house. When her mother made it clear that she herself would not be going too, Beatrice admitted, with feigned non-chalance, that she would mind this, and suggested that Daddy come to see her at her house instead. Once again we addressed the difficulty in not being able to make your parents get back together again, however much you tried. Beatrice's mother reminded her of the arguments they used to have – "Don't talk about arguments – you know I hate arguments!" said Beatrice, waving her hand across her mother's face, as though to wipe away her words.

Suddenly, out of the blue, Beatrice said "I was sad when the bird died". This emerged as a reference to a pigeon she and her mother had found injured in the road, that had subsequently died. There seemed to me to be a connection between the discussion of the 'death' of her parents' relationship, and this actual death, and we discussed this link, particularly in view of the hope that you can hang on to for a long time that eventually something that seems as though it has gone will come back. Beatrice then began playing in the play house, examining some of the puzzles and games. She commented on the fact that some of the pieces were missing – "There are lots of lost things here" – and her mother added "Yes, this is a place for lost souls". It felt as though a long cherished hope had been laid to rest, and that there was now some acknowledgement that something important had been lost, relinquished. The play room, with its collection of "lost" things, seemed to be an appropriate place to bury the body. Like Angela, Beatrice had started to let go of something idealised, hoped for, and dreamed of, and that, having done so, she was ready to think about moving forward. Beatrice's last drawing was a complicated pattern of brightly coloured shapes, which all fitted together. She left the office in a calm, poised state of mind, with no hint of mania or regression, taking both her drawings with her.

Contact between Beatrice and her father was eventually put to the test and established, although it took place in Beatrice's home town rather than in her father's house. Tensions continued between the parents but Beatrice seemed able to manage the situation, and her mother became more sensitive to her predicament.

## Carla

Like Beatrice, Carla, who featured significantly in Chapter V, also tended to move between two 'personae' in response to her parents' separation. Although her way of adapting was generally to become adult and parental towards her mother and little sister, despite the fact that she was only four, in the presence of someone she could perceive as genuinely grown up, she tended to retreat into babyhood, almost as a signal that all was not as it seemed. At our first meeting, she climbed onto my lap within a very short space of time, drinking from a baby's feeding cup, and cooing. During difficult periods of discussion about her parents' situation, or about contact, she would move backwards and forwards between her mother and myself, making a series of noises ranging from baby sounds to the cries of wild animals – denial, avoidance and disbelief characteristic of the early stage of grief. During the diversion that this created, she would curl up in a foetal position, and rock backwards and forwards.

Throughout this first visit, I was struck by the contrast between Carla's extrovert, poised, grown-up behaviour – often accompanied by instructions or advice to either her mother and her sister – and the sudden backward leap into infancy, characterised by a sudden clutching of her comfort blanket, frantic thumb sucking, and the repetitive twirling of strands of her hair, which seemed to be a form of self comfort. A child who had been encouraged to grow up quickly, through circumstances beyond her control, Carla seemed to need to retreat at regular intervals, both to comfort herself, and to obtain appropriate attention from others.

Carla, as I have described in Chapter V, had come to see her mother as a fragile, vulnerable person who needed looking after. In contrast, Carla's father appeared more stable and robust, both to me, and, I suspect, to her. It was interesting to observe, therefore, that during a period of supervised contact, Carla once more became a baby, curling up on her father's lap, sucking her thumb, and stroking her hair. She also soiled herself on this occasion, as though letting go of an important grown up accomplishment, to confirm her identity as a baby. This sudden failure of control was often a feature of these retreating children, burdened with adult worries, who had opted to be grown up, long before their time.

## Sally

Sally, another parental child who also appeared in Chapter V, reacted in a similar way. At seven, she was articulate, worldly wise, and confident in her analysis of her parents' situation. She knew all about the breakdown of her parents' marriage, could comment on the maintenance and property issues, and offered succinct criticism of the behaviour of the adults concerned. The giveaway was the fact that she regularly wet the bed. When we discussed this, she explained, in a very grown up way, that this was because she was worried about the fact that her father wanted both the children to go and live with him. She did not intend to do it – it just happened, and often after her return from contact. Although very adult and matter of fact on the surface, Sally would often reveal her vulnerable, baby side through her attachment to her toys. On one occasion, having introduced me to two of her favourites – her babies, as she called them – she informed me that "they have both gone out of the room now because they didn't understand what was happening". When I made the connection between their predicament and her own, Sally was able to acknowledge the similarities. I was subsequently struck, in play sessions, by the frequency with which I was left to baby sit for Sally's "babies" as though I could be entrusted to care for the baby part of herself.

## Sarah, Hugh and Anna

For some of the children in the sample, retreat was made possible by the presence of another child in the family who was able to act out some of the other reactions. Paul, encountered first in Chapter V, enabled Peter to retreat into a depressed state in which he became much younger than his years; Sophie performed a similar function for Sean, as Holly did for Emma (see Chapter VIII). Often retreat was signalled by primitive wailing, and bouts of incessant noise and chanting, as Kathy, and Tanya have demonstrated in Chapter V. Curling up, thumb sucking and the sudden need for cuddles were also common features among these children.

Sarah, Hugh and Anna were thirteen, nine and four, respectively, when their parents separated. This had been precipitated by their mother, after several years of a difficult and frustrating marriage, which, despite withstanding many other vicissitudes, appeared to flounder once the youngest child had become a little more independent. This had also coincided with a move to a new area, involving a larger mortgage for a bigger house. All the children had been very unsettled by what had happened and very upset by their father's obvious distress. For Sarah and Hugh, the situation was further compounded by the fact that they had been adopted as babies, and this crisis seemed to resurrect uncertainties and insecurities about what would happen to them, and who wanted them most. Sarah was so angry with her mother for, as she saw it, splitting up the family, that at one stage she talked in terms of going off to find her real mother, since she clearly felt she might be an improvement on the current model.

Both parents wanted all three children to be placed in their sole care and a welfare report was ordered. I first met the children at their mother's home. Sarah appeared, on the surface, the most aloof, playing the role of a Greek chorus, by presenting a running commentary on what everyone else was doing and saying. Her hostility towards her mother was very evident, and she rarely missed an opportunity to criticise, contradict, or imply that something was being said or done for my benefit – "You don't usually do that mum.... you don't usually say that, mum.... you don't normally allow them to behave like that". Under the layers of sarcasm and derision, there was clearly a troubled, angry young woman, who apparently, by her own admission, spent hours in her room, as though to hide from the events occurring around her. Sarah accepted my presence in a calm, aloof manner, confirming her understanding of my role, which she saw as "being there to assess the family situation".

Anna, at the other end of the developmental spectrum, was an energetic, exuberant four year old, who ran about constantly, with her thumb in her mouth, clutching her comfort blanket. Occasionally she would make repetitive wailing noises, or pretend she either could not talk or could not understand what was being said to her. She often made close physical contact with me, and made the most of being a baby, by claiming everyone's attention as often as possible.

Hugh, meanwhile seemed to be carrying the uncertainty and the confusion for the trio. A skinny, dreamy looking child, he seemed to be unable to get anything right, incurring criticism from both Sarah and his mother, whatever he did. He seemed strangely reconciled to this role, although occasionally directed flashes of anger at Sarah, when the provocation became too great.

Sarah's envy of Anna's apparently oblivious baby state was almost palpable. She often glared at her with disgust when she was being particularly regressed, and alternated between being fairly maternal, to being intensely rejecting, much to Anna's bewilderment. Whenever the children's mother did anything for Anna, Sarah would retort "You never did that for me when I was a baby".

When I saw the children with their father, Anna's behaviour became even more regressed than before. She constantly climbed onto his lap for cuddles, screamed incessantly if he did not do as she asked, sucked her thumb constantly, and ran around making growly, animal noises, rather reminiscent of primitive baby sounds. Interestingly, Sarah too had become more regressed, perhaps feeling that her father was grown up enough to allow her to retreat for a while, relieved of the burden of monitoring and checking on her mother. She would often suck her thumb, and there were moments when she would completely forget her other self, and enter into a game, in a genuinely playful spirit. Clearly for Sarah, an occasional retreat from the demands of adolescence was made all the more necessary as she coped with the crisis between her parents, and the responsibility she felt it placed on her.

Blos (1962) has drawn attention to adolescence as a "second individuation process" which has much in common with the first, occurring in the first three years of life. Because the two stages have so much in common – struggles with separation, physical changes, vulnerability of personality – it is hardly surprising to find the three year old Sarah inside her teenaged body. For several of the older children in the sample, this was a necessary reaction at a time of great stress – a reaction often misunderstood and frowned upon by exasperated parents who were relying on the fact that they had at least one grown up child who could cope with what was happening in the family. In these families, as in Sarah's, it was important to help the parents free the adolescent, allowing some retreat, just as it was important to alert them to the messages that their actual four year old was giving them about the degree of stress she was experiencing.

Eventually, in this case, the parents became so concerned about the effects their conflict was having on their children that they decided to reconcile.

## Neil and Simon

Neil and Simon were nine and five respectively when their mother decided to divorce their father. She had initially decided to take this action some three years before, and a very difficult period of acrimony had ensued. As a result of the tension engendered by this, she had experienced considerable stress, and had been hospitalised for a period for what was described as a "mild manic depressive illness". Because of this, she decided not to proceed with the divorce, since she feared she might lose the children.

When she initiated proceedings a second time, the children's father initially sought a reconciliation, but discovering this was fruitless, chose to conclude that his wife was once again suffering from a mental illness, and applied for custody of the children. It was at this point that I became involved with the family. At that stage they were all still living together in the same house, ostensibly for the sake of the children. However, it was apparent that a battle was going on between the parents over domestic tasks, and general child care, with each competing with the other.

On the occasion of my first visit, in order to see both parents and children, the tension in the home was palpable, despite the ostentatious smell of what I was told was father's home baking. Neil appeared to be a calm, poised child who seemed equally at ease with both his parents, and very protective of his younger brother. Simon seemed to be a charming, friendly five year old, although was so anxious that he tended to simply copy or echo everything that Neil said.

Our initial discussion focused on my role and the idea of a visit to the office for a couple of private discussions about what was happening at home. This was accepted calmly by both children, who were well aware of the issues. What also became apparent, however, was the degree to which they were being told pejorative things by each parent about the other. This had led to considerable confusion, they told me. Not surprisingly, it emerged that Simon was having difficulty concentrating at school, and was also regularly wetting the bed.

When I saw the children with both their parents, Simon became quite regressed, sucking his finger and curling up on his father's lap. Mother revealed that father often slept with Simon at night to comfort him, and indeed it was apparent from Simon's demeanour that he seemed desperate for cuddles and reassurance, gaining considerable comfort from being held in a foetal position on his father's lap.

Visits to the office revealed that Neil was being burdened by constant criticism of his mother, on one occasion complaining to me that she was not doing her fair share of the housework – a preoccupation I found unusual in a child of nine. It seemed to me as though, while he was grappling with all this strange information, probably coming at him from both sides, Simon was free to retreat from the arena of battle, often refusing to talk, pretending he had forgotten how, or making baby noises. This was particularly apparent when I saw the family together. Simon moved between myself and his parents, wailing and droning, increasing the volume until it was very difficult to hear anything that was being said. We talked about this in terms of the need to block out the painful nature of the discussion, and how much easier it would be to pretend it was not happening. It was also a way of deflecting attention away from the subject in the hope that it might be forgotten. The degree of Simon's distress enabled me to help the parents to look at ways in which they could reduce some of the arguments, competitiveness, and brain washing that had been taking place, and we focused on altering arrangements so that conflict could be reduced. The parents were also able to 'hear' for the first time, what the situation was doing to their children. Unfortunately, however, the parents continued in their legal battle, which was fought out in court to the bitter end. Mother ultimately 'won'.

## Summary: The Retreating Child

Retreat, then, for the children in this chapter, was a necessary way of leaving the field of battle, as well as a means of alerting the adults in their lives that something very unbearable was happening to them. Like despair, retreat as a mode of adaptation spanned a considerable age range and included both boys and girls. Much of the behaviour described in this chapter was characteristic of both the early and acute stages of the grieving process.

In terms of their development, all the children in this chapter should have theoretically mastered their first individuation process, resolving the tasks presented by Erikson's second stage of psychological growth in which the battle between autonomy and shame and doubt takes place. By the same token, all should have passed through Freud's oral and anal stages. Significantly, for all these children, mastery of developmental tasks associated with these stages had lapsed to some degree and all were exhibiting behaviours characteristic of much younger children.

In this contect, oral comforting in the form of thumb sucking was common; transitional objects also featured, perhaps as a way of hanging on to what was lost, to a previous phase of life when things seemed better. Regression as a defence against pain and anxiety was clearly operating for these children, as was denial that anything was really wrong, and the strong need to blot out reality with noise and diversion.

For parents, retreating children posed a number of problems. Already fraught and anxious, parents who thought they had children who had reached a reasonable level of autonomy suddenly found themselves the object of increased emotional demands, atypical behaviour and even wet beds or soiled pants. One of the major tasks I felt needed to be undertaken was to help parents understand this behaviour for what it was – natural, understandable separation anxiety and regression in the face of uncertainty and loss – while at the same time avoiding the trap of leaving them feeling persecuted and guilty for what they had supposedly 'done' to their children.

Once again, conflict between the parents of the children in this group was particularly high. Why it was that, in response to this, these children tended to regress more than to despair, is not clear to me, although the commencement of the official 'battle' tended to be more recent and this was, perhaps, significant. Children were experiencing a relatively new shock – retreat was the immediate instinctive reaction to this.

Working with these children once again required the ability to create a holding environment where behaviour could be accepted and contained, so that some kind of understanding, interpretation and translation could be conveyed to parents. In the countertransference I often felt an enormous sense of responsibility to protect, recue, cuddle, and fix. I was also often made to feel like the ideal mother, with the attendant expectation to make things right. Perhaps most powerful was a frequent sense of being filled with my own sense of loss and longing for a safe, predictable childhood that was gone. This enabled me to get a sense of the degree of desperation, yearning and longing which these children seemed to be experiencing, and to begin to help children towards the glimmer of an acceptance of what had been, and what might be to come.

# Chapter VIII: The Angry Child: Raging at the Pillars of Fire and Cloud

My mother groan'd! My father wept.
Into the dangerous world I leapt:
Helpless, naked, piping loud:
Like a fiend hid in a cloud.

William Blake: Infant Sorrow, from
Songs of Innocence and Experience

The anger was unthinkable, but it was not a thinking thing. It took charge of him and shook him. He was a rabbit in its jaws.

Peter Carey: Oscar and Lucinda

There can be little doubt that the emotions generated by marriage, separation and divorce might prompt many to sing their own versions of Blake's 'Songs of Innocence and Experience' particularly since relationships are so often conceived to the tune of the former state, and are ended as a result of the latter. The 'infant' referred to in the poem does indeed leap into a dangerous world at birth; the world of divorce, however, lends an additional dimension to everyday fears and resurrects all those primitive reactions associated with early experiences in infancy. The child of divorce is indeed "helpless, naked" and frequently "piping loud", though not always heard. This chapter is about such children – those whose principal response to separation and divorce is loud, protesting anger, borne of sorrow and frustration, and those whose angry feelings are so frightening that they have to be hidden and contained – "like a fiend, hid in a cloud" – or so overwhelming, and unthinkable that they seem to possess and entrap.

Grown up logic can often seem unfathomable and deeply flawed to a child, particularly when related to unpleasant, painful events. Separating parents will often tell a child that, although they are parting, the child is still loved and cherished by both. The child, quite understandably, wonders how this can be so, if the outcome is to turn his or her life upside-down – "if you really loved me, you'd stay together!" – is the perennial cry. The anger generated by what appears to be a hollow expression of concern which obviously masks a grown up wish to do what they want (or what one of them wants) – as usual – is often overwhelming, fearsome, and terrifying. A

145

murderous rage that has no bounds can be very difficult to carry
around with you....

The ability to express anger is not only a healthy and necessary
form of release, but it is crucial in terms of sound psychic
development for that expression to be permitted, accepted and
managed in childhood, by loving parents who are not destroyed or
damaged by it. The fear of chaos and disintegration as a result of
expressing anger, or the anxiety that one's anger will decimate its
object, quite apart from any other innocent obstacle in its path, is a
powerful force from infancy onwards (Klein 1940; 1957). Anger also
comprises many other elements – fear, sorrow, depression, love,
ambivalence – though is often expressed in ways which mask some of
its deeper aspects and can provoke the opposite reaction to that most
needed and desired at the time.

For the divorced child anger is a very tricky affair. No longer is
there a safe place where this feeling can be contained, processed, and
enabled to explode harmlessly – always assuming, of course, that the
child had a containing place to begin with. The world has become a
dangerous, unpredictable place where anything can happen – after
all, one parent has left home for some reason, so conceivably the
other could also leave at any second. Perhaps the child had
something to do with the parent's departure? If this was the case,
then it was clearly important to tread carefully, and not cause any
trouble, in order to preserve the parent that is left. Getting angry,
therefore, might not be a very good idea....

Once again, what Jewett (1984) refers to as "magical thinking"
often operates in such circumstances. Because parents are often so
angry themselves, any expression of anger by the child will often be
met with anger in return, so it becomes far safer to keep such
feelings hidden, since they are clearly so 'bad' and unbearable to
others. This reinforces the importance of being good as a way of
retrieving what is lost, almost as though bad feelings make you feel
so bad that you have to be extra good, to compensate. Feelings,
however, don't always simply go away because we want them to.

In my work with children of divorce, I encountered anger of
several different kinds, although many overlapped and comprised
additional features which I have dealt with elsewhere. This anger
was often felt, initially, rather than seen, or had been expressed in
ways not immediately obvious. I also encountered children who I felt
may well have been angry in their own right, but who were living in
such an angry atmosphere that it was sometimes hard to separate
their anger, from the projected anger of the parent/s. At times it
seemed as though adult lumps of feeling had been planted in the
children, so that they could carry the parental anger back and forth
during visits and fuel the marital war. Children became grenades,
Trojan horses, Cassandras. I felt that there was a need to free them

from this burden. I wondered whether acknowledging the child's anger in the context of several prearranged sessions might enable the child to begin to feel a little safer about setting it free. My theory was that if this intense feeling could be released in a safe place where it could be heard and accepted, this would then help children to express it to their parents with more confidence and less fear, thus, hopefully relieving them of the burden of carrying it around. Sometimes it seemed to work; at other times I was not so sure.

In considering this powerful emotion – anger – looking at it as a response to separation and loss, is perhaps the most obvious starting point. This is, of course, an extremely well documented reaction to a range of circumstances, as well as being an essential stage in the mourning process (Parkes 1972; Bowlby 1973; Jewett 1984). For divorced children, the situation is compounded by the fact that the experience of separation and loss is often regularly re-enacted and reinforced through the process of contact. As I have already suggested, in the early stages after the separation, this can become increasingly unbearable for both parents and children, and can often be a major reason behind a contact parent's decision to terminate contact, or a custodial parent's rationale for blocking it. When this painful re-enactment occurs in the context of intense parental conflict, the child's position becomes very difficult. How do you hang on to the middle of your rainbow, when your parents are pulling at each end?

## Joshua

Joshua was three when his parents separated, after a long and protracted period of acrimony, which included tempestuous arguments, outbursts of violence and, on one occasion, his mother's theatrical attempt to cut her wrists. I was constantly reassured by both Joshua's parents that he had been protected from witnessing many of the scenes between them, although probably remembered his mother's sudden departure from the home without him. Since the separation he had apparently shown no signs of distress, behaved well and was described as a happy child who really had no idea about the impending battle for his care. He appeared to have accepted his present circumstances with equanimity.

Joshua lived with his father and spent two and a half days a week with his mother. From my discussions with them, it was evident that his parents continued to feel both intense love and extreme hatred towards one another, characterised by frequent angry exchanges in front of their son, which both described to me in graphic detail. Joshua moved between them in an atmosphere of barely suppressed fury, and considerable pain.

When I met Joshua for the first time his parents had been apart for four months. His father reported that he had become rather clingy of late and seemed to become anxious whenever he left him to go out for the evening. During our first encounter Joshua fixed me with his dark wary eyes, accepting the explanation I gave him about who I was and why I had come without comment. He clung compulsively to his father, asking him, from time to time, whether he was going away, or going out. His father responded somewhat impatiently to this, remarking to me that "he wants to know where I am going every time I move an inch!" It was apparent that Joshua was both aware of, and sensitive to his father's unflattering, sotto voce comments to me about his mother.

Joshua had been born into a complicated family structure. Both his parents had been married before, and each brought children to the relationship. When his mother left, Joshua also lost a brother and a sister and the house, as a consequence, felt half empty to him. In addition everyone had changed bedrooms. As Joshua showed me round, explaining, rather sadly, who used to sleep where and who slept there now, he seemed lost and bewildered. As he tenderly stroked the hall wall, he looked at me and said: "There are cracks here now".

Joshua's world had become divided into the big house – Daddy's – and the little house – Mummy's. In the former he was expected to be quite grown up and he seemed to manage this well most of the time, appearing poised, responsible and obedient. In the little house he became Mummy's baby, often being cradled in her arms, sucking his thumb. During the time I worked with Joshua one of his favourite toys emerged as a Gobot – a robot that could be turned into an aeroplane and back again. This seemed to symbolise Joshua's plight quite graphically, and we regularly talked about how like a Gobot Joshua had had to become, having to change from one thing to another. At times he clearly felt strong, powerful and in control of his difficult predicament. At others, he seemed to experience a longing to take flight, and escape a very painful situation that made him very angry.

I saw Joshua four times, at both his homes, before I sensed he might be ready to come to the office to see me alone. Grown-ups, for Joshua, must have seemed, on the basis of his experience, strange, unpredictable creatures who gave no explanation for their actions. It was important therefore to give him time to make a thorough assessment of me. On this first occasion, Joshua was brought to the office by his mother and it was agreed that after his time with me, she would join us so that we could all talk together. I was surprised when Joshua agreed to be left alone with me, but thought it might be useful to acknowledge the worried looks he had given me at our previous meetings. "I was thinking of tigers," he said. I wondered aloud if perhaps he saw me as fierce and dangerous and did not know what I might do. He seemed to consider this but it was hard to know what he thought about it.

Joshua spent most of his first visit to the office drawing. He drew lots of pictures of crocodiles who, he said were all feeling sick and were either enclosed by gates, or stuck in jungles. He himself, he said, had been sick only that morning, and this identification with the crocodiles seemed to me to suggest that the pictures might be about some powerful, dangerous part of himself that was either being forcibly contained, or had to be kept in check for fear of what it might do. I also explored the possibility that Joshua felt he himself was stuck in the middle of something dangerous and frightening and might also have dangerous and frightening feelings. One of the crocodiles was being eaten by a bee and this led to a discussion about the way in which small things could be very powerful. Joshua reminded me that he himself was big – certainly not a baby, since he did not like them – and this seemed as though it might be linked to his need to be big and strong, in order to cope with what was happening around him.

After a while, Joshua's attention was drawn to a little wooden figure in the playroom whom he ultimately named Little Joshua, as he was Big Joshua. We talked about how Little Joshua might be feeling, whether he needed someone to look out for him and who that someone should be. Joshua elected me for this role, telling me, I think, as he did so, that there was a fragile part of himself that needed a bit of armour plating at this point. I made a point of holding the little wooden man very tenderly throughout the rest of the session, to try to convey that I was taking my responsibility seriously and was capable of holding on to the vulnerable part of Joshua.

As the session progressed, Joshua became increasingly boisterous, throwing toys and cushions across the playroom, and pretending to be he-man who, he said, was tough and strong. Something seemed to have been liberated and it looked as though some of the rage and anger that he was experiencing between his parents and that was inside him, as a consequence of the conflict he was in, was coming to the surface. Glancing into the play house, he remarked on the jumble of things inside and concluded that "there is something going on in there" but was unable to say more about it.

At the end of a session that lasted nearly an hour, Joshua's mother joined us. His energetic, often violent treatment of the things in the playroom increased significantly after her arrival, and, as she talked about her feelings for his father, he constantly moved between us making more and more noise.

By our second session, Joshua's anger was taking a more specific form. His father brought him to the office on this occasion, and he was accompanied by a Gobot. He was eager to come up to my room and parted unceremoniously from his father – "You can go home if you like". This session took place in my office, as opposed to the playroom, although all the playthings which had been available on the previous occasion were in evidence. The difference was that in my office there was a little dolls' house, rather than a big play house, and I wanted somehow to link this with Joshua's own experience of two houses, large and small. I explained that we were to spend time in another room so that he could see the other house that we had here.

Joshua, who seemed eager and excited about being at the office again, began by demonstrating to me how a Gobot worked and made the robot part of him shoot various things in the room. He explained that the Gobot was feeling very angry, because someone had made him angry – almost as though this anger had been put inside him by someone else. He explained that two other Gobots had been fighting and this had made him very angry. I suggested that perhaps Joshua felt a little like the Gobot when he heard his parents arguing. Joshua immediately adopted a menacing position and shouted into the space in front of him "Stop it! Stop arguing! Be quiet!" He then transformed the Gobot into an aeroplane and flew it about. I talked about how good it would be if Joshua could fly away whenever he heard his parents shouting at one another and he agreed.

Once again, Joshua drew several crocodiles. At the beginning of the session he told me they were all being sick – one, he explained, was ill because "he had been arguing too much" and, throughout the session, from time to time, the Gobot would resume his homicidal activities. By the end of the session, however, Joshua informed me that the crocodile was feeling much better. The Gobot's spirits had also improved – "He's not angry anymore," said Joshua. "He's going to point his gun downwards and he is not going to shoot anybody."

Joshua played briefly with the figures and animals in the dolls' house, and this enabled us to talk about the people in his two houses. Joshua recalled a holiday when they had all been together – he flew the Gobot-plane about talking about them all being on board. We acknowledged the sadness of not being together any more and talked about the empty rooms in the house, which he had shown me on an earlier visit. Joshua continued to mention anger, using the Gobot once again to reflect this and act it out for him. When Joshua rejoined his father he was calm but subdued and I wondered whether perhaps now that some of his anger had gone, he was beginning to move towards the next painful stage of the mourning process.

Soon after these sessions Joshua's mother reported to me that Joshua was becoming increasingly angry with her during periods of contact. This seemed to be the start of Joshua's struggle with his anger about her departure, and the mixture of love and fury he was feeling towards her. As we continued to work, Joshua and his mother were able to talk about this, and he continued to come to the office to unload and sort out some of his confusion, and let out more of his anger. We then discussed these difficult feelings with the relevant parent.

## Ben and Claire

Ben's anger was also to do with mourning the loss of the departed parent. However it was also about the fact that this parent – in his case his father – had apparently given up and gone away without a real struggle (at least from Ben's point of view) and his strong belief that his mother was responsible for what had happened. His mixed feelings towards her were quite graphically projected onto me during the course of a morning in the playroom, when I miraculously survived fire, flood, and gunshot wounds interspersed with very warm contact and a request to move into the office with me. It was also apparent that for Ben there was, in addition, a sense that there might be something bad about him that had made his father hate him enough to leave, and as a consequence his anger was often turned on himself, both in the form of self mutilation (scraping areas of skin until they bled) which Jewett (op.cit.) identifies as a possible reaction in the acute stage of grief, and by being so aggressive at nursery school, according to both his mother and his teacher, that he alienated other children.

Ben's world, like Joshua's, felt like a dangerous, unpredictable place. Grown ups with whom he had felt safe, and who had provided boundaries for him had become angry, moody, inconsistent people who had developed separate sets of goal posts for him – and then kept moving them. There was a lot of shouting in Ben's house; sometimes there was fighting too. Ben's father, an alcoholic, often looked strange, sounded funny and fell over things. Ben got frightened, confused and angry and started hitting his sister – after all, Mummy and Daddy were hitting one another. How baffling, then, to be told off for something they were doing themselves. When you are only four it's difficult to work out exactly what it all means.

When I first met Ben and his sister Claire, who was six, their parents had been apart for a year. Claire seemed to be dealing with the situation by cutting off from her father and identifying closely with her mother. It seemed to be Ben's task to carry her anger as well as his own. The parents' separation had been preceded by a protracted period of violence and arguing. Ultimately the father had had to be removed by court order, and since that time, despite a genuine love for his children, his contact had been erratic, and, when he had visited, his drinking often caused confusion for the children and alarm to their mother.

As is my practice, I first met the children at their home. Ben made a strong bid for my attention almost immediately and it soon became apparent that he was troubled, and preoccupied with what had happened to him, and was feeling some anger about the injustice he felt his father had experienced at the hands of his mother. He began to play, making a circle with bricks and building up the sides with great care. "This is Daddy's house," he said, "but Daddy hasn't got a key anymore – he can't get in."

Ben did not appear to understand why this was the case but suddenly announced "I hate Mummy", as if making some connection between his father's departure and something his mother had done.

"This is his house! This is his house!" he insisted, in quite a desperate way, as though saying it with emphasis would make it true once more. "I wish I had gone with him," he said sadly. "I hate it here – this house hates me." I tried to encourage him to say more about this awful feeling but he only repeated "I just know this house hates me".

There seemed to me to be several things that might be happening here. I wondered whether Ben was feeling guilt and self hatred about the fact that his oedipal fantasy appeared to have come true and that he had indeed got rid of his father, and feared that the damage would be irrevocable. In order to deal with this, it seemed to me that the bad feelings he was having then got projected both onto the house and his mother. By the same token, from a Kleinian perspective, Ben could also be seen as grappling with the consequences of the depressive anxiety that the realisation of mixed feelings brings with it, by using projection as a manic defence against this. Ben was looking increasingly confused, as though many things were going on in his mind. When I commented on this his explanation was simple – "My heart doesn't know what it feels like inside". Claire then knocked down the house he had made with such care and he ran to his mother for comfort.

When Ben and Claire visited the playroom for the first time, much of their energy was directed towards establishing two separate "houses", having tussles about who had taken whose furniture, and demonstrating how impossible it was for them to live together. In the game it was in fact Ben who commandeered the best house and the most contents, in contrast to what had happened to his father. We did, however, all end up in the play house at one stage, whereupon Ben soon became preoccupied with a threat of fire. He then decided that the house had caught fire and that "You are going to burn to death". He told me there was nothing I could do about this, although he suggested that I could get out of the house if I wanted to. Unfortunately, though, the fire was intent on pursuing me everywhere I went – "The fire's going to get you there you know!" – and although Ben was quite affable about this he clearly felt very passionately about burning me to death. While Claire placidly drew a careful picture of her parents, Ben was creating my next punishment. Bringing his drawing up to me he explained "this is all water, and this bit at the bottom is your bicycle, and this", pointing to a squiggle at the bottom of the page, "is you and you're drowning, you're going to drown".

I said I had a feeling that Ben was very angry and maybe that made him want to destroy everyone around him. I guessed that his possible fear that even thinking angry thoughts, irrespective of anything else he might do, feels powerful enough to whiz out and zap its object, and reflected on what a powerful yet frightening feeling that was. I tried to help him to see that I had survived fire and flood, and that perhaps people did survive his anger, after all. Ben made no comment but continued to play, periodically shooting me in the head, and then asking if he could stay with me at the office, because he liked it there.

In contrast to Joshua, it was harder to assess the effects on Ben of being given the opportunity to express his anger and have it accepted. According to both his mother and his nursery school teacher, however, he did seem to become less aggressive at school and stopped mutilating himself.

## Cathy

A significant source of anger for many of the children in my sample was the fact that they were being fought over, rather than for, and that this placed them in what they found to be an intolerable position. The children's notion of fairness frequently came into play, and they sought to resolve the conflict by suggesting imaginative arrangements whereby they could be shared equally between their parents – a week with each, parents living next door to one another, a year with each and so on. This preoccupation with fairness is characteristic of Piaget's third stage of development, and is linked with the need for things to be one way or another and a reluctance to accept ambiguity (Piaget 1969). Kathy, aged eight, was quite clear that it was now her father's turn to have her – "We lived with mum before". She expressed considerable anger about the fact that her mother and father were fighting over her, because of what they wanted, whereas, as she put it, "It should be what's best for us, not them".

During the course of our session she became increasingly boisterous, running round the room, pretending to fly a plane full of people to Disneyland. Her noise level also increased dramatically, eventually becoming a singsong chant of "No, no, no!" It felt to me that this was a means, adopted by several of the other children I saw, of shutting out the reality of what was happening – a whirl of distraction which, again, seemed to be a characteristic response to loss. Like Joshua, she talked about feeling sick, which felt to be something to do with wanting to get rid of the bad, angry feeling inside, although by the time she left the office she said the sick feeling had gone. Like Ben, she seemed reluctant to leave a safe place where powerful feelings could be expressed and where there appeared to be some sense that they might be acknowledged, accepted and contained.

## Camilla

Camilla, also aged eight, and first encountered in Chapter V expressed anger about the same predicament, but in quite a different way. Not for Camilla the energetic enactment of frustration and a wish to escape the field of battle. She dealt with it by adopting a prematurely adult, sophisticated, rather detached manner, discussing her parents with me as though they were rather irritating, wayward children squabbling over a plaything. Camilla's parents continued to live together during the divorce proceedings. Camilla would sit demurely in her chair, describing how when one parent said one thing, the other would say the opposite, and the way in which they would both call to her from different parts of the house, leaving her literally stuck in the middle, unsure of which way to go. As the sessions progressed she was increasingly able to talk – albeit in a calm, ladylike way – about her anger both towards her father for making her keep secrets from her mother, and towards her mother for relying so heavily on her. As this surfaced, particularly after her father's imprisonment for drugs offences, she began to express her anger more directly and I was able to help her to talk to both her parents individually about it.

## Diana and Naomi

Equally significant, however, were the smaller group of children who were angry because they felt they were not being fought for hard enough. Diana and Naomi were eleven and eight when their father applied for their custody. The parents had in fact been divorced for two years but they continued to have regular battles over contact, exacerbated by considerable geographical hurdles and intense mutual intolerance. The fact that Diana and Naomi were deeply attached to their father caused tension in their relationships with both their mother and their step-father and their increasing discomfort at home rapidly communicated itself to their father, prompting his application.

Both children expressed sadness about the breakdown of their parents' marriage, but were clearly becoming increasingly angry and exasperated by their inability to be friends for their sakes. "I wish I had a magic wand to wave it all back to the way it was. It's a pity it isn't like a video that you can put back into the machine and wind back to the place when it was last good," said Naomi, on one occasion. They were also angry about the fact that any contact, however, minimal, with their father was 'punished' by their mother's displeasure, and that she had threatened to send them back to him as a punishment for bad behaviour. Diana was able to see that her mother was hurt and angry too; Naomi just felt pain and fury.

Both girls explained that they were unable to express their anger at home, except to one another. They were concerned about the effects such expression might have and fearful that it could only make things worse. Implicit in this, I felt, was a fear of being rejected by everyone.

Notwithstanding, Naomi continued to exhibit behaviour which was clearly meant to sound the alarm about how intolerable she was finding the situation. When I visited her at her father's home during a period of contact, she talked at great length about her desire to commit suicide, explaining that she had attempted this at Christmas (two months previously) by throwing herself off a chair so she would hit her head. Despite the calm way in which she told this story, I felt that it needed to be taken seriously, not just in terms of what it seemed to say about her unhappiness, but also because it seemed to be an indication of rage turned inwards to an alarming degree. Unfortunately both parents simply saw it as an attention seeking gesture.

Although the children's mother went through the motions of fighting to keep them, it was apparent, both to me and to the children, that she and her husband were half-hearted about this. When their mother finally agreed to let them go, Diana and Naomi felt intensely rejected, since although they were clear that they wanted to live with their father, they had hoped that their mother would understand that they still loved her, and that she would be sad to lose them. They had wanted her to part with them with reluctance, rather than with the indecent haste that characterised the transfer – almost as though their presence had become so uncomfortable that they had to be removed as soon as possible. Their sense of being unwanted by her caused them to retreat considerably in the period before they left, and it was only when I saw them at their father's home that they were able to begin to talk about their feelings of hatred and anger, on the one hand, and the pain of losing their mother, on the other. Here it was once again difficult to separate the children's own anger from the anger of the parents. It almost seemed as though their mother had to have them removed so they would take these powerful feelings out of the house with them.

## Holly and Emma

Holly and Emma were twelve and seven when their parents decided to divorce, although, like Camilla's parents, they continued to live in the same house. Because of the dynamics of the marital relationship, their mother felt that the only way she could begin a new life was to get as far away from their father as possible, and she decided to emigrate to the other side of the world. She told me that she had decided she would take Emma with her but would leave Holly with her father. When I first met Holly and Emma at their home, soon after proceedings had been initiated, it was clear that they were choosing to deal with the situation by pretending it wasn't happening – after all, their parents were still living together, despite all this talk of divorce, so perhaps they had changed their minds....

They were both very apprehensive about coming to talk to me on their own, and I saw this as both a dread of having to face what was really happening by talking about it, and a fear that powerful feelings might be unleashed as a result. Holly adopted a calm, matter of fact approach to the whole issue, but acknowledged her anger about the effects of her parents' decision, and, most importantly, the proposed separation from Emma. During this discussion I found myself feeling increasingly desperate and anxious; I suspect that this was what Holly was actually feeling and that it was being transmitted to me in the counter-transference. I therefore used the way she was making me feel to try and explore the possibility that underneath her calm exterior something very different was stirring. Holly, however, was determined to maintain her rather academic, practical approach to the issue, almost as a denial that it contained an emotional component.

In contrast, Emma conveyed a sense of mutinous fury – she looked like someone barely controlling enormous rage and pain, but whenever I tried to explore any of the potentially worrying elements of her situation, she denied she could remember anything about anything – a common response to this situation. I commented that it was clearly much easier to forget painful incidents and painful thoughts, but that it all goes inside somehow and hurts very badly. She admitted that this sometimes happened to her and that she was in fact very angry with her mother – she said she had tried to persuade her to stay, but it was hopeless, and she doubted that I would be any more successful, so was angry with me as well. She explained that when she felt really angry, she went in to her room, slammed the door, and lay on the bed until the anger went away; sometimes she cried. Emma clearly felt very strongly that she was being forced to make a choice between her parents and that this was intolerable. She was desperate for this decision to be made for her, and angry that no one seemed to care enought to do so.

What seemed to emerge poignantly was both children's anger about the fact that their parents were doing this to them, and that their mother could calmly contemplate going to the other end of the world without Holly. Although Holly was expressing a definite wish to stay with her father, there was an equally strong wish, in my view, that by doing so she would be able to hang onto her mother. Holly's fury was about the fact that her love for her mother was not powerful enough to stop her leaving, and that she had simply accepted Holly's decision to stay without protest or struggle. Emma's anger was about being forced to choose and the fact that, whatever happened, at best she would be losing one parent, and at worst her sister as well.

Again it was hard to know whether releasing these feelings helped, but it did make it possible to enable the children's mother to consider their needs rather than simply her own. In addition, I found that the intense feelings which I experienced during my sessions with Holly and Emma helped me to appreciate more clearly what the impact of their separation might have, and I argued very strongly against this in my report. The mother ultimately agreed that both children should remain with their father.

## Oliver

Oliver was two when his parents separated. Initially he lived with his mother, but when she had a breakdown, his father took over his care, and he remained with him for the next two years. Oliver had regular contact with his mother during this period, but handovers were often accompanied by arguments and on one occasion his mother physically attacked his father. As his mother's health improved, she made repeated requests for Oliver's return, and eventually applied to the court for custody. Although his father had a strong desire to keep Oliver, and originally intended to fight the case, he suddenly capitulated, apparently overcome by guilt about depriving his ex-wife of her son. Oliver was therefore duly handed back to his mother without explanation or preparation.

After a few months however, Oliver's father began to be concerned about the situation once more. Oliver made repeated requests to return to him, became increasingly spiteful and generally seemed unsettled and confused. This was reflected in his conduct at school, where he was described as pale, quiet and anxious, and exhibiting a new found capacity for deceit. He had also been heard to say "I'm so worried....I mustn't tell anyone". As a result, his father felt the situation should be explored once more.

I visited Oliver three times at home before inviting him into the office to see me alone. What I found was a mature, poised, very anxious four year old whose deep, husky voice contributed to the impression that he was old beyond his years. He seemed very protective towards his mother and when anything difficult was being discussed, he would create a diversion. He also became very angry with his mother when she said anything pejorative about his father or his paternal grandmother, with whom his father lived – "Don't say that word," he yelled, when she described someone as destructive. On one occasion he confessed to me that he had dreamt that his father was dead. This seemed to me to be telling me something about Oliver's destructive urges – perhaps he was so angry with Daddy for giving him back to Mummy that he feared his anger had killed him off. Once again, I was struck by the way this child made me feel – vulnerable, very childlike, powerless, desperate and overwhelmed by the desire to rescue and protect. These feelings, I believe, told me something crucial about Oliver's experience, and helped me to begin to try to understand his communication later on, when expressed through play.

When Oliver was brought to the office for the first time by his mother, he seemed full of excited anticipation. He went straight to the dolls' house and began an elaborate game which lasted almost an hour. Oliver's play seemed to me both to indicate his confusion about his change of home, his awareness of his mother's fragility and the sense that he was now in some way responsible for her. In his game, which centred round a Mummy, Daddy and baby who lived in my dolls' house, the baby suddenly disappeared – "The Mummy can't handle it at all – she is upset and crying," he said, "but the Daddy can handle it – he's big, fat, and strong". The entire household was also, at one point, threatened by the invasion of a monster who assumed the guise of a baby in order to gain entry. This seemed to me a graphic statement about Oliver's powerful destructive feelings and the threat they posed to the status quo. How can he leave a mother who can't cope? Father seems able to manage without him – how is this possible? Dealing with both questions seemed to be the source of Oliver's anger and confusion.

At the end of the session Oliver made the baby move rapidly around the house in what seemed like a frantic, desperate way – "The baby is naughty – he doesn't want to leave". I told him I had noticed the baby's anxiety about his mother, and his anger and confusion about the changes that had taken place and reassured him that I would look after the baby for him till we met again. He spent some time settling the occupants more comfortably in the house, decided they would be alright and finally agreed to leave, after considerable persuasion from his mother.

Our next encounter was at his father's home, where I arrived, accompanied by the "baby" from the dolls' house, to convey, as I had tried to do with Joshua, that the vulnerable part of him and been noticed and was being kept in mind. Oliver was in fact able to use the baby in a powerful way to demonstrate to his father some of his needs and anxieties and he was also able to give graphic expression to his anger. Oliver said he was glad to see the baby and had thought it was a good idea to bring him as "he didn't like living with Mummy". He told his father he wanted to live with him because he didn't like living with his Mummy either – "There is more happiness here....I could be her good luck at weekends....God could look after her in the week".

In his frustration he threatened he would not return to Mummy, but would get a flat of his own, insisting he would live there alone and manage very well. This seemed to me to reflect a sense that he might be feeling abandoned by everyone – indeed unsure that anyone could provide him with the security he needed – so he might as well take care of himself. I remarked that at this very difficult time, he must be feeling very worried and that no-one was listening to him and taking him seriously, and that this was why our talks were important, since they allowed him to have his say. I was also suddenly overwhelmed by a feeling that maybe no-one wanted this child, deep down, and that this was the fear that he was communicating to me in the counter-transference. This awareness froze me completely, since I felt unable to reassure him that this was not the case, but balked from putting this feeling into words. In the end, I took it away with me, and subsequently used it to talk to both parents about what the conflict was doing to their child. As it turned out, however, this did not help much.

Oliver then initiated a sword fight with his father, leaping round the room brandishing his weapon – "I'm going to fight to live here! I'm going to fight everybody!" He rushed over to his father to give him a sword so he could fight too, but despite the tremendous energy and encouragement Oliver gave him, his father's efforts struck us both as extremely half hearted. At one point Oliver actually threatened his father with his sword – "You're evil – I'm going to chop off your head!" When father mildly asked why he was evil, Oliver's reply was simple. "Because you took me back to Mummy," he said.

During the course of this session Oliver was able to tell his father how angry he was, and request some explanation for what had happened. It was perhaps significant that his play with the baby centred round placing it in dangerous situations from which it was rescued by a powerful he-man figure – presumably the powerful, ideal father of his fantasy. Oliver's father unfortunately either failed to hear the message, or was unable to do so, or perhaps simply lacked the courage to enter into the battleground, as required. Despite his continuing concerns about the situation, Oliver's father felt unable to pursue his application to have his son returned to his care. The court felt that the situation should be monitored, however, and I was therefore able to continue to work with Oliver to try and resolve some of his angry feelings.

## Robert

The final group of angry children I wish to discuss contained those who were not only expressing anger of their own, but demonstrated particularly clearly that they did not only have their own anger to manage, but were also carrying the burden of a parent's projected rage. Such children often seemed to be used as an instrument of destruction, by a parent who, outwardly, often seemed the epitome of calm, sweet reason; they seemed doomed to wage war on a departed spouse until liberated from this duty by the resolution of the conflict.

The power of this projection frequently caused intensely mixed feelings in the children towards the angry parent, but left them feeling they had no choice in the matter. Such children were often prematurely adult, assuming responsibility for the 'abandoned' parent, with a strong need to avenge the wrongs done to him or her. This burdensome responsibility often engendered yet another source of angry feelings, when the child realised there was no longer any room to be a child. Although having an adult role bestowed upon you can be flattering, it is also horrifying to be confronted by someone you once saw as strong and a source of reliable support looking to you to meet all their needs, fulfil all their desires. Upholding the broken end of the arch is, as I have already suggested, a tiring and inappropriate job for a child.

Robert was an eloquent representative of children in this position. He and his mother were a sad young couple aged eight and twenty-nine when I first met them. Robert's father had left them some two years before, but a hope had remained, encouraged by him, that a reconciliation might be possible. When this didn't take place, and he moved in with another woman and her son, Robert and his mother sought comfort from one another. Robert's mother's fragility had by then been forcibly brought home to him by a suicide attempt she had made; he soon became man of the house, a charming companion and raconteur, culinary critic, and assessor of mother's friends, clothes, working hours and so on. They frequently slept together and Robert would often talk about what "We" think of Daddy. Clearly on one level, Robert's oedial fantasy had come true – father had disappeared and he had mother all to himself. However, this was not to prove as ideal as might be imagined.

Notwithstanding, Robert had established a successful relationship with his father, to whom he remained attached. It was therefore worrying when this bond began to deteriorate, and the father/son relationship worsened to a point when it seemed all contact must cease. Robert admitted that he had started to behave badly during visits, using his not inconsiderable intelligence to bait his father – "I'm getting very sarcastic," he told me. "It's my only defence". As an example of this, he recounted an exchange in which his father asked him what he should wear, what he would look good in. "A coffin," was Robert's swift reply.

This prompted me to speculate aloud about how difficult it must be to be full of angry, murderous feelings but scared to let them out for fear of what might happen. Robert, more angry with me than I had ever seen him said "That's certainly true in my case", going on to observe that some people don't need to be sarcastic, as they could show their anger out in the open. What began to emerge with considerable power – I certainly felt quite frightened at times – were his murderous feelings and his fantasies about his own destructive capacity. I felt that if I was feeling frightened by this then Robert probably was too, and as a consequence it was important to name this fear and look at it in real terms.

During this session, Robert's anger towards both his parents was palpable, and the two lots often became intertwined. In the course of a discussion about Robert's anger towards his father, he sat on his mother's lap, curled up like a baby, occasionally biting her finger. At one point he said "I'd like to strangle Daddy" and grabbed his mother round the throat. "Sorry," he said "wrong person." I wondered if it was. Robert then got off his mother's lap and roamed about the room, pummelling cushions and strangling a shawl I keep in the office. Much of what he said was spoken in a voice choked with the force of his feelings, and he became furious with me when I made links between anger and pain, and the fear of anger getting out of control. He was however able both to talk about and enact his love/hate feelings for his mother. "I'll always love you," he said, then called her a bitch.

Work with Robert involved several interrelated elements. It seemed important to reach out to the child part of him which was slowly being overwhelmed by adult responsibilities and preoccupations. The office provided him with a place where he could actually be a child, and he often chose to play with toys more suited to a younger child – cuddly toys, dolls, wooden animals – which suggested the need to regress as a response to the feelings of anger and loss he was experiencing. It also seemed crucial to help him to come to terms with the permanence of his parents' separation, and, in this context, helping him create a genogram (see Chapter IV), where he could consider the people in his life and his relationship to them, proved useful. The genogram he made was always present during our sessions; on one occasion when he was particularly angry and frustrated with coping with his parents' separateness he considered tearing it down the middle, until his mother observed that he would tear himself down the middle in the process. Most pressing of all, however, seemed to be to help Robert tackle his anger, explore it, release it, recognise which bits of it were his and which his mother's, and, equally importantly, help him to face the fact that he was as angry with his mother as he was with his father.

What began to emerge was Robert's need to punish his father for what he had done, both to him and to his mother, and that much of his bad behaviour was motivated by his desire to break up his father's new relationship so that he would return home, begging for mercy, whereupon, he said "Me and Mummy will kick him in the teeth". His mother was evidently still very hurt and derived a certain bitter satisfaction from the fact that Robert was giving his father such difficulty. The added, albeit unspoken additional advantage to breaking up his father's relationship, however, was that his father's imagined return would also release Robert from his onerous responsibility towards his mother. On the rare occasions when mother felt she should offer the odd word of restraint, in the course of one of Robert's outbursts, he would give her a knowing look and on one occasion actually said "Why do you say one thing at home and another in Miss Kroll's office, Mummy?"

By the same token, Robert was struggling with the love he also had for both parents as well as the hate and the destructive potential of the latter. During this period, Robert retreated to a very early stage, preoccupied with sending his father shit through the post, and dreaming up other torments, all involving excreta – "Send him a nappy as he's so full of shit". During one session Robert was in tears for most of the time, talking about his love and hate, how much he'd been hurt by his father, but how his mother had hurt him just as much – "I'm confused, I'm in the middle," he sobbed.

As sessions progressed, Robert's anger gave way to sorrow, resignation, and something that felt to me very much like exhaustion – again, characteristics of the grieving child identified by Jewett as suggesting a move towards the beginnings of an acceptance of the loss. His accounts of dastardly deeds performed at his father's home began to lack energy and conviction, and as we began to clarify whose anger was whose and which belonged where, the situation started to improve, particularly when his mother became able to own the anger that was hers. Finally Robert came to his own conclusion about the situation. "We've punished him in every possible way," he told me. "There's no more need to punish him – he's been punished enough." As he said this, he glanced at his mother, as though seeking her permission to abandon the fight. This coincided with his mother's new relationship, thus apparently freeing Robert from his vendetta.

## Summary: The Angry Child

Anger, then, for all the children in this chapter was a live and often frightening and disturbing feeling. It was a reaction that seemed to span the whole age range of the children in the sample, from three year olds to adolescents. Equally, it was expressed by both girls and boys, although generally speaking, boys tended to enact it, while girls discussed it. I was struck by the fact that, although many of the 'angry' children had experienced the loss of a parent some considerable time before, they were still in this very acute stage of the grieving process. Clearly, the continued presence of conflict was significant in ensuring that the children remained stuck in this position. By the same token, contact, which regularly resurrected the original parting, helped to fan the flames. Angry parents, too, projected their feelings onto their children, so that the fury was carried backwards and forwards, attracting more animosity in its wake. Anger became a giant snowball with an enormous, weighty stone at its centre.

Not all the children were able to talk about this dangerous emotion. Defence mechanisms were carefully developed, particularly by some of the girls, so that I was left with a sense of a well of feelings carefully concealed by an air of insouciance, a patina of maturity. There was real fear abroad about what this anger might do, and the degree to which it could become out of control and destroy its object. Once it was expressed, it was often hard to know what the consequences might be.

For some children, like Joshua and Ben, the release of anger seemed to lead to a positive change in a relatively short time; for Robert, however, the resolution of these feelings took much longer, due to his mother's investment in it.

Anger for me, as the worker, was also a tricky affair. I often felt quite overwhelmed by the strength of children's feelings, and that I was absorbing their pain to a considerable extent. I found myself feeling very angry towards their parents, and being inextricably drawn in to the destructive fantasies they were experiencing. After sessions with these children, I would frequently spend time talking to their parents, trying to put aside some of the rage that had been projected into me, so that I could work with the adults concerned, as an adult professional, as opposed to an angry three year old. This was not easy at times, and forcefully brought home to me the wisdom of the emphasis that both Olden (1953) and Lieberman (1979) place on the importance of being of a child's world but not in it, so that the professional self continues to function.

Despite these tensions, however, working with the countertransference was essential in enabling me to appreciate just what the children's experience might be like, and how frightening life could

feel. This, in turn, provided me with some useful information to use in my work with parents to enable them to focus more clearly on their children's states of mind. In addition, from the child's point of view, fiends could come out from behind clouds, at least for a while, enabling some of the anger to be released harmlessly, and some of the burden to be laid down.

# Chapter IX:
# Journey's End or
# New Beginnings?

In my end is my beginning.

T.S. Eliot: Four Quartets – East Coker

Wisdom denotes the pursuing of the best ends by the best means.

Francis Hutcheson: Inquiry into the Original
of Our Ideas of Beauty and Virtue

In this final chapter, I reach my journey's end only to discover new voyages which need to be embarked upon, before the position of children, in relation to separation and divorce, can both be fully recognised, and appropriately attended to by professionals who are enabled to be suitably equipped for the task. As more and more partnerships and marriages fail, more and more children may experience the pain and damage that an acrimonious separation can cause. What can or should be done to help and support children in this position? What are the best means to achieve the best ends?

The children with whom I worked told me, in many ways, what it was like to be in the throes of parental conflict, what they needed, what they mourned and how painful, difficult and confusing life could feel. With their help, as I have illustrated, I was able to construct a typology of children's adaptations, while developing a theoretical approach to assist me to embark on direct, individual work with them. This seems an appropriate moment to examine whether this typology was helpful and if so, both how and why.

## The Typology: Does It Help?

Categorisation is always problematic, because some 'categories' don't/won't fit, or seem to belong in more than one place. So it was with the children I met. However, the value of the categories, blurred though the boundaries between them may be, was that they provided some guidelines, a starting point that helped the process of thinking about how and where the child might be in terms of his/her capacity and ability to cope with what was happening. This in turn assisted me to help parents appreciate what their child was feeling, thinking and fearing; sometimes, as a result they were enabled to turn their attention to them more squarely, despite their own pain,

165

anger and grief.

Two questions arise from this process, however. Why did some children adapt in one way rather than another and how did the type of adaptation affect the response that the child might need from either worker or parent? The first question is difficult to answer categorically and the evidence is by no means conclusive. It would appear, however, that many of the parental children described in Chapter V had parents who had retreated into a childlike state, thus suggesting a role exchange – at least this created the illusion of some kind of adultness, which may have served as some kind of reassurance for the child, albeit of a somewhat hollow nature. The angry children encountered in Chapter VIII often had particularly angry parents, and were therefore expressing not only their anger, but someone else's too; the same might be said of despairing children in Chapter VI. The link between the retreating children in Chapter VII and their parents' state of mind was more difficult to fathom; what did seem to emerge, however, was the level of protracted conflict extant for many of these children, and their desire to retreat from the battleground.

All four types of adaptation represented protective states of 'being' at a difficult time. Two seemed to be types of identification – one with the parent/adult self and one with the infant self – and two reflected strong states of feeling – anger and despair. In terms of gender and age, adaptations were spread, with no clear correlation emerging. A larger study would have been required to explore links between age, gender and adaptation more rigorously.

Given that all these reactions seemed to have tied in very closely with stages of mourning, why should the type of response differ, since what is relevant is that they were all experiencing loss in some way? This, in my view, begs the question of loss and the experience of separation and divorce as a *process* – the stage, or state of 'being' in which the child may be found says something important about this process and the way in which it is being managed. It also gives clues about the appropriate reaction and approach required from both parents and professionals involved with them. The continuum of mourning, from denial to anger to depression and finally acceptance, and the oscillation between different protective states, requires a parallel continuum of response, so that the child can be helped through the maze of post-separation emotions, and led out to safety. Denial, perhaps the most difficult and worrying stage, should not be ignored – although on the one hand it supplies what Jewett (1984) would describe as "a reprieve from the pain", on the other hand, if it goes on too long, it can cause problems with other losses. Anger, far from being troublesome, needs to be seen as the healthiest reaction to loss and needs to be permitted to be expressed. It also requires both containing and validating. Despair and retreat also need to be accepted and understood; they also require the capacity in the worker and the parent to stay with the pain that these reactions may bring.

Identifying where a child was in this process sometimes enabled predictions to be made about what might happen next. Parents could therefore be prepared for a rush of anger or a period of despair, and be helped to accept, understand and support, rather than punish or ignore. Equally, a child's state could often be seen as a reflection of the parents' plight, which could then be attended to more purposefully.

The combination of a theoretical model and a range of play techniques gave me the opportunity to learn a great deal about how young children work, and what they thought and felt at a very stressful point in their lives. I discovered that, given some time of their own, in a safe place, even very small children were able to tell their stories, irrespective of verbal and cognitive skills. Games and toys facilitated this process, as did drawing, enactment games and empathic silence. Play, however, had to be set within a conceptual framework – I needed some theoretical bearings in order to help me make sense of what was happening and so enable real work to take place. Most children appeared to welcome the chance to spend some time reflecting on what was happening, asking questions that dared not be asked of parents, and releasing some of the difficult or powerful feelings they were experiencing. Some children seemed to feel considerably better at the end of the contact than they had at the beginning. I believe that this might have been because they felt heard, that someone had listened to what they had to say, and that they had had the chance to explore painful things without the fear that someone's feelings would be hurt or something awful would happen. My approach to the issue of confidentiality seemed to work. At no time did I find that my approach to this caused problems which were not surmountable. I felt that I was doing my job, promoting the interests of the child, not simply by working with the parents to diminish conflict and resolve issues, but by offering child clients a professional service.

## Assessment and Role

A devil's advocate would now perhaps pose three questions. How did this work assist assessment, which after all is often one of the purposes of intervention, whether or not it culminates in a court report? Surely all this took a long time – what about the issue of delay in going back to court, which goes against the best interests of the child, particularly now the Children Act 1989 is in place? What about role confusion – therapist, observer, investigator or what?

In terms of assessment, I considered that the depth of my

approach enabled me to make a clearer representation of the child's position to the court, and that the time spent with the child on an individual basis lent significant credibility to my recommendations. I cannot pretend that the approach did not mean that reports took longer to prepare. However this was never a cause for complaint either by the agency or the courts, since the delay was generally negligible. Indeed there were times when delay was actually constructive, since this allowed tempers to cool, arrangements to be tried out, some reflection to take place, and more time for children to be seen and heard. It is not realistic for parents to resolve their difficulties according to a court timetable; arrangements or agreements forged in haste do not always stand the test of time. Workers in this field often achieve resolutions in haste and repent at leisure, since the couple will inevitably have to return for further sessions, when the so called agreement falls apart. The Children Act, however, does come to the rescue here. As Cantwell (1992) observes:

> "The more precise concept of constructive delay can now be used....to reassure courts that it is not likely to be in the child's best interest to rush towards settlement....if the feelings of the parents are still too raw or too painful. Much better....to think about the therapy by consent opportunities provided by the six month Family Assistance Order."

This seems to underline the crucial point so often missed – that disintegrating relationships disintegrate at their own pace, and workers have to respect the needs of clients to resolve some of the painful issues in their own time. This may take longer, and may be more costly in terms of workers' time, agency resources; by the same token, engaging with the children may require more training, more specific and specialist supervision. At the end of the day, however, such preventative, child centred work must surely be worth the extra cost and effort, if one considers the long term consequences of not resolving the manifold problems that the breakdown of a relationship can cause for the family.

The confusion in terms of role was one which clearly had to be embraced, and tolerated although the roles of reporter, investigator, authority figure, assessor and therapist did not seem incompatible, since in my view balancing these facets very much reflected the everyday predicament of any statutory social worker. This mixture of role and tasks seems to me to be at the very core of professional social work identity – it is attempts to over-simplify rather than conflate which are most likely to cause problems. From my experience, parents and children, provided they were clear about what I was trying to do and why, were able to manage this encounter with a many headed creature, without undue difficulty.

In an ideal world, a service would exist that would offer specialist help for children caught in parental crossfire, provided by practitioners experienced in working not only with the effects of marital conflict but with loss – and of course, directly with children. In the meantime such children may be encountered in a range of settings, and it therefore becomes essential for any relevant professional – teachers, health visitors, nursery staff, child minders, social workers, conciliators, court welfare officers, guardians – to become sensitised to behaviours which could say something important about the impact that the separation process may be having. There is a limit to how loudly some children are able to shout, to sound the alarm that all is not well; perhaps it is time for professionals to develop more acute hearing.

The emphasis on working with the family system, in the context of family breakdown, needs to be reconsidered. After all, how can any really useful work be done without talking to the children themselves, as individual human beings, as clients of a service in their own right, rather than as appendages? Surely we are not to return to the days, so deplored by inquiries into the deaths of children in care when children's needs were catered for by pouring resources into parents, as though, by some magical process of osmosis, the child would automatically receive support at second hand?

## Listening to Children

Most striking is the extent to which the children get lost in the muddle. Children are a problem for many social workers; they are not at all sure what they should be doing in relation to them and how this might be accomplished. Sometimes they are seen – but not for long; sometimes they are seen but not heard. Workers who do feel it is important to offer children a service feel hampered by lack of time and expertise. Excuses and rationales for not having direct, meaningful contact with children abound. The real reasons, as I have suggested, are both more complex and more prosaic, primarily reflecting institutional defences against worker pain.

The advent of the Children Act appears to have had little impact on the approach to children. Demonstrable adherence to the Children Act 'welfare checklist' including establishing the child's views and wishes, is not accompanied by guidelines as to how establishing these should best be done. There is still a prevailing assumption in social work circles that if you can get parents to agree, then you do not need to speak to the child. This approach denies the child access to what may be the only source of impartial help likely to be available, as well as presupposing that what parents want is the same as that desired by their offspring. Parental responsibility, as emphasised by the Children Act, must surely embrace the responsibility to consider the wishes and feelings of children as separate entities.

Of course, establishing a child's view – their real feelings, as opposed to the views that parents wish them to express – is a tricky business and there is indeed a danger in placing too much weight on what children say. However this does not seem a reasonable argument for avoiding discussion about their views and attempting to understand how the experience of their parents' separation is affecting them. Canvassing a child's opinion does not automatically presuppose acting on it. It is possible, and indeed essential, to see a child without handing them the power to decide their own fate. Clearly the type of situation that arose in a recently reported case (Phillips 1993) in which a child felt forced to choose between her parents, in the pressurising and intimidating atmosphere of the court environment, and then had her hard wrung and hesitant preference acted upon without further investigation, is to be utterly deplored. This approach clearly short-changes the child's right to have his/her wishes and feelings taken into account by the court, and flies in the face of both the spirit and letter of the new act.

How can this rising tide be stemmed? How can this movement away from child-centred practice be checked? I believe that a new approach is needed, and needed quickly before the inexorable waves of checklists, assessment forms and other mechanistic devices drown all the imagination, skill and energy that still hovers hopefully in the breasts of social workers across the land. How might it be done differently? How might the task be achieved, while still keeping children at the centre of the work, with access to a real service which acknowledges their needs?

## A 'Starter Kit' for Practice: Four Essential Building Blocks

I believe that the approach I used offers a way forward and could provide a 'starter kit' for this kind of work. What I did during this project was to respond to what I felt and experienced as a gap, in terms of what the agency was offering to child clients, which fitted with the courts' paramountcy principle. In order to do this, I had to think about children in a different way. I had to learn how children worked, how they thought, how they communicated and how to make sense of all that they told me. I had to find different ways of making contact with them, allow them to teach me, take risks and experiment. In Chapters II, III and IV I have presented the strands of my approach in detail. What I want to do now is to present a synthesis of this and to set out an approach that can be easily taken up, run with and made use of by workers who still believe that what child-centred social work is still about is children.

At the heart of my approach are four essential building blocks – a child-centred philosophy, a theoretical reservoir, a tool bag of techniques, and access to appropriate training, supervision and support – which interlock with the 'Principles and Practice in Regulations and Guidance' (1990), produced by the Department of Health, that forms the central core of the Children Act and thus potentially provide the worker with the resources they need to do this work effectively.

At this stage, however, there is a danger. I am not offering a 'How To Do It' manual, set in tablets of stone, a checklist in disguise, requiring nothing more than routine application for success. This would be impossible. I offer, instead, a 'how to start thinking about it' guide, a professional synthesis, a set of principles, a range of complementary frameworks, rather as the authors of 'Principles and Practice in Regulations and Guidance' (D.O.H. op. cit.) have done and, unashamedly, I borrow their analogy:

"Principles are the colours on the social worker painter's palette. The range and quality of colour helps to produce a good painting but it is the painter's skill which makes or mars the picture." (D.O.H. 1990)

Understanding the principle is the first step; harnessing this to individual skills and applying this potent mixture differentially to individual clients is the art.

### i. A Child Centred Philosophy

A child-centred philosophy is perhaps the obvious starting point. This sounds very laudable and grand, but what exactly does it mean? It starts, perhaps, with a respect for children, with a belief in the value of child-centred work and a readiness to embrace the complexities and distress that this might involve, on both a professional and a personal level. I think it is a way of placing children alongside adults as clients in their own right, as individuals who also need to have their say, as equals in terms of their entitlement, as people, to be seen and heard. I believe that children are a disadvantaged group, in terms of the service they receive. They are discriminated against on the basis of their age and they are prey to assumptions made by adults regarding their levels of awareness and understanding. If a genuinely anti-discriminatory service is to be provided by social work agencies, then children have to join the long list of groups vulnerable to misunderstanding, stereotyping and oppression. The Children Act, with its emphasis on ascertaining the wishes and feelings of the child, gives a clear message in relation to this issue, a fact which is seen as significant by legal commentators (Freeman 1992) and which is underlined by the 'Principles and

Practice' guidance:

> "Young people's wishes must be elicited and taken seriously.
> Even quite young children should be enabled to contribute to
> decisions about their lives in an age appropriate way. Learning to
> make a well informed choice is an important aspect of growing up
> and must involve more than just sitting in on reviews and
> conferences at which adults have all the power and make
> decisions." (D.O.H. 1990)

In the context of divorce focused work, it is apparent that some
approaches militate against the child having any power since, as I
have already observed, many are only seen as part of the family
system, rather than as individuals in their own right. Once again, it
is important to emphasise that this is not to say that the decision
making should be left in their hands – far from it – but rather that
their views should contribute to the debate, and that their feelings
about the experience should be known about. Implicit in this is that
children are deserving of the respect, time, attention and thought-
fulness required to elicit their views, which, as the guidance
observes:

> "....involves direct, highly skilled and probably time consuming
> work with children especially if they are very young...." (D.O.H.
> 1990)

In this context, as Freeman (1992) makes clear, a range of issues
need consideration, relating to communication skills, objectivity,
style of questioning and appropriateness of methods used. Children,
like adults, have their own boundaries and their own time scale,
their own ways of conveying their thoughts and feelings. A child-
centred approach has to embrace and respect these differences.

Getting in touch with one's own inner child can be a good way of
beginning the process of getting alongside the child client, a way of
recalling what we knew, what we understood, what we thought of
grown-ups and what we needed from them at different ages. This
can often be a painful process, but elicits the kind of self knowledge
that enables us to know something important about the work being
undertaken. It also enables the creation of a safe place where
children can feel welcomed, prepared for and understood – the
provision of what Winnicott (1960) has called "holding", with the
added dimension provided by Bion's notion of containment (1959;
1962), where strong feelings can be explored, detoxified in the
context of a dynamic relationship between child and worker, and
made safer.

A child-centred philosophy and approach, however, cannot take
place in a vacuum. Most children belong somewhere and to
somebody, and child clients of separating parents are all too aware of

the implications of this. Part of the wider context has to be the making of useful and open relationships with parents – the development of working partnerships so strongly advocated by the Children Act – despite the atmosphere of wariness and suspicion which often characterises the worker/parent relationship. This should include the recognition of parents' needs as individuals, including respect for their separateness as well as their co-parenting role, which ought to include choice about how, when and with whom they are seen, in the context of any kind of intervention, including report preparation. Clearly partnership is harder to achieve if parents feel coerced into working in a way that they find uncomfortable or stressful. It also has implications for the work done with children and how that is undertaken. I consider that a crucial aspect of the worker's role is to make it clear to parents why they want to see and speak to their children, and what they will *not* be saying ("Which parent do you want to live with?" for example) as well as what they will be trying to achieve. The aim should be to enhance and facilitate communication between parents and their children, interpreting, if necessary, the needs and feelings of each to the other, and using the work with individuals to inform an understanding of the family system as a whole. The fear – in the minds of both parents and sometimes workers too – is often that the worker either will, or will be seen to be competing with or replacing parents, if special time with children is sought. Openness, in the context of partnership, is clearly essential to alleviate such fears, as is the worker's capacity to look inside the self and explore the motives within. Are we really anxious about being seen as alternative 'good parents' or are we defending against the pain of making real contact with a child's distress and sense of loss? I would argue that the latter is more likely to be the case.

All this takes time – time to actually be with people, time to allow them to tell their story, discharge some of the pain, distress and anger that separation and divorce brings in its wake, time to think about what has taken place and make sense of it, and time to talk to others and share impressions, as well as explore confusions and uncertainty. The amount of time taken needs to be considered in the context of both long and short term goals – a thorough assessment and a speedy decision are not always compatible, and the pace at which people are able to enter into a working partnership with a professional does not always accord with a court's timetable. It was after all a lack of thinking, breathing time that contributed to many of the tragedies revealed by the inquiries into the deaths of children in care. Thinking time is crucial.

## ii.　A Theoretical Reservoir

Once a set of principles and a way of thinking about children is established, both a practical and a theoretical perspective need to be considered to provide frameworks for thought and understanding – a reservoir of ideas that can be drawn upon and used to make sense of the world of children, the things they do and the things they say.

On a practical level, relative size becomes important, in terms of getting on the same level as the child client rather than towering over them; tone of voice also needs to be considered. How do we talk to children? What voice do we need? How can we be authentic rather than patronising? What did we, as children, make of grown-ups who seemed to speak in one voice to other grown-ups and in another, several octaves higher, to us? An awareness of a child's time scale and sense of time passing is essential, particularly when loss and change are realities – a week without contact between a small child and a parent can feel like a lifetime. Language needs to be both age appropriate and sensitive to the way different words are used to mean different things, depending on background and culture.

At a theoretical level, I see there being two sets of ideas that overlap with and inform one another, providing a knowledge base that can be drawn upon, using the theories and perspectives which fit together most happily with the worker's own philosophy and style. The first of these sets of knowledge is comprised of developmental perspectives – physical, cognitive, psychological, psycho-sexual and psycho-social; the second relates to feelings and how to understand them, work with them, make sense of them, involving psychodynamic concepts, attachment and mourning theory, ideas about the significance and interpretation of play. These divisions are, of course, somewhat artificial, as some theories straddle both categories, but they are useful in providing two different but complementary sets of windows through which the child's inner and outer world can be observed. It is these elements of the second building block to which I now turn.

As a starting point, it is important to know what children should/should not be able to do or understand at different ages, and the kinds of developmental tasks with which they may be wrestling which might influence their fears and preoccupations. A working knowledge of child development on a physical level is essential, since this enables some assessment to be made about developmental delay or regression – both possible responses to loss and emotional stress. It is also important to know about age appropriate play and what a child might be expected to understand, in terms of concepts and ideas. Both Sheridan (1986) and Fahlberg (1982) provide invaluable guidance in these areas – sufficiently specific and yet realistically general in terms of likely physical attainment.

Thinking about a child's cognitive and overall psychological development, from a range of standpoints, helps to build up a picture of the growing child moving through stages of development, each presenting its own set of hurdles and challenges which have to be overcome before the next stage can be entered. The task for the worker is to think about where the child might be according to the frameworks that make the most sense, decide what fits, and therefore what can be learned about where a child might be and how they are, in every sense. The important thing is to get an idea of what might be going on for the child on a number of levels. It is also useful to reflect on the fact that chronological age and developmental age may be at odds, communicating something which may be significant.

The central elements of my approach were a combination of psychodynamic concepts, rooted in Kleinian and object relations theory, and attachment and mourning theory. I felt that the ideas provided by these frameworks provided a way of thinking about children's experience with reference to both their inner world and anxieties, as well as those related to the real world outside. Outward manifestations, through stories, play and drawing, provide possible clues to inside feelings; an awareness of the importance and significance of transitional objects sheds light on a child's use of such objects to entrust an important part of the self to the worker. Being open, in the counter-transference, to the way a child makes you feel often indicates something crucial about how they are feeling themselves – a piece of information that can enable real understanding and empathy to take place, and can assist in an increase in awareness between children and their parents. This perspective offers, in my view, both a contrast and a complement to those already described. Although it could be argued that Klein's 'positions' – fluid states of being, within which the individual oscillates throughout life – and the anxieties and defences that accompany them, are incompatible with more schematic, developmental frameworks, I did not find this to be the case, and consider that a mixture of these perspectives, depending on personal inclination, is a viable option.

What, in my opinion, is non-negotiable, however, is a working knowledge of attachment theory, and mourning theory, as it relates to children. Children whose parents are parting are, by definition, experiencing or are about to experience separation and loss. It is very hard to understand the impact of separation without knowledge of attachment theory, and this, for me, provided a crucial theoretical core, as did the stages of mourning in children.

In this context, of course, the whole issue of interpretation becomes relevant, as does the way it can be used. I think that, in the first instance, interpretation is a silent activity undertaken for the benefit of the worker, to clarify thinking – it goes on in one's head and can be acted on; telling anyone else about it is not always necessary, relevant or helpful. Having said that, as I have demonstrated in Chapters V-VII, there are times when interpretations can be usefully shared with children; there is risk involved, but if you are wrong children are very quick to let you know, and if you strike a chord, something useful can often come of it. The value of an interpretation is that it provides the worker with hunches and hypotheses about what might be going on, clues rather than definitive answers. These can then be presented to children as exactly what they are – clues and hunches; you can wonder if things are as you suspect, you can ponder, you can guess. Most things are open to a range of interpretations, and I have described the kinds of struggles I have had in this area; this is not so much a quest for truth as an exploration. As a tool, it belongs on the voyage rather than at the destination.

At this point, then, the worker has developed a capacity to think about the child – what I call a child centred philosophy – a reservoir of theoretical knowledge from which to draw and an understanding, within this context, of what a child at a certain age might know and understand, as well as what they can or should be able to do. Reflections on one's own memory, understanding and awareness at a similar age is an essential addition, provided of course that the worker is able to be the worker and the child simultaneously. The first two building blocks are now in place.

### iii. Techniques in General and the Art of 'Being' in Particular....

The third building block relates to techniques that might be usefully employed to facilitate the dialogue that now takes place between worker and child. I think that the first technique to develop should be some way to give oneself over to the time with the child, clearing statutory thoughts and court dates from the mind, so that the time spent is actually spent *with* the other person, rather than fighting off other preoccupations that clutter up the mind – the next appointment, the next report, the fact that you only have half an hour and you need all this information.... The second technique is to develop the art of 'being' rather than 'doing' – although clearly 'doing' at times is essential. What I am advocating here, as I did in Chapter III, is the capacity in the worker to open themselves up to the experience of being with a child (or an adult, for that matter), in a state that can perhaps best be described as one of listening stillness, in which the urge to do, fix, reassure, telephone, write things down is resisted and, instead, the worker has to really *be*, so that the child's feelings can be known about. 'Doing' will be necessary, but as a purposeful activity, rather than as a defence; 'being' is an important quality to cultivate. The problem is: how can social workers learn this particular skill, when there is such an emphasis on 'doing'? How can the space be made? How can they be supported to stay with this, as a valid activity? I learned what 'being' really was – as well as how to observe properly – by undertaking child observation. Even when undertaken for a short period, this is an invaluable training and learning opportunity and I would argue that it should form part of every social worker's training, whether at pre-qualifying or post-qualifying level. If child observation is not possible, an awareness of the importance of thoughtful, listening stillness and the skills associated with it can be achieved through practice and application, in the context of appropriate professional support.

In terms of practical techniques, any use of play, drawing, or any other imaginative work with children rests on the assumption, alluded to earlier, that outward manifestations are reflections of the inner world and that play, for children, represents an expression of the unconscious, with symbolic significance, rather as free associations and dreams do for adults. For play of any kind to work, all participants have to feel comfortable with it. Each individual worker needs to find her/his own way of feeling comfortable with children, as well as feeling comfortable with the idea of play as work – work that worker and the child can do together. By the same token, it is important to share the imaginative life of children; it is helpful to retain a sense of and belief in magic and make believe, with a readiness to accept that children go in and out of fantasy, often without warning, in their own way, and can sometimes leave one there, unexpectedly, feeling rather silly. What Jewett (1984) calls "magical thinking" also needs to be kept in mind, both in terms of children's capacity for omnipotence and in relation to a belief in magical solutions to complex problems.

A range of possible techniques has been described in Chapter IV; they are not definitive and they cannot be used in every situation in the same way, since the worker needs to make them her or his own. They also need time in which they can be tried out, and time in which the activity can be engaged in in a meaningful way. It is clearly essential, when using a complex and potentially emotional tool like the circle game, that there is enough time to deal with what emerges from it. Games and techniques are valuable in providing a safe way of making contact, and potential apertures through which inner thoughts and feelings might be glimpsed.

### iv. Training, Support and Supervision

All this does not come together overnight. Training, support, supervision and a sense that expertise is valued in a specialist context are all essentials and it is to this final building block that I now turn. What do workers need in terms of training? What do they need from their colleagues, managers and agencies in order to enable this kind of work to be undertaken?

Let us look at training first. It would seem axiomatic to provide child development teaching to all students undertaking social work training at pre-qualifying level, irrespective of their prospective specialism. This not only facilitates a grasp of how children work but also enables workers to respond to, understand and work with the child part of the adult, so often activated or resurrected by the traumatic events which bring them to the attention of social work agencies. Such teaching should ideally be reinforced by, and integrated within a 'direct work with children and young people' sequence for those likely to be working with children at any professional level, or in any professional context. The teaching sequences I describe could combine various theoretical frameworks related to children in different age groups, with experiential work and role play enabling students to gain awareness of their own feelings, and to enter the world of their child clients.

By the same token, as I suggested earlier, a child study sequence, which provides the opportunity for a period of direct observation of children, should also form part of the generic first year Diploma in Social Work Training (DipSW), as indeed it already does in several social work departments. This would square well with the renewed emphasis in social work education on observation skills, and adopting a non-judgemental stance in relation to individuals, as well as developing a capacity to 'be' rather than to 'do' – all skills which can be transferred to a wide range of other areas of practice. From my own experience of child study seminars at DipSW level, I am aware of how hard it is for students to stop and think about whose needs they are really meeting when they leap into action. The sequence enables them to dig deep in to their own feelings of helplessness, sorrow and smallness, faced with the magnitude of the experiences they have to encounter.

At post-qualifying level, training has to address the continuing needs, on both a practical and an emotional level, of those who choose child-centred areas of practice. I am regularly concerned and amazed to discover the degree of insecurity among experienced social workers, who, faced with a child client, feel deskilled, ill equipped and out of their depth. The model outlined for pre-qualifying training, in this context, could form the basis for a 'refresher' in relation to child development; theory harnessed to an experiential element, the skills associated with communicating with children, and case discussion would seem to be a sound place to start. Training, however, cannot take place in a vacuum – once the process of exploration in this area begins it needs to be nurtured and supported through group discussion, case presentation seminars, debate and feedback. A climate needs to be provided in which difficult issues can be explored and discussed by people struggling with the same dilemmas. By this means, skills can be enhanced, expertise valued and supported.

## New Beginnings?

Perhaps it is indeed time to go 'back to basics', as is the current fashion. I believe that agencies need to rethink what social work is all about – fast. In responding to the chaos created by poverty, homelessness, oppression of every kind, unemployment, rising crime, drug and alcohol abuse, AIDS, the disintegration of 'the nuclear family', child abuse in many forms, moral 'panics', and the increasing divorce rate, there is a move towards devices that control and manage rather than listen and explore. There is a tendency to over-simplify, often through the use of worker- or manager-led approaches that deny or ignore the complex needs of people for whom the service was designed in the first place. The thinking, feeling, contemplative and imaginative social worker who wants to spend time making an assessment, talking to clients, being uncertain and struggling with that feeling is in danger of becoming the social work equivalent of the dinosaur.

Yet the Children Act demands such workers, requires just these qualities and skills if all the complex tasks identified are to be accomplished. As a consequence, child centred agencies and their managers need to attend not only to case management but also to practice – the encouragement of skills development, of openness about the impact of the work, of further training, as well as the celebration and validation of expertise.

Social work seems to have forgotten that people are its greatest resource and that they need taking care of. To work with children in need, in pain, in distress, in whatever context, and to attend to them properly, the worker needs to be attended to as well. Social workers with the commitment and training to work in the way I have described need to be enabled to develop, and need to be replenished, in order to survive. The social work tradition requires people to be thoughtful, reflective, willing to learn and to grow, to take risks, to be prepared to explore the child's world and to be able to integrate the knowledge skills and values laid down by the Children Act. To do all this, though, you need help, when you get stuck, from someone who knows what they are talking about. Perhaps it is time for the return of the Senior Practitioner who gets promoted on the basis of practice expertise rather than management ability.

My fear, however, is that social work will turn its face increasingly away from the child as an individual, and continue to focus on either the parents or the family system as a whole, unless research can convince the powers that be that there may be another way. There is clearly no perfect way to do this work, but a climate needs to be created in which different approaches can be more thoughtfully combined. I believe my model and approach offer a different, challenging way of thinking about the task and the role of the

professional who deals with children in whatever context, and I
believe that I have demonstrated that a short term therapeutic
service can be provided in the context of a statutory task. I also
consider that this is a model which could equally well be employed
by any professional involved in child-centred work, whether child
protection, working with accommodated children or children in
care, Guardian ad Litem work, fostering and adoption, conciliation,
and mediation, as well as in the context of family centres, nurseries
and residential child care provision. As I have discovered, working
with children in distress is far from easy, and, as I have already
suggested, it is tempting to try to manage the complex nature of it by
over-simplification, labelling, the use of mechanistic devices such as
'checklists'. Perhaps there is a need to stand back from this
approach, and think more positively about ways of working with
muddle, learning to make sense of the chaos and confusion of
people's lives.

I believe that if more workers who are involved with children
experiencing separation and divorce were enabled to undertake this
work in the way I have described, this could generate a considerable
body of clinical knowledge which could tell us a great deal about
children and divorce, on a wider scale, embracing a greater variety of
experience and incorporating a more diverse population, in terms of
race and class. Such a wealth of information could make a significant
contribution, both in terms of understanding the needs of such
children and enabling appropriate provision to be made for them, if
required, in terms of support and counselling. Practice and policy
has to respond to the growing needs of families in transition.
Divorce, as I have already observed, is what might be called a
growth area; it has many victims, but the most vulnerable and
powerless of them all are the children, who are denied any real
service at a time of significant need.

For children of divorce, then, "the space beneath, between" is not
always safe or comfortable. In the midst of acrimony and conflict,
someone needs to be there for the child, to "uphold the broken end
of the arch" for them, just for a while. The experience of children
has to be considered; their stories must be heard, if an appropriate
assessment of their needs is to be made. I hope I have demonstrated
that, for any worker involved in this field, this is an important and
valid activity – a conclusion which, not surprisingly, "makes me end
where I began" (Donne 1633).

# Bibliography

Adcock, M. (1988) 'Assessing Children's Needs' in J. Aldgate & J. Simmonds eds. (1988) *Direct Work with Children*: Batsford Academic

Aldgate, J. (1988) 'Work with Children Experiencing Separation & Loss: A Theoretical Framework' in J. Aldgate & J. Simmonds eds. (1988) op. cit.

Aldgate, J. & Simmonds J. eds. (1988) *Direct Work with Children: A Guide for Social Work Practitioners*: Batsford Academic

Axline, V. M. (1964) *Dibs – In Search of Self*: Penguin

Axline, V. M. (1964) 'The Eight Basic Principles' in M. Hawarth ed . (1964) *Child Psychotherapy*: Basic Books

Banks, E. & Mumford, S. (1988) 'Meeting the Needs of Workers' in J. Aldgate & J. Simmonds eds. (1988) op. cit.

Bick, E. (1964) 'Notes on Infant Observation in Psychoanalytic Training' in *International Journal of Psycho-analysis* No. 45.

Biestek, F. P. (1972) *The Casework Relationship*: George Allen & Unwin

Biller, H. B. (1974) *Paternal Deprivation*: Lexington Books

Bion,W. (1959) 'Attacks on Linking' in *International Journal of Psycho-Analysis* 40

Bion, W. (1962) *Learning from Experience*: Heinemann

Black, D. & Urbanowicz, M. A. (1987) 'Family Intervention with Bereaved Children' in *Journal of Child Psychology & Psychiatry* Vol. 28 No. 3

Black, D. (1984) 'Helping the Children of Divorce' in *Modern Medicine 29*

Blake, W. (1794) *Songs of Innocence & of Experience 1789–1794*: Oxford University Press/Trianon Press 1992 Edition

Block, J. H., Block, J. & Gjerde, P. F. (1986) 'The Personality of the Child Prior to Divorce' in *Child Development 57*

Block, J. H. Block, J. & Gjerde, P. F. (1988) 'Parental Functioning & the Home Environment in Families of Divorce' in *Journal of The American Academy of Child & Adolescent Psychiatry 27*

Blom-Cooper, L. et al (1985) *A Child in Trust : Report of The Panel of Inquiry into the Circumstances Surrounding the Death of Jasmine Beckford*: London Borough of Brent

Blom-Cooper, L. et al (1987) *A Child in Mind – Protection of Children in a Responsible Society: The Report of the Commission of Inquiry into the Circumstances Surrounding the Death of Kimberley Carlile*: London Borough of Greenwich *Study of the Child* 1987 No. 22

Bowlby, J. (1969) *Attachment*: Hogarth

Bowlby, J. (1973) *Loss: Sadness & Depression*: Hogarth

Bowlby, J. (1980) *Separation: Anxiety & Anger*: Hogarth

Bowlby, J. (1979) *The Making & Breaking of Affectional Bonds*: Tavistock Publications

Brookes, S. (1991) 'Bion's Concept of Containment in Marital Work' in *Journal of Social Work Practice Vol. 5. No. 2*

Burgoyne, J., Ormrod, R. & Richards, M. P. M. (1987) *Divorce Matters*: Penguin

Burnham, J. (1986) *Family Therapy*: Routledge

Butler-Sloss, Lord Justice E. (1988) *The Cleveland Report*: HMSO

Cantwell, B. (1992) 'Welfare Reports After The Children Act: Setting A New Agenda' in *Probation Journal*, September 1992

Cantwell, B. & Trinder, L. (1993) 'Listening To Children: The Impact of the Children Act 1989 on the Work of Family Court Welfare Teams' in *Probation Journal, December 1993: 189–192*

Carey, P. (1988) *Oscar & Lucinda*: Faber & Faber

Cherlin, A. J., Furstenburg, P. L., Chase-Lonsdale, K. E., Kiernan, K. E. et. al. (1991) 'Longitudinal Studies of Effects of Divorce on Children in Great Britain & the United States' in *Science 7.6.91*

Clulow, C. (1990) 'Training Implications of The Children Act 1989: The Checklist & Divorce Proceedings' in *Family Law* July 1990

Clulow, C. & Vincent, C. (1987) *In the Child's Best Interests?: Divorce Court Welfare & the Search for a Settlement*: Sweet & Maxwell

Cockett, M. & Tripp, J. (1994) 'Children Living in Reordered Families' in *Social Policy Research Findings* No. 45: Joseph Rowntree Foundation

Curnock, K. & Hardiker, P. (1979) *Towards Practice Theory: Skills & Methods in Social Assessments*: Routledge Kegan Paul

Dallos, R. (1991) *Family Belief Systems, Therapy & Change*: Oxford University Press

Danziger, D. (1992) *Lost Hearts: Talking About Divorce*: Bloomsbury

Davies, H. G. (1992) 'Welfare Reports: An Expanded Checklist – The Importance of Core Information' in *Family Law*, May 1992

Davis, G. (1982) 'Conciliation: A Dilemma for the Divorce Court Welfare Service' in *Probation Journal* Vol. 29. No. 4. December 1982

Davis, G. (1985) 'The Theft of Conciliation' in *Probation Journal* Vol. 32. No. 1 March 1985

Davis, G., Macleod, A. & Murch, M. (1983) 'Undefended Divorce:Should Section 41 of the Matrimonial Causes Act 1973 be Repealed?' in *Modern Law Review 46. (22)*

Daws, D. & Boston M. eds. (1977) *The Child Psychotherapist & the Problems of Young People*: Wildwood House

Department of Health (1990) *The Care of Children:Principles and Practice in Regulations and Guidance*: HMSO

Denzin, N. K. (1978) *Sociological Methods: A Sourcebook*: McGraw Hill

Di Leo, J. (1979) *Young Children & Their Drawings*: Constable

Donne, J. (1633) 'A Valediction: Forbidding Mourning' in *The Oxford Book of Seventeenth Century Verse*: Clarendon Press (1968)

Dryden, J. (1678) *All For Love* A & C Black (1975)

Dunn, J. (1990) *Separate Lives: Why Siblings are So Different*: Basic Books

Eekelaar, J. (1991) *Regulating Divorce*: Clarendon Press

Eekelaar, J. & Clive, E. M. (1977) *Custody After Divorce*: Centre for Socio-Legal Studies

Egan, G. (1975) *The Skilled Helper: A Systematic Approach to Effective Helping*: Brooks/Cole

Eliot, T. S. (1944) *Four Quartets*: Faber and Faber

Elliott, J., Ochiltree, G., Richards, M., Sinclair, C. & Tasker, F. (1990) 'Divorce and Children: A British Challenge to the Wallerstein View' in *Family Law*, August 1990 Vol. 20

Elliott, J. & Richards, M. P. M. (1991) 'Children & Divorce: Educational Performance & Behaviour Before & After Parental Separation' in *International Journal of Law & The Family*, 5

Emery, R. E. (1988) *Marriage, Divorce and Children's Adjustment*: Sage

Erikson, E. H. (1965) *Childhood & Society*: Penguin

Fahlberg, V. (1982) *Child Development*: BAAF

Fenby, J, (1992) 'Welfare Reports: Levels of Agreement & Parental Views' in *Probation Journal* December 1992

Ferard, M. L. & Hunnubun, N. K. (1962) *The Caseworker's Use of Relationships*: Tavistock Publications

Ferri, E. (1976) *Growing Up in a One Parent Family*: NFER

Foden, A. & Wells, T. (1990) 'Unresolved Attachment: Role & Organisational Ambiguities for the Divorce Court Welfare Officer' in *Family Law*, May 1990

Fraiberg, S. (1952) 'Some Aspects of Casework with Children I: Understanding the Child Client' in E. Holgate ed. (1972) *Communicating with Children*: Longman

Freud, A. (1936) *The Ego & The Mechanisms of Defense*: New York International University Press

Freud, S. (1900) *The Interpretation of Dreams*: SE Vols. 4 & 5

Freud, S. (1901) *The Psychopathology of Everyday Life*: SE Vol. 6

Freud, S. (1905) Three Essays on the Theory of Sexuality: SE. Vol. 7

Freud, S. (1917) *Mourning & Melancholia*: SE. Vol. 14

Furstenberg, F. F., Peterson, J. L., Nord, C. W. & Zill, N. (1983) 'The Life Course of Children of Divorce' in *American Sociological Review* 48

Furstenberg, F. F., Morgan, S. P. & Allison, P. D. (1987) 'Paternal Participation and Children's Wellbeing after Marital Dissolution' in *American Sociological Review* 52

Garrett, A. (1942) *'Interviewing: Its Principles & Methods': Family Service Association of America*

George, V. & Wilding, P. (1972) *Motherless Families*: Routledge & Kegan Paul

Gibran, K. (1972): *The Prophet*: Heinemann

Godden, R. (1963) *The Battle of the Villa Fiorita*: Pan

Goldsmith, O. (1992) *The First Wives' Club*: Heinemann

Goldstein, J., Freud, A. & Solnit, A. J (1973) *Beyond the Best Interests of the Child*: The Free Press

Goldstein, J., Freud, A. & Solnit, A. J (1980) *Before the Best Interests of the Child*: Burnett Brothers

Gorell Barnes, G. (1991) 'Step-Families in Context: The Post Divorce Process' in *The Association of Child Psychology & Psychiatry Newsletter*, November 1991

Gorell Barnes, G. (1991) 'The Role of the Extended Family' in *Family Policy Bulletin*, December 1991

Gorell Barnes, G. (1991) 'Ambiguities in Post Divorce relationships' in *Journal of Social Work Practice* Vol. 5. No. 2

Gorell Barnes, G. (1992) 'Getting it Right The Second Time Around' Plenary Address, International Family Therapy Association Conference on Divorce & Remarriage, April 1992

Griffiths, P. (1993) *Decision Making in Divorce Court Welfare Work*: PhD thesis, in progress

Guardian (1991) 'Finding Fault' 26.9.91. Guardian Newspapers Ltd. Guardian (1992) 'Frendly Divorce for Princess Royal & Capt. Mark Philips' 14.4.92. Guardian Newspapers Ltd.

Guardian (1992) 'Unfair for Fathers?' 8.7.92. Guardian Newspapers Ltd. Guardian (1992) 'Second Child Wins Divorce from Parents' 12.11.92. Guardian Newspapers Ltd.

Guardian (1993) 'Looking Out for Children's Wishes & Welfare In Court Warfare' Letters Page 18.2.93. Guardian Newspapers Ltd.

Harris Williams, M. ed. (1987) *Collected Papers of Martha Harris and Esther Bick*: Clunie

Hawarth, M. ed (1964) *Child Psychotherapy: Practice & Theory*: Basic Books

Haynes, J. (1981) *Divorce Mediation*: Springer

Haynes, J. & Haynes, G. (1989) *Mediating Divorce: A Casebook of Successful Strategies for Successful Family Negotiations*: Josey Bass

Hetherington, E. M. (1984) 'Stress and Coping in Children and Families' in A. Doyle, D. Gold & D. S. Moskovitz eds. *Children and Families under Stress, New Directions for Child Development* No. 24: Jossey-Bass

Hetherington, E. M. (1989a) 'Coping with Family Transitions: Winners, Losers & Survivors' in *Child Development* 60

Hetherington, E. M. (1989b) 'Marital Transitions: A Child's Perspective' in *American Psychologist* 44

Hetherington, E. M. & Arasteh, J. eds (1988) *The Impact of Divorce, Single Parenting & Step Parenting on Children*: Lawrence Erlbaum

Hetherington, E. M., Cox, M. & Cox, R. (1978) 'The Aftermath of Divorce' in J. H. Stevens & M. Mathews eds. *Mother Child, Father Child Relations*: Washington National Association for the Education of Young Children

Hetherington, E. M., Cox, M. & Cox, R. (1979) 'Play & Social Interaction in Children Following Divorce' in *Journal of Social Issues* 35

Hetherington, E. M., Cox, M. & Cox, R . (1982) 'The Effects of Divorce on Parents & Children' in M. E. Lamb ed. *Non Traditional Families: Parenting & Child Development*

Hetherington, E. M., Stanley-Hagan, M. & Anderson, E. R. (1989) 'Marital Transitions' in *American Psychology* 44
Hinshelwood, R. D. (1991) *A Dictionary of Kleinian Thought*: Free Association Books
H.M.S.O. (1989) *The Children Act 1989*
H.M.S.O. (1989) *An Introduction to The Children Act 1989*
Hobhouse, J. (1992) *The Furies*: Bloomsbury
Hodges, W. F. (1986) *Intervention for Children in Divorce: Custody, Access & Psychotherapy*: John Wiley & Sons
Hoffman, A . (1992) *Turtle Moon*: Macmillan
Home Office (1992) *Draft Strategy Document: Probation Service Work in Serving the Needs of Children Involved in Separation or Divorce*: Home Office C6 Division
Howard, J. & Shepherd, G. (1987) *Conciliation, Children & Divorce*: Batsford Academic
Hoxter, S. (1977) 'Play & Communication' in M. Boston & D. Daws ed. *The Child Psychotherapist & the Problems of Young People*
Hutcheson, F. *Inquiry into the Original of Our Ideas of Beauty and Virtue*
Hutten, J. (1977) *Short Term Contracts in Social Work*: Routledge & Kegan Paul
Hollis, F. (1964) *Casework: A Psychosocial Therapy*: Random House
Hopkirk, E. (1988) 'Introducing Direct Work with Children to Area Teams in Social Services Departments' in J. Aldgate & J. Simmonds eds. op. cit.
Independent (1992) 'Court Will Decide Girl's Separation From Family' 7.1.92. Newspaper Publishing PLC.
Independent on Sunday (1992) 'For The Sake of the Children' 5.4.92. Newspaper Publishing PLC.
Isaacs, M. B., Leon, G. & Donohue, A. M. (1987) 'Who are the Normal Children of Divorce? On the Need to Specify Population' in *Journal of Divorce* 1987 No. 10
Isaacs, M. B., Leon, G. & Kline, M. (1987) 'When is the Parent out of the Picture? Different Custody, Different Perceptions' in *Family Process* March 1987 No. 26
Jackson, C. (1992) 'Reporting on Children: The Guardian ad Litem, The Court Welfare Officer & The Children Act 1989' in *Family Law*, June 1992
Jacobson, D. S. (1978) 'The Impact of Marital Separation/Divorce; Interpersonal Hostility & Child Adjustment' in *Journal of Divorce* 2
James, H. (1897) *What Maisie Knew*: Penguin 1984
James, A. & Hay, W. (1992) *Court Welfare Work: Research, Practice & Development*: University of Hull
James, A. L. & Wilson, K. (1983) 'Divorce Court Welfare Work: Present & Future' in *Probation Journal* Vol. 30. No. 2
Jewett, C. (1984) *Helping Children Cope with Separation & Loss*: Batsford Academic/ BAAF
Johnston, J. R., Campbell, L. E. G. & Mayes, S. S (1985) 'Latency Children in Post Separation & Divorce Disputes' in *Journal of Child Psychiatry* Vol. 24 No. 5
Johnston, J. R., Kline, M. & Tchann, J. M. (1989) 'Ongoing Post Divorce Conflict' in *American Journal of Orthopsychiatry* 59
Jones, A., Kroll, B., Pitts, J., Smith, P. & Weise, J. (1992) *The Probation Handbook*: Longman
Jordan, W. (1970) *Client-Worker Transactions*: Routledge & Kegan Paul
Kelly, J. & Emery, R. (1989) 'Second Chances: Men, Women & Children a Decade after Divorce' (Book Review) in *Family Law*, December 1990
Kiernan, K. (1991) 'What About the Children?' in *Family Policy Bulletin*, December.
Kiernan, K. (1992) 'The Impact of Family Disruption in Childhood on Transitions made in Young Adult Life' in *Population Studies* Vol. 46
Kiernan, K. & Wicks, M. (1990) *Family Change & Future Policy*: Family Policy Studies Centre
Klein, M. (1926) 'The Psychological Principles of Infant Analysis' in J. Mitchell ed. (1986) *The Selected Melanie Klein*: Penguin
Klein, M. (1932) *The Psycho-analysis of Children*: Hogarth Press
Klein, M. (1940) *Mourning – Its Relation to Manic Depressive States* in J.Mitchell ed. op.cit.

Klein, M. (1952) 'On Observing the Behaviour of Young Infants' in *Developments in Psychoanalysis*: Hogarth Press

Klein, M. (1955) 'The Psycho-Analytic Play Technique: Its History and Significance' in J. Mitchell ed. op.cit.

Klein, M. (1957) *Envy & Gratitude: A Study of Unconscious Sources*: Tavistock

Klein, M. (1961) *Narrative of a Child Analysis*: Hogarth Press

Klein, M. (1963) *Our Adult World & Its Roots in Infancy & Other Essays*: Heinemann

Kline, M., Johnston, J. & Tschann, J. (1991) 'The Long Shadow of Marital Conflict: A Model of Children's Post Divorce Adjustment' in *The Journal of The Marriage & The Family*, May 1991 No. 53

Kline, P. (1984) *Psychology and Freudian Theory: An Introduction*: Methuen

Krementz, J. (1985) *How It Feels When Parents Divorce*: Gollantz

Kroger, J. (1989) *Identity in Adolescence: The Balance between Self and Other*: Routledge

Kurdek, L. A. ed. (1983) *Children & Divorce*: Josey-Bayy

Kurdek, L. A. & Siesky, A. E. (1980) 'Children's Perceptions of their Parents' Divorce' in *Journal of Divorce* 1980 3 (4)

La Fontaine, J. de (1668) *Fables*: Peguin Classics Edition 1982

Lawrence, D. H. (1950) 'Piano' in *D. H. Lawrence: Selected Poems*: Penguin 1968 Edition

Leobuchhandlung (1964) *Springs of Oriental Wisdom*: Herder & Herder

Lieberman, F. (1979) *Social Work with Children*: Human Sciences Press

London Borough of Lambeth (1987) *Whose Child? The Report of the Public Inquiry in the Death of Tyra Henry*: London Borough of Lambeth

Lonsdale, G., Elfer, P. & Ballard, R. (1979) *Children, Grief & Social Work*: Basil Blackwell

Lund, M. (1984) 'Research on Children & Divorce' in *Family Law* 1984: Vol 14 No. 7

Maidment, S. (1976) 'A Study in Child Custody' in *Family Law* Vol. 6. No. 7 & Vol. 6. No. 8

Maidment, S. (1984) *Child Custody & Divorce; The Law in Social Context*: Croom Helm

Mattinson, J. & Sinclair, I. (1979) *Mate & Stalemate*: Basil Blackwell

May, T (1991) *Probation: Politics, Policy & Practice*: Open University Press

McGredie, G. & Horrox, A. (1985) *Voices in the Dark; Children & Divorce*: Unwin

McGurk, H. & Glachan, M. 'Children's Conception of the Continuity of Parenthood following Divorce' in *Journal of Child Psychology and Psychiatry* 1987 Vol. 28 No. 33

Miller, L., Rustin, M., Rustin, M. & Shuttleworth, J. (1989) eds *Closely Observed Infants*: Duckworth

Mitchell, A. (1981) *Someone to Turn To: Experiences of Help before Divorce*: Aberdeen University Press

Mitchell, A. (1985) *Children in the Middle*: Tavistock

Mitchell, J. ed. (1986) *The Selected Melanie Klein*: Penguin

Mnookin, R. H. (1979) *Bargaining in the Shadow of the Law: The Case of Divorce*: Oxford Centre for Socio-Legal Studies

Moore, B. E. & Fine, B. D. eds. (1990) *Psychoanalytic Terms & Concepts*: The American Psychoanalytic Association

Murch, M. (1980) *Justice, Welfare & Divorce*: Sweet & Maxwell

Murray, N. (1992) 'Jackie-v-Mum and Dad' in *Community Care* 3.12.92

Neal, J. H. ( 1983) 'Children's Understanding of their Parents' Divorce' in L. A. Kurdek ed. *Children & Divorce* op. cit.

Nelson-Jones, R. (1988) *Practical Counselling & Helping Skills*: Cassell

Oaklander, V. (1978) *Windows to Our Children*: Real People Press

Office of Population Censuses & Surveys (1974) *Marriage & Divorce Statistics*: HMSO

Olden, C. (1953) 'On Adult Empathy with Children' in *Psychoanalytic Study of the Child 8*

Parkes, C. M. (1972) *Bereavement: Studies of Grief in Adult Life*: Tavistock

Parkinson, L. (1986) *Conciliation in Separation & Divorce: Finding Common Ground*: Croom Helm

Parkinson, L. . (1987) *Separation, Divorce and Families*: Macmillan

Payne, M. (1991) *Modern Social Work Theory: A Critical Introduction*: Macmillan

Phillips, M. (1993) 'Ninety Minutes to Lose a Daughter' in *The Guardian* 13.2.93

Piaget, J. (1969) *The Psychology of the Child*: Routledge & Kegan Paul

Pincus, L. (1976) *Death & The Family: The Importance of Mourning*: Faber

Pirani, A. (1989) *The Absent Father*: Arkana

Preston-Shoot, M. & Agass, D. (1990) *Making Sense of Social Work*: Macmillan

Proust, M. (1922) *Remembrance of Things Past*: Chatto & Windus 1971

Racker, H. (1968) *Transference & Countertransference*: Karnac

Rahe, R. H., McKean, J. D. & Arthur, R. J. (1967) 'A Longitudinal Study of Life Change & Illness Patterns' in *Journal of Psychosomatic Research* 10

Randall, P. (1990) 'A Child's Eye View' in *Community Care* 14.3.90

Rappaport, L. (1967) 'Crisis Oriented Short Term Treatment' in *Social Service Review* 41: March

Reid, W. J. & Shyne, A. W. (1969) *Brief & Extended Casework*: Columbia University Press

Richards, M. P. M. (1982) 'Post Divorce Arrangements for Children: A Psychological Perspective' in *Journal of Social Welfare Law* 4

Richards, M. P. M. (1984) 'Separation, Divorce & Remarriage: The Experiences of Children' in Guy ed *Relating to Marriage*: Rugby National Marriage Guidance Council

Richards, M. P. M. (1986) ' Behind the Best Interests of the Child: An Examination of The Arguments of Goldstein, Freud & Solnit concerning Custody & Access at Divorce' in *Journal of Social Welfare Law* 8

Richards, M. P. M. (1990) 'Parental Divorce & Children' in Tonge, B. T., Burrows, G. D. & Werry, J. S. eds. (1990) *Handbook of Studies in Child Psychiatry*: Elsevier Science Publications

Richards, M. P. M. (1990) 'Divorce Cambridge Style: New Developments in Conciliation' in *Family Law* November 1990

Richards, M. P. M. (1991) 'Divorce Research Today' in *Family Law*, February 1990 Vol. 21

Richards, M. P. M. (1991) 'Helping Children to Cope' in *Family Policy Bulletin*, December 1991

Richards, M. P. M. & Dyson, M (1982) *Separation, Divorce and the Development of Children: A Review*: Cambridge Child Care and Development Group

Rickford, F. (1993) 'A Private Function' in *Social Work Today* 14.1.93

Roberts, M. (1990) 'Systems or Selves? Some Ethical Issues in Family Mediation' in *Journal of Family Welfare Law*

Robinson, M. (1991) *Family Transformations through Divorce & Remarriage*: Routledge

Rose, P. ed. (1993) *Social Trends*: HMSO

Rosenbluth, D. (1965) 'The Kleinian Theory of Depression' in *Journal of Child Psychotherapy* Vol. 1. No. 3

Ruszczynski, S. (1992) 'Notes Towards a Psychoanalytic Understanding of the Couple Relationship' in *Psychoanalytic Psychotherapy* Vol. 6. No. 1

Rutter, M. (1971) 'Parent-Child Separation: Psychological Effects on Children' in *Journal of Child Psychology & Psychiatry* 12

Rutter, M. (1975) *Helping Troubled Children*: Penguin

Rutter, M. (1981) *Maternal Deprivation Reassessed* (Second Edition): Penguin

Rutter, M. (1985) 'Resilience in the Face of Adversity' in *British Journal of Psychiatry* Vol. 147

Rutter, M. (1987) 'Psychosocial Resilience & Protective Mechanisms' in *American Journal of Orthopsychiatry* 57

Salzberger-Wittenberg, I. (1970) *Psychoanalytic Insight & Relationships: A Kleinian Approach*: Routledge Kegan Paul

Seale, S. (1984) *Children in Divorce:A Study of Information Available to the Scottish Courts on Children involved in Divorce Actions*: Edinburgh Scottish Office Central Research Unit

Segal, H. (1988) *Introduction to the Work of Melanie Klein*: Karnac Books

Shakespeare, W. (1604) *Othello*: Arden Shakespeare Edition 1971

Shakespeare, W. (1605) *King Lear*: Arden Shakespeare Edition 1972

Sheridan, M. (1968) *The Developmental Progress of Infants & Young Children* (Second Edition): HMSO

Sheridan, M. (1980) *From Birth to Five Years*: NFER/Nelson

Sheridan, M. (1986) 'Chart Illustrating the Developmental Progress of Infants & Young Children' in BAAF ed. (1986) *Working with Children*: BAAF

Stone, N. (1991) *Family Court Welfare Law*: University of East Anglia

Storr, A. (1989) *Freud*: Oxford University Press

Sunday Times (1991) 'Children of Divoce Suffer in Adult Life' 15.9.91. Times Newspapers Ltd

Trowell, J. & Miles, G. (1991) 'The Contribution of Observation Training to Professional Development in Social Work' in *Journal of Social Work Practice* Vol. 5 No. 1

Tugendhat, J. (1990) *What Teenagers Can Tell Us about Divorce and Step-Families*: Bloomsbury

Wadsworth, M., Maclean, M., Kuh, D. & Rogers, B. (1990) 'Children of Divorced & Separated Parents: Summary & Review of Findings from a Long term Follow Up Study in the U. K.' in *Family Practice* Vol. 7. No. 1

Walczak, Y. & Burns, S. (1984) *Divorce: The Child's Point of View*: Harper Row

Wallerstein, J. S. (1984) 'Children of Divorce: Preliminary report of a ten year follow-up of young children' in *American Journal of Orthopsychiatry*

Wallerstein, J. S. (1985) 'The Overburdened Child : Some Long Term Consequences of Divorce' in *American Journal of Social Work* March/April 1985

Wallerstein, J. S (1991) 'The Long Term Effects of Divorce on Children: A Review' in *The Journal of Child and Adolescent Psychiatry* 30:3

Wallerstein, J. S. & Blakeslee, J. (1989) *Second Chances*: Corgi

Wallerstein, J. S. & Kelly, J. B. (1980) *Surviving the Breakup: How Children & Parents Cope with Divorce*: Grant McIntyre

Wilkinson, M. (1981) *Children & Divorce*: Blackwell

Winnicott, C. (1986) 'Face to Face with Children' in BAAF ed (1986) *Working with Children*: BAAF

Winnicott, D. W. (1960) 'The Theory of the Parent Infant Relationship' in *The Maturational Process & The Facilitating Environment*: Hogarth 1971

Winnicott, D. W. (1964) *The Child, The Family & The Outside World*: Penguin

Winnicott, D. W. (1971) *Therapeutic Consultations in Child Psychiatry*: Hogarth Press

Winnicott, D. W. (1971) *Playing & Reality*: Penguin

Winnicott, D. W. (1977) *The Piggle*: Hogarth Press

Winnicott, D. W. (1979) *The Making & Breaking Of Affectional Bonds*: Tavistock

Wyld, N. (1992) 'Stifled Voices' in *Community Care*, 29.10.92

Yeats, W. B. (1928) 'Among School Children' in *W. B. Yeats: Collected Poems*: Papermac 1982 Edition